A Royal Family

1660 The Year of Restoration
Prince Rupert of the Rhine
Restoration England

Charles I and Henrietta Maria Departing for the Chase, by Mytens

Patrick Morrah

A ROYAL FAMILY

Charles I and his family

Constable   London

First published in Great Britain 1982
by Constable and Company Ltd
10 Orange Street London WC2H 7EG
Copyright © 1982 by Patrick Morrah
ISBN 0 09 463560 9
Set in Monophoto Baskerville 11pt by
Servis Filmsetting Ltd, Manchester
Printed in Great Britain by
Ebenezer Baylis and Son Ltd
The Trinity Press, Worcester
and London

For

MARY BARBER

Contents

Note on Dates and Names   1

Introduction: The Family   2

1 The Father, 1600–25   5

2 Raising a Family, 1625–42   25

3 Separated by War, 1642–6   61

4 In the Depths, 1646–50   92

5 Haven in Holland, 1650–8   122

6 Turn of the Tide, 1658–60   160

7 Year of Destiny, 1660–1   180

8 Eldest and Youngest, 1661–70   204

9 Two Brothers, 1670–85   234

10 Lone Survivor, 1685–1701   260

References   266

Bibliography   275

Index   278

Illustrations

Charles I and Henrietta Maria Departing for the Chase by Mytens
(*by Gracious permission of H.M. The Queen*) *frontispiece*

Henry Prince of Wales. Miniature by Isaac Oliver   3
(*by Gracious permission of H.M. The Queen*)

Elizabeth of Bohemia, by Honthorst   3
(*National Portrait Gallery*)

James I by Mytens   33
(*National Portrait Gallery*)

Anne of Denmark by Marcus Gheeraerts   33
(*by kind permission of the Marquess of Tavistock*)

The five eldest children of Charles I, by Van Dyck   42
(*by Gracious permission of H.M. The Queen*)

Charles I and Henrietta Maria dining in public, by   43
Houckgeest
(*by Gracious permission of H.M. The Queen*)

Execution of King Charles I, engraving   116
(*Bibliotheque Nationale, Paris*)

Mary of Orange, by Hanneman   124
(*by Gracious permission of H.M. The Queen*)

Le Grande Mademoiselle, by Bourguignon   131
(*Musée de Versailles*)

James Duke of York, by Lely   155
(*National Portrait Gallery*)

Charles II, miniature by Samuel Cooper   181
(*Mauritshuis Museum, The Hague*)

Henry Duke of Gloucester, after Luttehuys 188
(*National Portrait Gallery*)

Coronation of Charles II engraving 205
(*British Museum*)

Catherine of Braganza, by Lely 211
(*By Gracious permission of H.M. The Queen*)

Henrietta, Duchess of Orleans, miniature by Samuel Cooper 218
(*Victoria and Albert Museum*)

Mary of Modena by Wissing 242
(*National Portrait Gallery*)

Coronation of James II and Mary of Modena 261
(*British Museum*)

Note on Dates and Names

In the seventeenth century there was a difference of ten days between the Old Style of dating employed in England and the New Style (based on the Gregorian Calendar) in general use on the European continent. I have used the Old Style in all cases. The year is taken as starting on 1 January. Officially it began on 25 March, but the custom now followed was already widely practised.

As in previous books I have followed no precise rule in the spelling of names. I have endeavoured to write them as one would expect to find them spelt today. Finding myself in a small minority, I have reluctantly abandoned my practice of alluding to the name of the royal house as Stewart rather than Stuart.

In the use of names I have tried to avoid pedantry. I have freely alluded to Henrietta Duchess of Orleans as 'Minette', the appellation by which she has become best known to posterity; this was in fact a pet name used only by her brother Charles, and by him only in a few letters.

As to spelling in general, when quoting from sources I have retained the words as I found them. In some cases they are modernized in the works consulted; in others left as in the originals. This inevitably leads to inconsistency, but consistency is difficult to attain.

Introduction: The Family

Until fairly recent generations members of English royal families have not been remarkable for mutual affection. Conditions and ambitions have often militated against good relations within the household.

With scanty evidence available it is hard to generalize about the Saxons. Alfred the Great, wise of judgement in this as in all matters, managed to bring up his family in harmony; other cases must be adjudged doubtful, though in general there is not much evidence of serious friction.

The Normans and early Plantagenets were more often than not at loggerheads. Occupancy of the throne was again and again disputed, the result being intrigue and armed rebellion. Henry I kept his eldest brother in captivity for nearly thirty years; Stephen and his cousin Matilda were involved in a protracted civil war; the sons of Henry II made their father's life a misery with their squabbles. Henry III was loyally served by his sons, but there was more friction in the days of the three Edwards. The female members of the family hardly came into the picture. With a few exceptions they existed only as pawns in the marriage game.

After Henry of Lancaster had dethroned, and almost certainly murdered, his first cousin Richard II, the family history moved towards the cut-throat conflicts known to later generations as the Wars of the Roses. The Tudors, few in number as they were, were usually bickering among themselves; Elizabeth I was free from family quarrels mainly because there was no family left to quarrel with.

In the eighteenth century the Hanoverians were notorious for their dislike of each other. In the nineteenth, with the decline of royal power and the consequent lack of reason for intrigue, royal

Henry Prince of Wales.
Miniature by Isaac Oliver

Elizabeth of Bohemia,
by Honthorst

relationships improved; but the household of Victoria was not entirely harmonious. In more recent years the brief reign and subsequent history of Edward VIII did not make for family concord, though this was an isolated case.

One royal house proved an exception to the general rule. Throughout most of the century in which the Stuarts ruled England the family lived in amity; happy relationships were broken only towards the end of the period when the two daughters of James II turned against their father. In particular the children of Charles I, involved as they were in trials and vicissitudes such as seldom afflict royalty, were devoted to each other. They had occasional minor differences, but in matters of moment they stuck together through thick and thin.

Their parents are entitled to much of the credit. The marriage of Charles of England and Henrietta Maria of France began in discord, but it developed into one of the great love matches of history. The deep affection in which they held each other was transmitted to their offspring.

In the following pages an attempt has been made to trace the story of the relationship throughout their lives between these children of Charles and Henrietta Maria. There were nine of them, but two died almost at birth and a third in early childhood. I have tried to concentrate as far as possible on the female members of the family, as their stories are less well known than those of their brothers. For this reason I have dealt in less detail with the period following the death of the last of the sisters in 1670. The course of events when only Charles II and his brother James were left alive will be familiar to most readers.

Public affairs must inevitably play a large part in a chronicle such as this, but I have endeavoured to keep them within bounds, narrating events only where they affect family relationships. Thus I have refrained from discussing the ethics of the Secret Treaty of Dover. Anybody interested in the justification of those tortuous negotiations may be referred to the last chapter of Cyril Hughes Hartmann's *The King my Brother*.

Nor have I gone into all the ins and outs of the Popish Plot, which has been the subject of extensive literature, or the Exclusion Crisis. These episodes have been fully but succinctly chronicled by, among others, Sir Arthur Bryant, Dr Maurice Ashley and Lady Antonia Fraser.

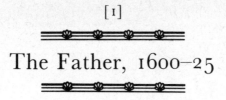

1

The Father, 1600–25

The boy who was to become known in history as England's most tragic monarch did not have the happiest of childhoods. For this his parents were less to blame than were the natural disabilities with which he was born. His father, the learned royal eccentric James VI of Scotland, had married, in 1589, the lively and lovely Princess Anne, daughter of King Frederick II of Denmark and Norway. Anne of Denmark was fifteen years old at the time, and it was not until five years later that she presented her husband with the first of the seven children to be born to them.

Of these seven children only three grew up. This was by no means unusual in that age of multitudinous infant mortality, which not even the superior care lavished on royal babies could do much to mitigate. But in the case of the family of the King and Queen of Scots the only two who appeared to enjoy the best of health and physique were the first to be born. Henry, the eldest, quickly caught the eye and the imagination of his contemporaries as a boy of the most brilliant promise. A splendid athlete with a more than adequate brain, quick and impulsive but a budding scholar always eager to learn, before entering his teens he shone forth as a future paragon of royalty.

His sister Elizabeth, two years his junior, resembled her mother in her beauty and her brother in her vitality. Like Henry she learned quickly and grew up fast, and even in her childhood she charmed the courts of Scotland and England with the liveliness of her personality.

The third child, a daughter named Margaret, born in 1599, lived only fifteen months. Then, on 19 November 1600, was born at the King's castle of Dunfermline the fourth of the family, a boy to replace the little sister he never knew.

So far there had been only one death in the royal family; but it was taken almost for granted that there would quickly be another. The new prince was so weak and sickly that he had to be baptized at birth, being given the name of Charles. A month later, to the surprise of his parents, he was still alive; so as the King's second son he was invested with the titles of Duke of Albany and Earl of Ross. But he was still not expected to live.

He did live however, surviving even the comparative neglect that was the inevitable lot of so unpromising an infant, a younger son at that; and in this he was luckier than the three later offspring of James and Anne who failed to meet the challenge. His survival may well have been mere chance; but it is possible that even at that early age some innate strength of spirit enabled him, in the teeth of every obstacle, to keep alive.

The obstacles were indeed formidable. At four years old young Charles could neither walk nor talk; he was 'so weak in his joints and especially his ankles, insomuch as many feared they were out of joint.'[1] The chances seemed to be that, in the unlikely event of his surviving childhood at all, he would grow up both crippled and mentally defective.

This he might well have done if his father had had his way. But whatever inner resources the little Duke of Albany may have possessed were reinforced by the fortunate chance that he fell into the hands of a practical and strong-minded Cornish-woman who had little patience with misconceived parental notions, though the parent in question were the King of Great Britain himself.

When Charles of Albany was a little less than two and a half years old the event for which his father had been waiting with ever growing eagerness at last took place. Queen Elizabeth I of England died at Richmond on 24 March 1603—the last day of 1602 according to the old calendar. To the end of her life the future of the English crown had been uncertain, the old queen refusing to name a successor. But by the time of her death it was tacitly assumed that the King of Scots, whose right according to the principles of heredity was indisputable, would succeed. He was in fact proclaimed King of England within a few hours of the Queen's death, but even before this an unofficial messenger had set out to give him the news. This was Sir Robert Carey, who had been watching events at the English court in King

James's interest. He had made his preparations: relays of horses had been posted along the road to the north. Evading the order that nobody should leave the palace, Sir Robert rode with furious speed for Scotland, and at Holyrood on 27 March achieved his object of being the first to tell his master that he was the ruler of two kingdoms.

The new sovereign lost no time in travelling south to his new realm, followed soon after by his wife and their two elder children. Charles was left behind; he was unimportant, and in any case was thought to be too weak to make the journey. His health, however, was improving slightly, and in August 1604 King James sent for him to join the royal family in London.

It was now that the King began to take an interest in his younger son. His was an affectionate nature, and he was in no way unmindful of parental responsibilities. But he had little knowledge or experience of children. His own early years had been harsh and lonely; he had known neither of his parents. His father, Lord Darnley, had died by violence before he was a year old, and shortly afterwards his mother, Mary Queen of Scots, had been driven out of her country into an exile that ended on an English scaffold. James never saw her again. He was brought up by governors and tutors, a king from infancy and in a sense almost an adult from his cradle.

He doted on his elder children, though he never gained their full confidence in return. And now, when the third began to claim his attention, he had to decide whom to entrust with his care. In Scotland the child had been looked after by Lord and Lady Fyvie at Dunfermline, but James wanted him to have an English upbringing; and it was now that he bethought him of Sir Robert Carey, who had rendered him such signal service at the moment of accession. He had so far done little to reward Sir Robert; it was a good opportunity to do so by confiding to him the care of his younger son.

It was the physical well-being of the little prince that first concerned King James, once he had decided that his son was not likely immediately to relieve him of his presence in this world. Charles's health was improving, but he was still very weak; he could walk a little, though unsteadily, and while he had begun to talk there was an obvious impediment in his speech. James was the prisoner of the medical theories of his time, and he designed to cure his awkward son by putting him in iron boots to strengthen his legs and cutting the string under his tongue to free him from his stammer.

Here Lady Carey put her foot down. Sir Robert's Cornish wife Elizabeth had a mind of her own; she had quickly gained the affection of her little charge, and she was not going to have him mutilated. 'Many a battle my wife had with the King', wrote her husband, 'but she still prevailed'.[2] James could be as obstinate as a mule, but he was no match for Lady Carey. Both the proposed remedies were abandoned, and Charles's infirmities gradually yielded to nature and the loving care of his lady guardian. He remained undersized, and his stammer was never completely eliminated; but he grew up a reasonably healthy boy who could hold his own with his contemporaries in walking and riding.

Prince Charles, who was created Duke of York soon after his father acquired his second kingdom, continued in the care of Sir Robert and Lady Carey until his twelfth year. He inevitably saw more of them than he did of his parents, but as time went on he became his mother's favourite. Unlike her husband, Anne of Denmark had enjoyed in her native country a lively and loving family life, and she herself was a fond mother; she was, moreover, more strongly attracted to her backward son than to his more extrovert elders. She and Lady Carey, rather than the tutors to whom his education was entrusted, were principally responsible for his development. As for himself, he was from his early years painstaking, earnest, and determined to prove himself worthy of his royal destiny.

He was naturally overshadowed by his dazzling elder brother, who himself regarded his junior with a somewhat patronizing affection. Henry, now Prince of Wales and the white hope of a nation which could never understand his father, thought his little brother, physically insignificant and intellectually serious as he was, fit only for an ecclesiastical career; it was said that he promised half humorously that when he was King he would make Charles his Archbishop of Canterbury.

The young duke himself would probably have looked forward to nothing more happily. He was from the first intensely religious, and in these early years he developed that deep love for the Church of England from which he never wavered. His father, the son of Catholic parents, was brought up as a Scots Presbyterian, and through all his theological deviations remained fundamentally rooted in the principles of that rigid Calvinistic creed. Queen Anne, a Scandinavian Lutheran by origin, became a Catholic not long after her marriage. Prince Charles, trained in Anglicanism at least from the time of his arrival in England, found in its tenets a completely satisfying creed to which he gave unswerving and lifelong devotion.

When the Duke of York was twelve years old he experienced a profound change in his life and prospects. In this winter of 1612–13 he lost both those two older members of the family who had so dominated his childhood. In one case it was in the normal course of events; in the other it was totally unexpected and tragic.

A spectacular and influential marriage had always been King James's hope for Princess Elizabeth. Various suitors had been considered, but the match when it came was a disappointment to Queen Anne and was to lead to great diplomatic complications in the future. The young Elector Palatine of the Rhine, Frederick V, though not a powerful prince, was a graceful youth of distinguished ancestry and sound Protestant principles. James I gave his blessing to the union, and elaborate wedding ceremonies were planned. Then, just as the celebrations were getting under way, the Prince of Wales was taken ill. Fever developed (it is generally believed to have been typhoid), and on 6 November 1612, he died. The Princess's marriage was postponed, but the ceremony took place early in the new year and the bridal couple left for Heidelberg.

Charles's whole existence was altered. Even under the care of the Careys he had been a withdrawn and lonely child. Now he was lonelier than ever. But the Prince of Wales's death had made him his father's heir, and he had to face the prospect of future responsibilities that he had hardly envisaged. Henry, the object of his awed admiration, had seemed the picture of robust health, and it had been taken for granted that in the near future he would marry and become the ancestor of future sovereigns. Now he was dead, at the age of eighteen, and the burden of the future rested on the shoulders of the shy, shrinking, self-effacing boy who knew himself to be hopelessly inferior in all worldly qualities to the brilliant elder brother he had lost.

Prince Charles, however, had inner qualities of his own. He was conscientious and determined, and he set himself to fill the position which was so unexpectedly his with all the earnestness and gravity of his nature. At his sister's wedding he made his first public appearance as heir apparent, and he did so with a grace and dignity that surprised those who had hitherto regarded him as of no account. From then onwards he devoted himself to his royal duties in a manner that earned him the respect of all who came in contact with him.

He played his part conscientiously in court ceremonial, though the atmosphere of that court was alien to his temperament. James I came to England from a ruder, cruder country where he had reigned almost from birth in the teeth of opposition from boisterous nobles of little breeding and few manners. He had held his own among them, but the court he established was perforce graceless and uncouth. Once ensconced at Westminster, he seized eagerly on the ceremonial and magnificence associated with the régime of the great dead queen, but he tempered the splendour of it all with the more earthy customs with which he had grown up in Scotland. He yielded to none in extravagance, and the ritual of court life was as elaborate as it had ever been under Elizabeth. But grace and dignity were not among the King's virtues, and the drunkenness and bawdy behaviour of the courtiers, which increasingly pervaded palace life, earned no rebuke from the sovereign. James, moreover, was almost openly homosexual, and the sight of the King inebriately caressing and mauling his male favourites did not enhance the decorum of the Jacobean court.

All this was foreign to the outlook of the solemn, straitlaced young man who was now heir to the throne and in due course was created Prince of Wales. How much he loathed it was known only to himself but his disapproval was evident when he came himself to preside over the English court. He was, however, a dutiful son. Prince Henry, with very much a mind of his own, had been openly scornful of his father's habits and policies and established his own court where the monarch was freely criticized. Prince Charles, on the other hand, regarded his parents with filial respect, and however much he may have deplored their way of life it would have violated his conscience to show his feelings.

In any case there was genuine affection between the remaining members of the royal family, however much they differed in temperament. King James was a doting father and sentimental by nature, but he may even have felt some secret relief at the death of his magnificent elder son, who from early years had tended to overawe him. His new heir was more malleable; he could fuss over him and continue to treat him as a child. To the end of his own life he addressed his son as 'Baby Charles'.

So the Prince, always reserved and decorous, became less lonely, blossoming in his father's love. His relations with his mother had always been good, and after the death of his brother and the departure of his sister, to whom Queen Anne had also been devoted, she clung to her surviving son with a possessiveness which led to recriminations between her and his father. Relations between King and Queen had deteriorated with the years. James's homosexuality and Anne's Catholicism were naturally bones of contention, while James, deeply intellectual, had a poor opinion of his frivolous wife's mental capacity. In the circumstances it was perhaps surprising that they tolerated each other's foibles to the extent that they did. Both were warm-hearted and easy-going, and in spite of disputes over which should exercise the greater influence on the young prince they tended to come closer together once more in the later years of the Queen's life.

One effect of Prince Charles's growing participation in public life was that he now developed what was to prove one of his paramount interests, and one which he could pursue without fear of friction with either of his parents. This was the collection of works of art and the cultivation of artists, which was in due course to give him lasting fame as the greatest of English royal connoisseurs, on a level with such lavish patrons as Francis I of France and his own contemporary Philip IV of Spain.

James I's cultural interests were primarily literary. He was the most intellectual of all British monarchs, himself the author of a number of books; he was no mean poet, and his prose works were of genuine merit. At the same time he was not without interest in the visual arts. There was little of consequence in the way of native painting in England before the eighteenth century, apart from the peculiarly English product of the miniature; but Henry VIII had established a tradition of encouragement of foreign painting by his patronage of Hans Holbein. This tradition was pursued by James I, who was responsible for the introduction into England of a number of artists from the Low Countries; notable among them were Paul van Somer, Abraham van Blijenberch and Daniel Mytens, all of whom painted portraits of members of the British royal family, including Prince Charles himself.[3] At the same time the beginnings of a native tradition of painting can be discerned in the appearance of Cornelius Johnson, who was born in London, though of Dutch parentage and trained in Holland. All these artists were known at the English court at the time that Charles Prince of Wales was beginning to make his presence felt there.

Queen Anne's interest in artistic matters was greater than her husband's. She lacked his intellectual capacity, but she was a woman of taste and discernment; she was also, it may be added, as extravagant and as regardless of expense as was the King. Her prime interest was in jewellery, but more important for posterity was her passion for building. To her is due in considerable part the credit for the creation of beautiful houses in the Palladian style that is one of the glories of the seventeenth century. Above all she was the patron of the one indubitably great English artist of that period, the architect and designer Inigo Jones, himself an ardent disciple of Palladio. It was Jones, a titanic figure, who designed for her the Queen's House at Greenwich, to add to the palace buildings presented to her by the King. She never lived in it, as it was not completed in her lifetime; but it stands today as a monument to the taste of queen and architect alike.

When Inigo Jones, Surveyor of the King's Works and as such official architect to the Crown, was commissioned to build the Queen's House, he was already well known in the Jacobean court, and he had for many years been designing masques in which the Queen herself loved to appear as well as her ladies and courtiers. The masque was an importation from Italy. King James was hardly cosmopolitan by nature, though in his years in Scotland, where the 'Auld Alliance' was paramount, he studied French literature. In England there was more of a feeling for Italian culture. Jones had studied in Italy, and it was probably he who brought the idea of the masque to England. At any rate he was the leading figure in the production of a series of court masques which lasted through the reign of James I and into that of his son.

These productions—*The Masque of Blackness, The Masque of Hymen, The Masque of Beauty, The Queen's Masque* and others—were mostly staged in the Banqueting Hall of Whitehall Palace. They were lavish spectacles, of a literary and artistic standard that could not be equalled in the public theatres of the day. Not only was the incomparable Jones the designer of the scenery and costumes, but the words of most of the masques were written by Ben Jonson, who after Shakespeare's death was the country's leading poet and dramatist and even in the lifetime of his supreme contemporary ranked higher in public esteem. Jones and Jonson did not work harmoniously together. Both were strong characters, and each was jealous of the other. The dramatist, highly regarded by the King, thought it was the words that mattered in a masque; the designer, favourite of the Queen, was equally convinced that language was only an adjunct to his scenic masterpieces. But for many years their uneasy collaboration produced performances of grace and charm that few if any Italian courts could rival.[4]

How far the young Charles was influenced by his father's literary interests is uncertain. He was far from being James's intellectual equal, and there is no evidence that he set much store by the royal scholastic output, though one of the King's books, *Basilikon Doron*, instructions on kingship originally written for Prince Henry, was certainly required reading for the new heir. Nor does it appear that he had shared the general admiration for Ben Jonson. It is worth mentioning here, however, that at the end of Charles I's tragic life a book, *Eikon Basilike*, was to appear in his name which could challenge comparison with anything his father wrote. Controversy, however, has raged ever since on whether or not he had any real hand in its composition.

There is no such doubt of his appreciation of the artistic aspects of the court life of his parents. Here he was in his element. There might be a leaven of vulgarity in court ceremonial with which he was out of sympathy, but the beauty of the masques and the works of the court painters appealed as much to his aesthetic sensibilities as the stately homes that were going up under the influence of Queen Anne and Inigo Jones.

Apart from the Prince's parents there was another considerable artistic influence on him, that of the Earl of Arundel. Thomas Howard, the head of the most important clan in England after the royal family, was the grandson of that Duke of Norfolk who had been executed in 1572 for high treason, having been involved in the intrigues of Mary Queen of Scots. Thomas would himself have held that dukedom had it not been for the attainder passed on his grandfather. He was a proud, aloof figure, intensely conscious of his position at the head of the English aristocracy. He took little part in politics, his interests lying purely in the realms of art and culture; a young man at the accession of King James, he became the greatest art collector of the Jacobean age. At the same time, while his wealth and influence enabled him to form a magnificent collection of priceless pictures, he was somewhat indiscriminate in his taste, amassing a conglomeration of foreign and venerable curios not always remarkable for their artistic value.

Arundel's most ardent pupil was Henry Prince of Wales. That versatile prince included the appreciation of art among his innumerable interests and began to form a collection of his own. He might indeed have become himself the foremost royal connoisseur of Europe; as it was, his early death meant the passing of his mantle to his younger brother. Charles inherited the elder prince's collection, to which he went on adding, with a taste and discrimination all his own, till the political troubles began which were to lead him to the scaffold. Prince Henry was his predecessor and Thomas Howard his mentor. His patronage extended to all the countries of Europe, and his interests embraced the greatest names of the cultural world; his artistic programme, 'which he may be said to have taken over from the Earl of Arundel, was to align and marry the tradition of art in Britain to the European tradition. In this he succeeded and British painting has never been the same again.'[5]

Surrounded by such influences, Prince Charles grew to manhood. He remained shy and reserved, always unsure of himself. But he had found one overriding interest in life. He studied politics and prepared, as befitted the heir to the throne, for the day when he would be called to take his place at the head of the nation. But it was in art and outward beauty that his deepest instincts found fulfilment.

As he approached his twentieth year, a new influence entered his life. It was King James's regrettable habit to heap his favours on young men whose only attribute was the possession of good looks. Having established a favourite, he would load him with wealth and honours and allow him a position in the affairs of the country to which his qualities in no way entitled him. For some years the reigning minion was Robert Carr, a graceless youth whom the King created Earl of Somerset. But in 1616 Somerset became involved in a particularly unsavoury murder case, the victim being Sir Thomas Overbury who had opposed the earl's marriage to Frances Howard, daughter of the Earl of Suffolk. James saved his favourite from the block, but the tremendous scandal forced him to banish him from his presence. He had to look around for a successor, and he quickly found one in an altogether more formidable figure, George Villiers.

Villiers, the son of an obscure Leicestershire knight, was all that King James looked for in a protégé. He was tall, graceful, an Adonis in form and feature. He had all the desired social attributes; he danced beautifully, he was a fine horseman and an expert swordsman; he was musical and his manners were perfect. His mental qualities were not equal to those of his body, but he was reasonably intelligent and a good talker. He had no sense of money values, his extravagance matching that of the King. His judgement in public affairs was negligible; he was guilty on a number of occasions of almost criminal irresponsibility, and in the long run his career was politically disastrous for England. Yet he was not devoid of finer qualities. He was good-hearted, open and generous. He had public spirit, and while his mediocre mind led him into stupid errors he was a patriot at heart. Above all, he was a genuine connoisseur and a patron of art; the wealth his sovereign lavished on him enabled him to become the third great collector of the era, inferior only to Lord Arundel and Prince Charles.

George Villiers first appeared at court in 1614, at the age of twenty-two, impecunious but assisted by the intrigues of an ambitious widowed mother. His physical beauty immediately attracted the attention of the King, as Lady Villiers had intended it should, and when the fall of Somerset occurred two years later the young courtier was ready to take his place. From then on his rise was meteoric. In 1616, already a Gentleman of the Bedchamber, he was appointed to the important household office of Master of the Horse, given the Garter and created Viscount Villiers. In the following year James made him Earl of Buckingham, and two years later Marquess. Before the end of the reign he had reached the highest rank in the peerage.

James made no bones about his devotion to the young upstart—though the late Archbishop Mathew, an exceptionally acute historian, expressed the opinion that his 'relations with his last favourite were technically innocent.'[6] The King had always been addicted to caressing his minions in public; now, as he approached a premature senility, his behaviour became more nauseating than ever. Always fond of pet names, he called his new favourite 'Steenie',[7] slobbered over him at court, and wrote to him as his 'sweetheart' and his 'sweet and dear child'.

This conduct was not calculated to please the puritanical heir to the throne, and at first Prince Charles was understandably revolted. But Steenie Buckingham had a charm of his own, and with an eye to the future he set himself to win the friendship of the young man who would one day be his sovereign. Charles was an impressionable youth, and he was not proof against the blandishments of the now accomplished courtier, some eight years his senior. A point of contact was their mutual enthusiasm for art, of which Buckingham made the most. Once the defences of the enemy were dented, progress was rapid. By the early 1620s the Prince of Wales was almost as much the slave of the Marquess of Buckingham as was his father.

In March 1619 Prince Charles lost his mother. Anne of Denmark had been for the last few years an invalid, suffering increasingly from dropsy. She had remained devoted to her surviving son, and he was with her when she died at Hampton Court.

Her death left him closer than ever to Buckingham. It was becoming more evident with the years that the Prince was one who always tended to lean on some personality stronger than his own—a tendency that had its roots in his uncertain and unhealthy childhood. Queen Anne was not herself a particularly strong character, but she had a will of her own and she served her turn in this respect. Latterly at least she had probably more influence on Charles than had his father, who was sinking into maudlin sentimentality. He doted now on his 'Baby Charles', but it was a sickly and tearful doting and it exasperated the young man who would have welcomed the domination of a more forceful parent. Buckingham was able to exert his influence over both father and son, and so far as Charles was concerned he took the place of that revered elder brother who had died seven years before.

Yet Buckingham was not enough. He was a friend and a mentor, but nothing more; unlike his father Prince Charles had no trace of homosexuality in his make-up. He needed a feminine confidante to whom he could entrust his innermost thoughts, and as he was too virtuous to take a mistress it is plain that, consciously or unconsciously, he yearned for matrimony. This in any case was his clear destiny. It was his dynastic duty to marry, and the King and his ministers were busy seeking a bride for him. There were a number of candidates available; most of them were Catholic, but though the British people would have preferred a Protestant the matter did not worry the King, with his Stuart tolerance and his wish to bring all shades of opinion within his orbit.

For a time the favourite candidate was Christina, sister of the French King Louis XIII. As a small child she had been proposed as a bride for Prince Henry, and after his death, when a French alliance was still favoured, King James considered her for his second son. But international politics diverted his mind into other channels.

Princess Elizabeth's marriage to the Elector Palatine Frederick V, which at the time seemed to be of little diplomatic consequence, had proved to be one of the most momentous events of the century, with political and religious repercussions which involved England in continental affairs at the time of one of the greatest cataclysms of European history.

The spark that was to set the greater part of Europe aflame was lit in Bohemia, a far-away country of which the English in general knew nothing. The Bohemian monarchy was elective, but in the early years of the seventeenth century the crown was somewhat uneasily worn by the Holy Roman Emperor, ruling from Vienna. The Empire was Catholic, but there was a strong Protestant movement in Bohemia and the danger of revolt was ever present. In 1617 the elderly and ailing Emperor Matthias, hoping to ensure a peaceful succession, abdicated the Bohemian throne and arranged for the election of his cousin the Archduke Ferdinand of Styria, the accepted heir to the Empire. Matthias had been an easy and a tolerant ruler, but Ferdinand was fiercely Catholic and his election was the signal for the Protestants of Bohemia to throw off the imperial yoke and assert their independence. The result of their action was the prolonged and bloodthirsty struggle known as the Thirty Years War.

The war, at first of a local character, broke out in 1618. The following year Matthias died, and Ferdinand was duly elected Emperor; the imperial election had become a formality, and the crown was in effect hereditary in the Habsburg family. In the meantime Ferdinand's rule had been repudiated in Bohemia, and the Protestant party were looking for a new king. They decided on King James of England's son-in-law, the Elector Palatine, whose father, the Elector Frederick IV, had been the acknowledged leader of the Protestant princes of Germany.

Frederick's wisest friends—and they included his shrewd old father-in-law—were opposed to his accepting so dangerous an assignment. The Emperor was already in arms, and the chances that the Bohemian rebels could defeat the forces of Austria were poor. To the Protestants of Germany, however, it was a glorious challenge, and their enthusiasm (unsupported by adequate military backing) spread to England. The fascinating Princess Elizabeth was still a heroine to her father's subjects, and when her husband was threatened by the hated papist powers they shouted for a holy war. Their clamour was championed by Prince Charles and Buckingham. The Prince had always a romantic devotion to the sister whom he had last seen at her marriage and was destined never to see again. Buckingham saw in a Protestant crusade a chance to recapture his waning popularity.

Fired by all this mainly vocal support, and inspired with the thought of acquiring a genuine crown, the Elector Palatine, young and inexperienced as he was, accepted the Bohemian offer. He and his princess travelled in state to Prague and after a form of election were crowned. For a brief period they reigned in triumph.

Disaster was not long in following. The Emperor moved at his leisure, and in November 1620 the 'Winter King' of Bohemia was defeated at the Battle of the White Mountain and ignominiously ejected from Prague. Worse was to follow. The imperial forces, supported by Spanish and Bavarian, overran the Palatinate, and Frederick, having lost his elective crown, was deprived of his hereditary dominions as well. Henceforth the Winter King and Queen, with their ever growing family, were wandering exiles dependent on the charity of friends and relations.

King James, already losing his grip on affairs, was in a sad quandary. He had dreamed of being the arbiter of Europe, the architect of international peace. For this purpose he had made overtures to Spain, which since the previous century had been regarded as the inevitable foe of Great Britain. He was already contemplating a Spanish marriage for his son; the French Christina, whose candidacy had never been taken very seriously in Paris, had become the Duchess of Savoy. But now his subjects were demanding war against the Habsburg powers, Austria and Spain. The King was forced to temporize. He agreed to send an English force to fight for Frederick in the Palatinate. It was small, and it achieved nothing. But King James's dreams of peace were blighted. Moreover, to pay for the venture, he was forced to call a parliament; and parliaments had a habit of thwarting the royal aims.

For the time being the King had his way. Parliament would have liked a Protestant marriage for the Prince of Wales, but it was still recognized that such matters were part of the royal prerogative. James's solution was a different one. He was genuinely anxious to help his daughter and son-in-law, and still more to appear to be doing so; but he clung to his ideal of European peace. If, he thought, he pressed on with the Spanish alliance, the King of Spain might be induced to intercede with his Austrian cousin and bring about the restoration of at least the Palatine lands of the Elector. There was a suitable Spanish princess available, the Infanta Maria Anna, the young sister of King Philip IV.

Charles was happy to fall in with his father's plans, provided there was a chance of their providing help for his sister. For himself he was ready to fall in love with any prospective bride who might be suggested. As for Buckingham, that all-powerful favourite never had any consistent policy; he had been attacked in the new parliament and was prepared to back any line that was opposed to that of his critics.

The outcome of the royal designs was the musical-comedy journey of Charles and Buckingham to Madrid. The idea would appear to have originated in the fertile brain of the Spanish Ambassador to England, Don Diego Sarmiento de Acuna, Conde de Gondomar, one of the ablest diplomats of his age. He had acquired a considerable ascendancy over the mind of King James, and his overriding aim, which he constantly urged on both his own and the British monarch, was to bring England into the Spanish and Catholic camp. He worked assiduously to conclude the projected marriage, hoping that thereby Prince Charles might be induced to change his faith and that under a Catholic sovereign the penal laws would be abolished and England brought into the orbit of the Spanish and Austrian Habsburgs.

Gondomar, for all his astuteness, underestimated both the strength of English Protestantism and the Prince's personal devotion to the Church of England. But the return of England to the Roman fold always seemed a possibility to the Catholic powers of seventeenth-century Europe. Spanish manoeuvres, however, have never been remarkable for speed, and Gondomar found his designs for a momentous diplomatic revolution hampered by procrastination in Madrid. In these circumstances he instigated in the mind of Prince Charles the notion of taking the matter into his own hands and wooing the Infanta in person.

The Prince seized on the idea with avidity. Some thirty years earlier, King James in an uncharacteristic gesture had himself set out from Scotland to fetch the Princess Anne from her native Scandinavia. To emulate his father and bring back his own Iberian bride appealed to the most romantic instincts in the young man's nature.

To the King the plan was less appealing. In spite of his wish for an alliance, Spain was to him a sinister and mysterious land, and he feared his son might be kidnapped or held as hostage. The thought of losing Baby Charles, to say nothing of the beloved Steenie, who was determined to go with the Prince, obsessed him to the point of tears.

Buckingham, however, had been carried away with the idea of the Spanish adventure, and the King was as wax in the hands of his favourite. In February 1623 the Prince and the Marquess set off from Dover in highly publicized secrecy. They wore false beards and called themselves Jack and Tom Smith. Riding through France, where their transparent incognito was diplomatically respected, they reached Madrid on 7 March.

Their arrival embarrassed the Spanish authorities. Nevertheless the courtly King Philip was equal to the occasion. He received the pilgrims with grave dignity, and despite the rigid etiquette of the Spanish court Prince Charles was even allowed brief meetings with the Infanta, a sweet and lovely girl, with whom he immediately declared himself passionately in love. The masquerade was solemnly played out. Negotiations for the marriage were elaborately initiated, but as the months passed it gradually became clear that the Spaniards were not really interested. A dispensation was procured from Rome, but with conditions that would plainly be unacceptable. Not only was Maria to have complete freedom for the public exercise of her religion, with members of her household nominated by the King of Spain, but the Catholic body in England were to be granted open toleration. King James was to ask his parliament to repeal the penal laws under which that body suffered. However laudable such measures might be, there was not the slightest chance that, in the political and religious climate of England, they could be put into operation; and the Spanish government, in which the Conde-Duque Olivares was the leading figure, knew perfectly well that this was so. Gondomar's dream of Charles himself becoming a Catholic was tacitly ignored.

The solemn farce was protracted for six months, with Buckingham in particular becoming increasingly disillusioned. For Charles, however, whatever the political and matrimonial disappointments, the time spent in Madrid was not wasted. He was enchanted with the stately ceremonial of the Spanish court, which contrasted so glaringly with the sleaziness now pervading that of King James. Bishop Burnet summed it all up long afterwards. Prince Charles, he wrote, 'was much offended with king James's light and familiar way, which was the effect of hunting and drinking, on which occasions he was very apt to forget his dignity, and to break out into great indecencies: on the

other hand the solemn gravity of the court of Spain was more
suited to his own temper, which was sullen even to moroseness.' [8]
The foundations of the dignified court of Charles I were laid
during the Spanish visit of 1623.

More important still, from the point of view of Prince
Charles's cultural development, was the aesthetic aspect of
Spanish court life. Philip IV, an artist himself, ranks high in the
list of royal connoisseurs, enjoying as he did the wealth that
enabled him to indulge his tastes to the full. He was at this time
only eighteen years old, five years younger than his English
guest. He had succeeded his father, Philip III, two years before,
and was already adding to the splendid collection of pictures
accumulated by his Habsburg and Burgundian ancestors.
Velázquez, most illustrious of Spanish artists, was his court
painter.

Philip, moreover, was a most generous host. Prince Charles
during his visit received many valuable gifts, but no other
reached the level of the painting known as *The Venus of Pardo*,
which the Spanish monarch presented to him from among his
superb collection of Titians. This present enhanced Charles's
interest in the great Venetian master, who became his favourite
painter, and inspired him on this same visit to purchase the
Titian portrait of King Philip's ancestor the Emperor Charles
V. These were only two of the pictures he was able to take home
with him to England; they included also a sketch of himself
painted by Velázquez and a portrait by Bartolomé Gonzales of
his intended bride, the Infanta Maria.

Charles feasted his eyes on the treasures of Madrid, acquiring
a new knowledge of the great painters of Europe, particularly
Titian. Nor was it only in the capital that he added to his artistic
education. He visited other cities, including Valladolid where
he saw pictures by Raphael and Michelangelo.

It was this that made the protracted visit worth while. In the
realm of public affairs it was a story of failure and frustration. As
time went on it became evident that the Spaniards had no
intention of helping the Elector, did not want the English
marriage to take place, and were simply spinning out time with
characteristic courtesy; it was already virtually decided that
Maria would eventually marry within the Habsburg circle. On
the Spanish side it was soon realized that there was not the

slightest chance of Prince Charles embracing the Catholic faith.

In the circumstances it was only a matter of time before the whole venture was abandoned. Charles decided that he was not in love after all, Buckingham antagonized his hosts by quarrelling irresponsibly with Olivares, and at last, to the relief of the Spaniards, the two young men left for home, loaded with gifts and fêted to the last.

They were received in London with tremendous enthusiasm. The very idea of a Spanish alliance had always been unpopular, and the reaction to its collapse was frenzied delight. Charles was received as a conquering hero, and Buckingham, not hitherto loved by the commonalty, shared in the triumph. As for King James, who had conferred a dukedom on the favourite during his absence, he fell on his two 'sweet boys' with lachrymose delight. He had been reiterating with tearful lamentation that he would never see them again.

The national euphoria was accompanied by a jingoist bellicosity such as from time to time engulfs the people of Britain. Spain, the perfidious popish power, had tricked the English prince, abandoned his sister to her fate, and plotted to undermine his country's religion. Only war against the powers of evil would satisfy the popular conscience.

The Duke of Buckingham fell in with the national clamour, and under his all-pervading influence the Prince of Wales joined the warmongers. The King gave up the struggle. He had not changed his views, but he was rapidly sinking towards the grave. He could not resist the combined pressure of his son and his favourite; nor did he try to do so. At their insistence a new parliament was called in February 1624 (the last one had been quickly dissolved), and in his last extremity King James gave up his cherished right of retaining in his own hands the conduct of foreign policy. He asked for the advice of the House of Commons, and the result was the declaration of a totally futile and unnecessary war against Spain.

King James made, indeed, one feeble protest which was at least prophetic. Having been bullied into taking this final, fatal step, he turned on his son and heir, telling him that he would 'live to have his bellyful of Parliaments'.[9]

James VI and I died at his country house, Theobalds, on 27

March, 1625. He was only fifty-eight, but an old man in all but years. He had to all intents abdicated; the reign of Charles I began in effect from the moment he returned from Spain.

Charles was still unmarried; but he was not to remain so for long. During his journey through France on their way to Spain in 1623 the Prince and Buckingham had stopped in Paris, and in their transparent disguise had entered a gallery where they could watch a masque being rehearsed by members of the French court. Among the dancers was the thirteen-year-old sister of King Louis XIII, the Princess Henrietta Maria.

This was Charles's first sight of his future wife. Her elder sister Christina was now out of the running, and when the match with the Infanta fell through, and an alliance with France once more became desirable, it was proposed to marry the Prince to the younger French princess. Such was the position when King Charles succeeded to his father's throne. This time there was no hitch. Two months after King James's death a marriage ceremony by proxy took place at the Cathedral of Notre Dame in Paris. Early in June 1625 the new sovereign rode to Dover to meet his bride.

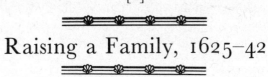

2

Raising a Family, 1625–42

The first meeting of the new King of Great Britain and his young French bride was described in detail by their contemporaries. 'She arrived at Dover on Sunday, about eight in the evening,' wrote one, 'lay there in the castle that night, whither the king rode on Monday morning from Canterbury, came thither after ten of the clock, and she being at meat, he stayed in the presence till she had done, which she advertised of, made short work, rose, went unto him, kneeled down at his feet, took and kissed his hand. The king took her up in his arms, kissed her, and talking with her, cast down his arms towards her feet (she, seeming higher than her height was, reaching to his shoulder,) which she soon perceiving, discovered and showed him her shoes, saying to this effect: "Sir, I stand upon mine own feet; I have no helps by art. Thus high I am, and am neither higher nor lower."' [1]

Henrietta, then, was a tiny princess. Charles I was a small man; his height has been estimated at between five foot and five foot four inches. Yet his child-bride came up only to his shoulder. The scene thus sketched of their meeting, corroborated by other eye-witnesses, shows her also to have been a child in mentality, warm, impulsive, anxious to please, naïvely conscious of her smallness but at the same time eager to measure up to the requirements of her solemn and stately young bridegroom.

The bridal pair dined together, and, after a second wedding ceremony, supped at Canterbury. There, says another correspondent, 'her majesty went to bed, and, some time after, his majesty followed her; but, being entered her bed-chamber, the first thing he did, he bolted all the doors round about, being seven, with his own hand, letting in but two of his bed-chamber to undress him, which being done, he bolted them out also. The next morning, he lay till seven o'clock, and was pleasant with the lords, that he had beguiled them, and hath ever since been very jocund.'[2]

On 16 June, while the bells rang and bonfires blazed in the streets, Charles and Henrietta rode to Gravesend, and from there went by river to London; on their way the Queen 'had the beautiful and stately view of part of our navy that is to go to sea, which gave her a volley of fifteen hundred great shot'.[3] At Whitehall Palace a sumptuous wedding feast was held, and on Tuesday, 21 June, 'was the marriage confirmed, declared to be lawfully and fully consummated, and the queen proclaimed queen'.[4]

Such was the official proclamation. Whether or not the marriage had been physically consummated must be left to the imagination. Henrietta Maria was only fifteen, and it was to be some years yet before she presented her husband with the first of their children.

The first meeting of the royal pair and its immediate aftermath present an idyllic scene of concord and hope—the union of two young people of worth and vitality eager to join with each other in shaping a new age. It was not long, however, before clouds began to gather and personal clashes to show that bridegroom and bride were not so closely attuned as each would have liked to believe.

The first cause of friction was religion, aggravated by Anglo-French differences. It was the religious question that first and foremost had led to the breakdown of the Spanish marriage project, and it was hoped that such difficulties would be obviated now. The marriage treaty had been negotiated rather hurriedly, and the details inadequately thought out; needless to say, this was largely the fault of Buckingham, who regarded the alliance with France as his brain-child and was out to brush aside all obstacles. Under the treaty Henrietta was to be allowed to bring with her a substantial French retinue, including a bishop and a quantity of priests. She was to have free exercise of her religion, with her own chapel in St James's, and King Charles promised for his part to alleviate the condition of his Catholic subjects, though what he was actually supposed to do in this direction was left conveniently vague.

It was hoped that concessions would smooth the way to an

amicable relationship. Contemporary observers thought it likely that in due course the King would be able to bring his bride into the communion of the Church of England. After all, she was the daughter of Henry of Navarre, who had not scrupled to change from Protestant to Catholic when this facilitated his succession to the French throne. One correspondent reported that, 'being asked, not long since, if she could abide an Huguenot, "Why not", said she; "was not my father one?"'[5]

It quickly became clear that such an idea was wishful thinking. Henrietta Maria, who soon showed that she was a wilful young lady who would never submit meekly to her husband's wishes, was in fact as fervent a Catholic as any Spanish infanta could be. Moreover, young and inexperienced as she was, she leaned heavily not only on her spiritual advisers but also on the older attendants of her own race, particularly the women, who had come with her from France.

There had been minor trouble even before the couple left Canterbury. It was concerned with questions of etiquette, always sources of dissension in the seventeenth century. The haughty French ladies were touchy over what they considered their right to proper precedence, and one in particular, Madame St George who had been one of Henrietta's gover-nesses, was furiously affronted when refused a place in the royal carriage which she claimed had been promised her by the Queen Mother of France.

Worse was to follow. The chapel at St. James's had been designed by Inigo Jones for the Infanta, and when the Spanish marriage faded out of the picture the work on building it was stopped. It was not yet ready for worship, and the Queen's priests—Oratorians under the leadership of the Bishop of Mende—made the unreadiness a grievance and protested that this and other articles of the treaty were not being observed. 'The Fathers of the Oratory, on their arrival in London,' wrote the Capuchin Father Cyprien de Gamache, a life-long attend-ant on Henrietta Maria and her family, 'were lodged in the suburb of St James, in sight of the royal residence, to which access was not obtained of the sentries without extreme difficulty by the Catholics, who repaired thither to attend divine service.'[6]

King Charles did what he could to keep the peace. At the

same time he was determined to be master in his own house, and in general the weight of his authority was exercised against the clerics and the Frenchwomen. Henrietta came ardently to their defence, and the result was the increasing estrangement of the royal couple, with tears and tantrums on Henrietta's side, dignified but angry recriminations on Charles's, and open quarrels that were often manifested in public. The climax came with the King's Coronation on Candlemas Day, 2 February 1626, when the Queen refused to be crowned in an Anglican ceremony or even to be present in Westminster Abbey.

King Charles's married life was becoming a burden to him, and the relations between him and his wife were approaching hatred. For it all he blamed the 'monsieurs', as he collectively dubbed the French attendants, clerical and lay, male and female. At last he decided that he could stand it no longer.

Before taking action he confided in his beloved friend. To Steenie Buckingham, who was about to visit France, he wrote on 20 November 1625:

I wrote to you by Ned Clarke that I thought I would have cause enough in short time to put away the monsieurs, either by attempting to steal away my wife, or by making plots with my own subjects. For the first, I cannot say certainly whether it was intended, but I am sure that it is intended; for the other, though I have good grounds to believe it, and am still hunting after it, yet seeing the maliciousness of the monsieurs, by making and fomenting discontentments in my wife, I could tarry no longer from advertising of you, that I mean to seek for no other grounds to cashier my monsieurs, having for this purpose sent you this other letter that you may, if you think good, advertise the Queen Mother with my intention; for this being an action that may have a show of hardness; I thought it was fit to take this way, that she to whom I have had many obligations may not take it unkindly, and likewise I think I have done you no wrong in my letter, though in some place I may seem to chide you. I pray you send me word with what speed you may, whether you like this course or not, for I shall put nothing of this in execution until I hear from you; in the meantime, I shall think of the convenient means to do this business with the best mind, but I am resolute; it must be done, and that shortly.[7]

The 'other letter' was a more diplomatically worded missive to the same effect, intended for the eyes of Henrietta's mother, Marie de Medici, widow of that Henry of Navarre who had become King Henry IV of France. It alluded to 'the unkind usages of my wife', but emphasized Charles's belief 'that it was not in her nature, but made by ill instruments'. The King underlined his obligations to Queen Marie, but the letter continued: 'You must, therefore, advertise my mother-in-law, that I must remove all those instruments that are causes of unkindness between her daughter and me, few or none of the servants being free of this fault in one kind or other; therefore I would be glad that she might find a means to make themselves suitors to be gone.'[8] Otherwise he would himself have to get rid of them.

Whatever remonstrances Buckingham may have made to the Queen Mother, they did not induce her to take the initiative in recalling the monsieurs to France. Marie de Medici was a formidable lady to whom it was not easy to dictate. The Duke might perhaps have done better with a younger queen, Louis XIII's wife Anne of Austria, to whom he had already paid court with a brazen openness that had caused scandal throughout France.

At the English court matters dragged on miserably till the summer of 1626. On 12 July Charles wrote a long letter to Buckingham detailing all his grievances against his wife and her followers, including the conduct of Madame St George. He reiterated his intention of throwing the monsieurs out, and charged his friend with the duty of telling both Marie de Medici and her son King Louis.

A month later he acted. Once again he made Buckingham his agent, sending him on 7 August a letter the uncharacteristic tone of which shows the extent of his exasperation:

I have received your letter by Dick Graem. This is my answer. I command you send all the French away to-morrow out of the town. If you can, by fair means (but stick not long in disputing), otherwise force them away; driving them away like so many wild beasts, until you have shipped them; and so the devil go with them! Let me hear no answer but of the performance of my command. So I rest

    Your faithful, constant, loving friend,

       Charles R.[9]

The King's peremptory orders were carried out, and the monsieurs were sent packing. There were of course violent repercussions, but not in the international context. Marie de Medici sent letters of pain and distress to her daughter, but Louis XIII and Cardinal Richelieu, who as his chief minister was the real ruler of France, were too busy with internal affairs to bother much about the grievances of the King's sister; they wanted the matter smoothed out as easily as possible.

It was in London that the fur flew. The Bishop of Mende, an arrogant young noble who had displayed a lack of tact throughout these sad events, protested that he was entitled to diplomatic privileges and could not leave unless King Louis sent for him; he was hustled out of the country just the same. Henrietta, who was left with three priests and half a dozen French attendants, wept so much that it was feared she would cry herself to death. It was even said that she put her fist through a glass window in her rage against the King. 'The women howled and lamented, as if they had been going to execution, but all in vain; for the yeomen of the guard . . . thrust them and all their country folk out of the queen's lodgings, and locked the doors after them.'[10]

The King, however, had acted wisely and chosen his moment well. Louis sent Marshal the Duc de Bassompière, a charming and accomplished soldier and diplomat, to London as Ambassador Extraordinary to straighten out the affair, and under his amiable influence the Queen calmed down. The way was open for the ultimate reconciliation of Charles and Henrietta.

The time when that should come, however, was not yet. Bassompière did his work well, bringing all his worldly wisdom to bear on the task of bringing the King and Queen together. He did not find it easy, for though Henrietta ceased to rage she did not cease to sulk. She was still only sixteen, self-centred and high-spirited, and she was not prepared to accept defeat with humility.

Relations between the royal couple appeared as bad as ever, if not worse. There had been two main causes of the estrangement. One had been the presence of the monsieurs, with all that it entailed. That had been disposed of. The second cause, perhaps the more potent of the two, remained. It was George Villiers, Duke of Buckingham.

Henrietta Maria had first met Buckingham in 1625 when King Charles had, inevitably, made him his agent in bringing his bride to England. It was at this time that that ineffable courtier had involved himself in a scandal touching the highest circles in France. He had already paid court to the Queen, Anne of Austria, and there were at least rumours that the attentions of the handsome Englishman had not been unwelcome. Now, in the course of the journey, he behaved with an indiscretion that only he could have achieved. Making an excuse to leave Henrietta at Boulogne, he dashed back to Amiens, where Queen Anne had parted with her sister-in-law; there he evaded the guards, forced his way into her bedroom, and declared his passion. He was repulsed, though some court gossips thought otherwise; and the scandal was hushed up as far as it could be.[11] Henrietta, however, soon heard all about it from her friend the Duchesse de Chevreuse.

The effect of such a revelation on the young girl, strictly brought up in morals and manners, can be imagined. She was impressed by Buckingham's magnificence and his courtly elegance, but a smouldering resentment that a man capable of such conduct should have been sent to conduct her to her husband remained.

In England he added to his irresponsibility. Secure in the confidence of his sovereign, he lost no chance of insulting that sovereign's bride, treating her as a child and lecturing her on how she should behave. It is clear that a real hatred sprang up between the two. Buckingham wanted no rival in Charles's affections and did what he could to aggravate the royal differences. Henrietta for her part bitterly resented her husband's dependence on his favourite. Buckingham had been chosen to bring her to England, a mission of which he had proved himself patently unworthy. It was his counsel, not hers, which influenced King Charles on every conceivable question. Buckingham had been Charles's adviser in the matter of her own attendants, and now it was he who was given the task of expelling them from England. He was all-powerful in politics, invincible in his arrogant power, and an object of impotent loathing to the frustrated queen.

The climax came in the summer of 1627 when Buckingham forced England into a senseless war with France, Henrietta's native and beloved country, to add to that with Spain which was still theoretically in being. The declared object was to assist the Huguenots of La Rochelle who were in revolt against King Louis. The real purpose, it was widely believed, was to provide naval and military glory for Buckingham.

The glory did not materialize. On 19 July Buckingham landed on the Ile de Ré with the design of relieving La Rochelle. The campaign that followed was an ignominious failure, though its commander behaved with personal gallantry. He came home with his tail between his legs.

He was received with derision by his countrymen at large, among whom his unpopularity was increasing. But the King held him in undiminished affection. Charles was delighted to have him back, and the favourite was once more completely in the royal confidence. He himself was resilient as always, and no improvement was discernible in his behaviour towards the Queen. A marital reconciliation seemed as far off as ever. But a *deus ex machina* was at hand. His name was John Felton.

Unperturbed by his failure, though concerned at the attacks made on him in Parliament, Buckingham planned a second expedition to relieve La Rochelle. On 23 August 1628, he was at Portsmouth preparing to embark when Felton, a disgruntled officer whose pay was in arrears, sprang on him as he came from his breakfast and stabbed him to the heart with a knife.

In a moment the great paladin who had been the virtual ruler of England for the past decade had disappeared from the scene. With all his splendour and charm and political ineptitude, his arrogance and elegance and generosity, he was no longer in being to delight his sovereign or plague his fellow-countrymen.

The effect of the murder on the relations between Charles I and his wife became apparent remarkably quickly. There had indeed been signs of a reconciliation during Buckingham's absence in 1627, but on his return there was a relapse. Now,

James I, by Mytens

Anne of Denmark,
by Marcus Gheeraerts

however, the whole situation changed, and it changed from one extreme to the other. King Charles was inconsolable when the news of his favourite's death reached him, but he found consolation almost at once, and found it in the most satisfactory place. Henrietta Maria was not always tactful, but on this occasion her conduct was above reproach. So far from gloating over the removal of her hated rival, she promptly and unequivocally expressed her grief not only to her husband but to the Villiers family. Charles was deeply touched; needing, as he always did, somebody to lean upon, he threw himself with love and gratitude into the arms of his wife.

Soon it was obvious to onlookers that the King and Queen, for the first time since their marriage three years before, were deeply and genuinely in love with one another. And it was not long before this new-found love bore fruit, though the first fruit failed to blossom. How far physical intimacy had already progressed was known only to the couple themselves; neither was of the type that parades the secrets of the bedroom. There had been rumours of a pregnancy before the death of Buckingham, but these were no more than court gossip. Now there was no doubt of the matter. At Christmas 1628 it was formally announced that the Queen was expecting a child.

The hopes were doomed to disappointment. The son that was so eagerly awaited was born prematurely at the Queen's palace at Greenwich in the early hours of 13 May 1629. So unexpected was the birth that no skilled medical care was available. The Greenwich town midwife, hurriedly sent for, 'swooned with fear as soon as she came into the queen's chamber, so as she was forced presently to be carried out'.[12] The baby was so small and puny that immediate baptism was thought necessary. Charles Duke of Cornwall, who if he had survived should have eventually succeeded to the throne, lived only for an hour.

Various causes were assigned to the disaster. In a news-letter sent from London to Sir Thomas Puckering the author wrote:

> . . . I can say no more of the cause thereof than, as the common report is, that she was frighted two or three days before with the fighting of two great dogs in her gallery, whereof the one belonged to my Lord of Dorchester, which is said to have come so near the queen, as that he did snatch at

her and pull her by the gown. Others say, that at her coming back by water from this town, where she had been about her devotions, by reason of the Ember-week, the Monday before, she making haste to rise from her seat at the landing afore the barge had touched the shore; the strength of that touch made her to bow backwards, as she rose upon her feet, that presently she felt a pain upon it which did not leave her till she was brought to bed. Others again impute it to the violence of her exercises, namely, her much walking and going up hill; and some will have this to be the more likely cause.[13]

One of these occurrencies may have been responsible for the tragedy. In any case the death of a newly-born baby, even in a royal family, was so frequent an event in that age that no prolonged distress was caused. Henrietta, now nineteen years old, was strong and buoyant; she soon recovered her strength and was ready for more child-bearing.

The birth of the second royal child took place almost exactly a year after that of the first. This time the circumstances were very different. During the fiasco of 1629 King Charles had been frantic with anxiety, continually hovering over the Queen and imploring their attendants to save her life at any cost. Now he made sure that nothing should go wrong if royal care could prevent it. Henrietta was pampered to a degree which would have seemed impossible a couple of years before. From the time when her pregnancy became certain she was provided with every possible medical attention, including that of Sir Theodore Mayerne, the most eminent physician of the day, who had ministered to both King James and Queen Anne. Marie de Medici was encouraged to send not only gifts but attendants to her daughter, who was even allowed the addition to her suite of ten French Capuchins to take the place of the expelled Oratorians. Their Superior was Father Leonard of Paris, and they included Father Cyprien de Gamache who in later years was to write the story of the mission.

On 29 May 1630, was born, in St James's Palace, the prince who was eventually to become King Charles II of Great Britain. He is reported to have been an ugly baby but, in contrast with his ill-fated elder brother, brimming over with health and vigour, large and strong and swarthy. On that afternoon King Charles rode to St Paul's to give thanks for the birth of an heir, and as he went a portent appeared in the heavens. A contemporary wrote:

> Prince *Charles* was borne, a little before one of the clock in the Afternoon; and the Bishop of *London* had the honour to see him before he was an hour old. At his Birth there appear'd a Star visible at that very time of the day, when the King rode to St Paul's Church, to give thanks to God, for the Queen's safe delivery of a Son. But this star then appearing, some say was the planet Venus; others Mercury, the Sign of *Merlin's* Prophecy. . . .[14]

The star was to become the symbol of the new prince's hope and glory. Thirty years later John Dryden, the leading poet of the age, was to write, in a paean apostrophizing the monarch newly restored to his father's throne, of 'that Star, that at your Birth shone out so bright, it stain'd the duller Suns Meridian light'.[15]

The birth of the new Duke of Cornwall marked the beginning of the happiest time in the lives of King Charles and Queen Henrietta Maria. The King had come truly into his own. Freed from the influence of Buckingham, he made peace with both Spain and France. The parliaments of his reign had been a continual thorn in his side, criticizing his policy and his choice of ministers and denying him money except on terms that he considered unacceptable. Now he decided that he could do without them. In March 1629 he had dissolved the third parliament of his reign and embarked on his eleven-year period of personal rule, during which, though perennially short of money, he valiantly endeavoured to 'live of his own'. For the moment at least he was eminently successful.

Domestically his bliss was complete. He had the complete love and trust of his wife, all trivial squabbles were at an end, and he was able to devote his attention to his cultural interests, to the development of his stately court, to music and to masques; above all to his incomparable art collection.

As for Henrietta, with the impetuous thoroughness of her nature she revelled in the new situation that had arisen. She now doted on her husband. 'A French Ambassador arrived in London', writes her best-known biographer, 'and sent home glowing descriptions of the King of England's devotion to his wife. Charles, after kissing Henrietta "a hundred times" in the course of an hour, said to the Marquis de Chateauneuf, "You do not see that in Turin, nor," lowering his voice, "in France." Henrietta, who confessed to the ambassador that she had felt a little jealous of her successful sister Christine, now courageously announced herself "Not only the happiest princess, but the happiest woman in the world."'[16]

It is the general view of historians that Charles I was without sexual experience when he married Henrietta; it is virtually certain that he was never unfaithful to her after they came together. From then on their relationship was mutually satisfying, and their love showed its fulfilment in the succession of children, not all equally healthy but on the whole above average, whose births followed that of the second Charles.

The next to be born was Mary, who first saw the light on 4 November 1631. Two years later came James, on 14 October 1633. He was followed after another two years by Elizabeth, born during a snowstorm on 28 December 1635. All these children were born in St James's Palace.

The four brothers and sisters, only five years separating the eldest from the youngest, were brought up very much together during their early years, and their parents lavished every possible care on their welfare. They moved in the stately ritual of the court between the royal residences of St James's, Whitehall, Greenwich and Richmond. The two girls were placed in the care of the Countess of Roxburgh as governess, but each had her own suite of attendants. Mary's consisted of a nurse, a lady of the bedchamber, a gentleman usher, three watchers, a physician, two pages of the backstairs, a sempstress, a laundress, a tailor and shoemaker, two grooms of the great chamber and one of the robes, five kitchen servants, four footmen, a coachman and a groom. When her education began the staff were joined by Monsieur d'Aranjou as French and writing master.

Meals were on a similar scale. A contemporary manuscript gives Mary's breakfast as fine bread, beer and ale, mutton or chicken. 'At dinner, the royal children sat at the same table, when Gascony wine, game and meats of different kinds, custard, pies, and tarts were their fare, with a slight change for fish days and fast days, on both of which they were still allowed the lighter meats. Their supper was an abridged edition of the dinner.'[17]

The fact that these small children throve on such fare is a tribute to their sturdiness. Mary was seriously ill at the age of a few weeks, but Dr Mayerne pulled her through. Otherwise the three eldest appear to have enjoyed excellent health. Elizabeth was less robust. She suffered from rickets, and the weakness in her legs was thought to be an inheritance from her father.

Charles, as the eldest son and the heir-apparent, naturally received the greatest attention. At first he was under the care of the Countess of Roxburgh; but Lady Roxburgh was a Catholic, and there were soon murmurings among influential Protestant circles. So when Princess Mary was born Charles was handed over to the impeccably Anglican Countess of Dorset, Lady Roxburgh being consoled for her dismissal by being put in charge of the baby princess.

Almost from the first Prince Charles was given his own miniature court at St James's, and by the time he was seven he had his governor and his tutor. The governor was William Cavendish, Earl of Newcastle, a splendid magnifico who could be described as the perfect courtier; skilled in all the accomplishments considered necessary for a gentleman, he was England's leading authority on horsemanship, while at the same time a devotee of poetry and music. Under his guidance the young prince quickly progressed in dancing, fencing, riding and all outdoor pursuits.

On the academic side he showed less enthusiasm. Scholarship was not in his line, and in this he never equalled his father, let alone his grandfather. Certainly he had every chance. His tutor was Dr Brian Duppa, Dean of Christ Church, Fellow of All Souls and soon to be Bishop of Chichester, a distinguished classicist at a time when classical scholarship was held to be the foundation of all knowledge. There is no evidence that Charles profited much from Duppa's labours, but he retained a deep affection for his tutor, as he did also for Newcastle.

His brother James, three years his junior, shared his education, while naturally playing second fiddle to the first-born. James was also a strong child, fair where his brother was dark and much better looking; he quickly became his mother's favourite. Little is known of the details of the education of the two brothers, but it appears that thus early they showed the widely different qualities that were to distinguish them throughout their lives. Charles was clever, quick-witted, but lazy, ready to dodge learning if he could. James was earnest, slow and stubborn, though also said to be gentler in his nature.

Elizabeth, the fourth of these four eldest children, shared the pursuits and training of her sister Mary, so far as the four-year differences in their ages and her own inferior health allowed. But she had her own suite of attendants, which included writing, music and dancing masters. Book learning was not considered of great importance for princesses at this time, less so apparently than in the previous century, when Lady Jane Grey and Elizabeth Tudor were brought up to a formidable standard of classical knowledge; Elizabeth Stuart, however, was to develop into the only intellectual of the family. Possibly her own infirmities, depriving her of her chance of outdoor activities, helped to incline her to studious pursuits.

More important than any formal education in the development of the royal children was the cultural atmosphere of the court in which they grew up. This was highly formal. The squalor and raffishness with which King James had delighted to surround himself was banished by his solemn and respectable son. Now everything was regulated according to a ceremonial ritual which made Whitehall as elegant a royal residence as any in Europe. 'From the Gentlemen of the Bedchamber to the waiters at the sideboard,' Dame Veronica Wedgwood has written, 'each man precisely knew where to be and when, at which table to take meat, when to attend prayers, when the King would rise, when sleep, when ride, when give audience, and who, with staff of office in hand or napkin on arm, should walk before him or stand behind his chair.'[18]

Such elaborate etiquette was of course a characteristic of royal courts. Philip IV's in Madrid was more formal still, and later in the century Louis XIV at Versailles was to bring the whole system to perfection. Where the court of Charles I particularly shone was as an artistic and intellectual centre. Here King Charles excelled Philip of Spain, who had indeed been one of his mentors, and in his personal artistic taste was the superior of the *Roi Soleil*. His own interests did not run notably towards literature, but poets and other writers found patronage from their sovereign and were themselves entertained by him. Music dominated the scene, and Inigo Jones's masques provided elegant and sophisticated spectacle. Nor were the sciences ignored; leading physicians such as Sir Theodore Mayerne and the eventually even more distinguished William Harvey, discoverer of the circulation of the blood, were to be seen in the royal presence.

It was, however, in the realm of the visual arts that Charles I outshone every monarch in English history, with few rivals among foreign sovereigns who were wealthier and had more opportunities. The collection inherited from his brother and developed during his father's reign now reached its glorious apogee.

Of his personal responsibility for assembling this splendid collection there can be no doubt. He of course had expert advisers, and his selection of such advisers is part of the merit of his achievement. Buckingham, who was a genuine connoisseur, and Arundel were among those who helped him. But all contemporaries were agreed on the King's taste and discrimination. Peter Paul Rubens, as fine a judge of such things as could be found in that age, described him as *'le prince le plus amateur de la peinture qui soit au monde'*.[19] The French word *amateur* implies a degree of taste and knowledge absent from its English adaptation. Concerning Whitehall the same illustrious Flemish artist said: 'When it comes to fine pictures I have never seen such a large number in one place as in the royal palace.'[20]

Rubens, as eminent a diplomat as he was a painter, was in England on an unofficial mission for King Philip (Flanders was a Spanish possession) in 1629–30. It was on this occasion that King Charles knighted him and commissioned him to design the vast allegorical painting which he had planned, as a memorial to his father, to decorate the ceiling of the new Banqueting House at Whitehall, recently completed by the inevitable Inigo Jones. This was Rubens's most important work in England, though naturally it was only partially painted by himself.

King Charles would have liked to make him his principal court painter, but Rubens, now in his fifties, was too much of a European, too important an international figure, to settle down as the servant of an English king. Instead the position went to a younger Fleming, Anthony Van Dyck.

The name of Van Dyck, who was one year older than his patron, is inseparably associated with the court of Charles I. What Velázquez was to King Philip, Van Dyck was to King Charles. He was not the great artist that the Spaniard was, but he was the most elegant of court painters, and his portraits have a charm and technical perfection which have seldom been equalled. He was undeniably a flatterer, here differing from Velázquez, and this must lead to wariness on the question of the actual looks of the King and Queen and members of their court. But few royal families have been so well served pictorially.

Van Dyck's time in England was short, for he was only forty-one when he died. But in the eight years or so that he spent in the country he was incessantly at work, most of the time on portraits. Among these, which give the court circle a lasting air of elegance, are several of the royal children. The most famous, one of those still in the royal collection, was painted in 1638 and shows the five eldest (the fifth, Princess Anne, was born in 1637). It is a striking and a richly coloured picture. Prince Charles occupies the centre. Clad in scarlet silk and delicate lace, he stands robust and self-confident, his left hand on the head of a mastiff which, docile under his touch, appears larger than himself. On the left of the picture stand Princess Mary, curly-haired and as pretty a child as the eye could wish to see, and Prince James in the feminine garments that younger boys were accustomed to wear. On the right the less spectacular Princess Elizabeth nurses her infant sister Anne.

Other fine continental artists made intermittent appearances at the King's court. Mytens was still painting; so was Cornelius Johnson. Alexander Keirincx, another Fleming known in England as Carings, worked for King Charles; others were the German Francis Klein and the Italian Orazio Gentileschi. There was still little sign of a genuine English tradition in painting, though William Dobson, 'the most distinguished purely British painter before Hogarth',[21] may have been at work in this period. His earliest known paintings date from a slightly later time. Only in the technique of the miniature are many native names to be found. Peter Oliver, son of the better-known Isaac Oliver, and John Hoskins found favour at court,

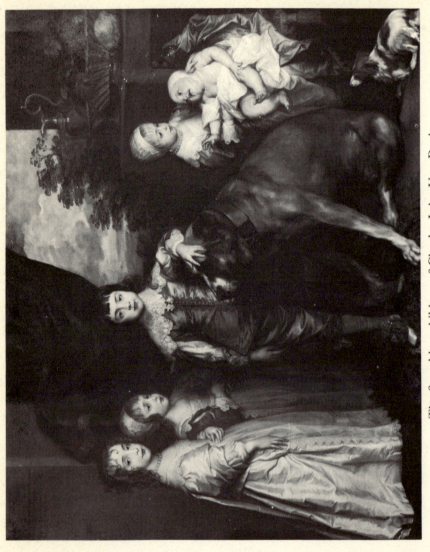

The five eldest children of Charles I, by Van Dyck

Charles I and Henrietta Maria dining in public, by Houckgeest

and at this time there first appeared Samuel Cooper, who in a long career was to eclipse them all.

The paintings owned by King Charles included selections from the works of most of the best-known artists of Europe. By 1630 he was the possessor of at least five Titians. Masterpieces by Raphael, Leonardo, Tintoretto and others of the great Italians also adorned his galleries. He had pictures by Dürer, Holbein, Rembrandt, Rubens and Velázquez. He scoured the Continent for additions to his collection. Buckingham had brought many to England, and the cosmopolitan collector Endymion Porter was also commissioned. Charles was never a rich monarch, but where pictures were concerned he was ready to spend the most his slender purse could afford, and his shrewd discrimination enabled him to get the best value for his money. His most spectacular purchase was of the entire collection of the Duke of Mantua, for which he paid £25,000 and which included, besides works by Titian, Raphael, Andrea del Sarto, Caravaggio and Correggio, the famous Mantegna paintings of 'The Triumph of Caesar'[22] still on display at Hampton Court.

Never had such artistic wealth been seen in England. These masterpieces adorned the walls of the various royal palaces— Hampton Court, Richmond, Nonsuch, Oatlands and the Queen's House at Greenwich, now completed by Inigo Jones; but the greater part were at the King's official residence, the straggling mass of buildings known as Whitehall, purloined a century before by Henry VIII from his over-mighty subject Cardinal Wolsey.

Such was the court in which King Charles's family grew up. It is not to be supposed that they were in daily sight of the masterpieces of European art. Royal children in the seventeenth century were not in constant contact with their parents, and the young Stuarts had courts of their own. Yet these too were Whitehalls in miniature, and the same aesthetic principles were followed. It is safe to assume that Prince Charles and his juniors found themselves ensconced in the artistic atmosphere of their royal parents. The influence of this heritage is intangible but was certainly considerable. None of the children ever possessed a knowledge of art comparable with that of Charles I, but the sense of culture and grace of manner that characterized all of them can be traced, at least in part, to the example presented by the cultivated court of Charles I.

The royal children passed a pleasant enough time in their early years, surrounded by luxury and by beauty and with a mother and father who, in contrast with many royal parents, were devoted to them, saw as much of them as they reasonably could, and watched over their welfare. They had their share of infant maladies, which in the age in which they lived meant considerable risk to their lives. At the age of three Prince Charles was seriously ill, as his sister Mary had been at an even tenderer age. It was apparently some sort of fever. His sturdy constitution pulled him through, not before great anxiety had been caused to his physicians and his parents. His experience left him with even more than the normal small boy's dislike of medicines, nauseous as those administered to him probably were. His mother's first letter to him reads:

> Charles, I am sore that I must begin my first Letter with chiding because I heere you will not take phisike. I hope it is onlei for this day and that to morrowe you will doe it, for yf you will not I most come to you, and make you take it, for it is for your healthe. I have given order to mylord Newcastell to send mi worde to night whether you will or not, therfore I hope you will not give mi the paines to goe and so I rest
> Your affectionat mother,
> Henriette Marie, R.[23]

It may be presumed that Charles at this age did not venture to defy his mother; but his reaction to her orders is delightfully characteristic of the individual he was to become. He soon afterwards sent the following letter, the first that survives from his pen, not to her but to his governor:

> My Lord,
> I would not have you take too much Phisick; for it doth allwaies make me worse, and I think it will do the like with you. I ride every day, and am ready to follow any other directions from you. Make hast to returne to him that loves you.
> Charles P.[24]

A habit of the young prince that impressed itself on those who surrounded him was that of carrying around with him a wooden bar or 'billet', to which he was so attached that he insisted on taking it to bed with him. Wiseacres at court predicted from this 'either that blockheads would one day be his favourites or else that he would rule with the club'.[25] An equally intelligent interpretation might have been that here again the child was father of the man. In later life King Charles II had playthings that he liked to take to bed with him; but they were not made of wood.

Prince James, styled Duke of York from his nursery days though not so invested till his tenth year, was the companion of his elder brother in work and play. The princesses likewise were mostly in each other's company, under the tuition of Lady Roxburgh. St James's Palace was their main residence, but in the summer of 1636 all four were removed to Richmond. There Charles and Henrietta visited them, and the Scottish Monsignor George Conn, who had just arrived as papal agent to the Queen, bore witness to the joy the children showed at the arrival of their mother and father. 'After a cheerful evening, the elder ones were allowed to sup with their parents, the Prince of Wales and Duke of York sitting on each side of their father, whilst the Lady Mary was placed next her mother; the little Elizabeth, yet too young to appear at table, was sent to bed.'[26]

Actually Charles's correct title at this time was Duke of Cornwall. He was not declared Prince of Wales till two years later, when he was eight. At the same time he was made a Knight of the Garter in the usual ceremony at Windsor Castle. His installation as Prince of Wales was postponed for the time being, and in the event, owing to the troubles that were soon to break out, never took place.

Meanwhile the third sister, Anne, named after her aunt the Queen of France, had been born in St James's Palace on 17 March 1637. It was a difficult birth, and the baby was delicate from the start. She had a constant feverish cough, and disease of the lungs was suspected.

A fourth daughter, Katharine, was born to Queen Henrietta Maria at Whitehall on 29 January 1639. This birth was even more difficult than the last, and Henrietta went through terrible agony. Nor was the result rewarding. The short life of the little princess was recorded by the author of *The Worthies of England*:

Catherine, fourth daughter to King Charles and Queen Mary, was born at Whitehall, (the queen mother being then at St James's), and survived not above half an hour after her baptizing; so that it is charity to mention her whose memory is likely to be lost, so short her continuance in this life. . . .[27]

The 'queen mother', Marie de Medici Queen Dowager of France, having fallen foul of Richelieu, had imposed herself on her daughter's court, where she was far from welcome. This commanding blonde dragon, whose portrait by Rubens shows, in Aldous Huxley's expressive phrase, 'a large, fleshy, gorge-ously bedizened barmaid',[28] took a possessive attitude towards her children; to everybody else she was singularly callous and cold-hearted. To Charles I she was a financial burden, and to his subjects a figure of loathing. She was an influential addition to the Catholic contingent at the English court, which was a source of increasing anxiety to the Protestant majority.

The royal children were brought up, in accordance with the King's beliefs, on the strictest Anglican principles. Charles I was by no means antagonistic to Rome. This was shown in his cordial friendship with, among others, Monsignor Conn, a cultured cosmopolitan. The two had many friendly discussions on religion, and Conn was always welcome in the royal circle. But the King's own beliefs were unswerving. The Anglican creed, in what would be now called its High Church aspect, was to him infallible. It was personified by William Laud, his most trusted ecclesiastical adviser, whom he had appointed to the Archbishopric of Canterbury in 1633. With Laud at his side King Charles was determined that all his children should be brought up to hold his own High Anglican views.

Queen Henrietta thought otherwise. Marriage had made no alteration to her staunchly Catholic faith, and she longed to have at least one Catholic child. It was the one question on which she and her husband profoundly differed. Just as his father had been tolerant of Queen Anne's Catholicism, so Charles was anxious to accommodate his wife so far as he could. He allowed her to have her priests, and her own chapel at Somerset House as well as that at St James's. But further than this he would not go.

Henrietta never acquiesced in this restriction, and throughout her married life she was perpetually trying to bring one or other of her offspring into her own faith. She had started by taking Prince Charles to Mass, but the King had immediately objected and she was forced to give in. Now she transferred her attention to Princess Mary. Here she found more fruitful ground. Mary was the fond pupil of the Catholic Lady Roxburgh, and Henrietta now found another abetter in her friend the Duchesse de Chevreuse, a dazzling beauty and a bold defier of convention, who on an earlier visit to England had scandalized the people of Richmond by swimming across the Thames. Madame de Chevreuse, moving in where the Queen no longer dared to tread, herself took Mary to Mass, and the princess responded by showing great devotion and by acquiring a rosary, which she habitually carried in her pocket and brought out when she was sure no Protestant was looking. The Queen assured her that in time she would be married to one of the great princes of Europe, the Emperor's son or the French Dauphin or the prince of Spain, and then she must change her faith. 'I have no objection,' replied Mary. 'Let me be taken to Mass; I shall be very glad to go.'[29] Such was her disposition at this time; her subsequent life was to take a different course.

On one occasion in 1637, during an absence of the King, Henrietta Maria took all her children to Vespers at Hampton Court. Princess Elizabeth was not yet two, and to keep her quiet her mother gave her a book of devotion. A few minutes later she was much edified to find the child engrossed with a picture of Christ's scourging at the pillar. 'Elizabeth exclaimed, "Poor man, poor man," and kissed the picture many times.'[30]

The Queen's efforts at proselytization had no apparent lasting effect; but this does not mean that no seed was sown. Only three generations back the Scottish Stewarts had been notable for their Catholic devotion, and their descendants were to return to the faith in the not far distant future. Most of the children of Charles I were to show at least an interest in it at some time or other of their lives.

In the meantime reports of the Queen's zeal leaked out, and the fear of popery gathered volume in the country at large.

And now, with the waning of the halcyon days of the 1630s,

clouds gathered with ever increasing gloom over England and over the Stuarts. The troubles that brought about the greatest disaster ever to overwhelm the British monarchy concern the present study only so far as they affected the relations between the various members of the royal family. A brief summary is necessary.

The causes were multifarious, but were primarily financial, religious and military. In doing without a parliament, an institution which when in being had become ever more conscious of its potential strength, King Charles had been thrown on his own resources for raising money to carry on the government of the kingdom. The income from the crown lands, on which in centuries past English kings had been expected to live and govern, were far from sufficient in the seventeenth century. Charles contrived to keep going by means of traditional import taxes known as tonnage and poundage and prerogative sources of revenue such as wardships; in addition he set his lawyers to the task of reviving old feudal dues such as fees for knighthoods. But his methods raised rumbles of discontent from the gentry this mulcted, and the climax came with the ship-money crisis of the mid-1630s.

The payment of ship money was a form of tax imposed to provide naval resources for the defence of the realm. It was by tradition the local responsibility of the maritime counties alone, but when Charles I proposed to raise a powerful navy, rendered necessary by the increasing strength at sea built up by possible enemies abroad, and also by raids on the coast by corsairs and pirates, he decided not unreasonably that the inland shires also could be asked to contribute to what concerned the country as a whole. There was immediate opposition, crystallized in the action of the wealthy landowner John Hampden, who refused to pay and challenged the royal policy in the courts. He lost his action, but only by a small majority of judges; and from then on the raising of revenue became more difficult.

By the end of the decade the King's financial position was becoming desperate, and it was at this time that he made the fatal error of going to war against his recalcitrant subjects in his native land. He had visited Scotland, and been crowned there, in 1633, and had taken note of the dour Presbyterianism that dominated the lives of the ruling classes. The Kirk of Scotland was entirely antagonistic to the Church of England as King Charles had established it, and he now determined to bring his northern kingdom ecclesiastically into line. In 1637, the same year in which Hampden's suit was heard, he imposed on Scotland a new prayer book embodying the full ceremonial of Anglican worship.

The result was calamitous. There were riots in Edinburgh, the Bishop was stripped of his vestments, and in 1638 the General Assembly of the Kirk issued the National Covenant abolishing episcopacy and denouncing 'the re-establishing of the Popish religion and tyranny'.

James I, who had spent the first thirty-seven years of his life in shrewd observation of his Scottish subjects, knew better than to stick his finger into so seething a hornets' nest. His son had left Scotland at the age of three, and he never began to understand the fierce and obstinate nature of its people. He decided to teach them a lesson by force of arms, and in 1639 he marched north in what later became known as the First Bishops' War.

It was the most ill-advised action of his life. He had neither an adequate army nor the means to pay one. He summoned the trained bands (the territorials of those days) of the northern counties, and advanced as far as Berwick-on-Tweed. There he was met by a determined force raised by the Covenanters, who had in the meantime seized Edinburgh. A truce was arranged, known as the Pacification of Berwick, which settled nothing and hardly even saved King Charles's face. He marched homewards in humiliation.

It was the beginning of the end. In England the Puritan opposition to what might be called the 'establishment', the power of the crown in politics and the High Church in religion, had been gathering strength, and its leaders, in particular the eminent parliamentarian John Pym, saw their opportunity. They were not as yet anti-monarchist, but they were prepared to join with the rebellious Scots in imposing shackles on the King. They would never let go.

Charles was in dire straits. But he had at least the sense, in this crisis of his reign, to send for the one man who might be able to extricate him from the morass into which he had plunged. He had already been in close touch with Thomas Viscount Wentworth, Lord Deputy of Ireland, who now received a concise missive from his sovereign containing the words: 'Come when you will, you shall be welcome.'[31]

Thomas Wentworth, who in a few months from this time was created Earl of Strafford, was a man of iron who had been sent to Ireland to bring order to that turbulent country. He had attained a great measure of success, and had made his name as a ruthless disciplinarian and an organizer and administrator of consummate ability. But he was hated by the Puritans. In the early parliaments of Charles I he had stood forward among those who opposed royal measures and claimed grievances against the King. Since then he had become the staunchest supporter of royal authority, and was regarded by the opposition as a traitor to their cause.

He arrived in England too late to do much for his King; but he set himself to bring what order he could out of chaos. King Charles had determined on another expedition to Scotland; it took place in the summer of 1640. Strafford had offered him the services of the army he maintained in Ireland: an offer that was to have momentous consequences. Secondly, realizing that no further hostilities could be carried on without funds, he advised his sovereign to call a parliament. The Short Parliament was of no help and was dissolved within a few weeks, but when the Second Bishops' War proved a greater fiasco than the first Strafford advised the King to summon another. He did so in full awareness that its members would soon be howling for his blood.

The assembly that was to become known as the Long Parliament met on 3 November 1640. Immediately John Pym and his accomplices embarked on their one paramount objective—the severing of Lord Strafford's head from his body. The King was powerless to prevent his faithful minister's impeachment on an absurd charge of high treason, and the accusation was carried to the House of Lords.

Before the trial could take place further events took place in the royal family. Henrietta gave birth to her eighth child at Oatlands on 8 July 1640. In contrast with the last two instances the birth was easy, and the son she bore was strong and healthy. He was named Henry and was soon to be created Duke of Gloucester.

Four months later, just as the Long Parliament was beginning its ominous sessions, the little Princess Anne died in her fourth year. She had always been delicate, but according to contemporaries showed bright promise. Thomas Fuller described her as 'a very pregnant lady above her age'—not perhaps the happiest turn of phrase. Speaking of her death, Fuller wrote:

> Being minded by those about her to call upon God, even when the pangs of death were upon her, 'I am not able,' said she, 'to say my long prayer (meaning the Lord's prayer), but will say my short one,—"Lighten mine eyes, O Lord, lest I sleep the sleep of death."' This done, the little lamb gave up the ghost. [32]

There was deep distress in the family, felt most deeply by the Queen. The elder Prince Charles and Princess Katharine had died almost at birth; such losses were regarded as in the natural order of things, and two in a family of eight was well below average. But Anne had lived long enough to win the affection of her parents and her elder brothers and sisters. A post-mortem examination was ordered, and Sir Theodore Mayerne certified that the death was natural, caused by consumption.

Grief for a lost child, however, was soon overshadowed by troubles on a larger scale. The trial of Lord Strafford by his peers opened in Westminster Hall on 22 March 1641. So momentous was the occasion that the King himself was present, though officially incognito; he sat in a box, sometimes with the Queen and Princess Mary, while the throne was left vacant. To the right of it, however, sat the ten-year-old Prince of Wales in his robes, present among the Lords by right as Duke of Cornwall.

For the last year or two Prince Charles had been largely withdrawn from the company of the younger members of the family. Preparing for man's estate, he was being educated with two boys slightly older than himself, the sons of his grandfather's and father's dead favourite; they were George second Duke of Buckingham, who was three years his senior, and his brother Lord Francis Villiers, posthumous son of the murdered duke. Charles was from this time increasingly in the confidence of his father, and it was felt that at this great crisis of the reign he should be publicly seen to be associated with the affairs of the kingdom.

Not even the crafty Pym could prove treason against a man whose only crime had been loyalty to his sovereign, and the impeachment failed. On 10 April the hearing was adjourned *sine die*, and the optimists hoped that this was the end of the affair. But Pym was not defeated; he brought in a bill of attainder. Proof was no longer needed; the bill had only to be passed by both Houses of Parliament, and of course receive the royal assent, and Strafford would be liable to the death penalty. There was a fierce debate, but Strafford's enemies got hold of his offer to King Charles of troops from Ireland. It was made to appear that he had intended to bring in an Irish army to reduce England, as opposed to Scotland, to obedience; anti-papist hysteria was worked up and the bill was passed in the Commons with a large majority.

The King made frantic efforts to save his servant's life, addressing the House of Lords in an abject speech and promising to dismiss Strafford from his counsels and strip him of his offices. It was all in vain. Pym and his gang incited the London mob to demonstrate outside the Parliament buildings, and the Lords passed the bill by 26 votes to 19.

The crisis now reached its climax. The King's signature had to be procured before Strafford could be executed, and if Charles could by any possible means avoid giving it he would do so. But Pym had stirred up the mob, and it hardly needed a helping push to see that they got completely out of hand. The King and Queen, with Prince Charles, were in Whitehall Palace; the other royal children at St James's. The screaming rabble stormed about Westminster, vowing death to the papist queen if Strafford was allowed to live. The King had only a small force of guards; at any moment the crazed mob might break in and his adored wife, if not he himself, be lynched. The murder of the children might well follow.

This was the situation on Sunday, 9 May 1641: 'a rabble of many thousand people'[33] threatening to storm Whitehall Palace; the King in an agony of apprehension and indecision, ready to seize on any device for saving Strafford's life; the Queen's ladies hiding in terror while the Queen herself, controlling her fears as best she could, 'gave way by turns to anger and tearful despair'.[34] Strafford himself was in the Tower of London, the Constable of which, Lord Newport, had declared that he would have his prisoner killed on his own authority if the King did not consent.[35]

King Charles could resist the threat of anarchy and murder

no longer. Next day he gave way. The Earl of Manchester and the Earl of Lindsey were sent to the House of Lords with his decision. A delegate from Parliament calmed the crowd by telling them that the King had surrendered, a plain indication that the riot was officially inspired; and King Charles signed the bill with tears in his eyes. 'My Lord of Strafford's condition is happier than mine' was his comment.[36]

He had not abandoned the struggle. The following morning he drafted a letter to Parliament pleading that the death sentence should be commuted to life imprisonment. He added a postscript, pitiful in its lameness: 'If he must die, it were a charity to reprieve him until Saturday.'[37]

At Henrietta's suggestion the young Prince of Wales was sent to take the letter in person to the House of Lords; she felt that the sight of the eleven-year-old boy, pleading for his father's honour, would soften the hearts of Strafford's persecutors. It did nothing of the sort. The letter was returned unopened, and the Prince summarily dismissed. On the following day the Earl of Strafford was beheaded on Tower Hill.

Thus King Charles abandoned to his enemies the greatest and most forceful champion of his rights. He had been subjected to almost unbearable pressures, but the betrayal haunted his conscience till the last moments of his life.

One thing was certain. The King had totally lost control of his kingdom, and he could never reassert it except by force of arms. From the day of Strafford's execution the country moved inexorably towards civil war.

In the meantime, however, a new development had occurred in the history of the King's children. It was connected with the crisis of the reign, and it brought Princess Mary into the limelight, making her for the moment the most important member of the royal family.

There had been hopes of a grand marriage for Mary. Matrimony was among the most important elements in diplomacy, and many a fruitful international alliance had been cemented through the agency of a marriageable royal princess. Charles and Henrietta had had grandiose ideas for Mary and for some time it was hoped that she would marry the Infante Baltasar Carlos, son and heir of Philip IV of Spain. This project came to nothing, and in any case the Infante was destined for an early death. But with troubles accumulating about him King Charles became reconciled to a humbler but perhaps more diplomatically advantageous match.

Henrietta's mother, Marie de Medici, was a born match-maker. When she left France in 1638 to deposit herself at her daughter's court she passed through Holland, and she took the opportunity to sound out the Stadtholder of the Netherlands, Prince Frederick Henry of Orange, on the possibility of a matrimonial alliance with the English royal family. The idea was that Frederick Henry's only son William, then aged twelve, should marry the two-year-old Elizabeth, second daughter of Charles I.

Frederick Henry was delighted by the prospect of such a marriage. The Orange dynasty was not recognized as royal. The northern Netherlands had attained independent status in the sixteenth-century revolt against the rule of Spain. In this bloody and long-drawn-out struggle William of Orange, 'William the Silent' as he came to be known, whose title was French but whose family was Dutch, assumed the leadership of the insurgents. Such was his prestige, and such the ability of his two sons, Maurice and Frederick Henry, that each in turn succeeded almost without question to the Stadtholdership, the quasi-royal position of head of government and commander-in-chief of the armed forces. The post, however, was not officially hereditary. The strongly republican States of the Netherlands, federated but each with its own administration, fiercely guarded their independence, and on the death of the Stadtholder his successor had to be elected by them all before assuming office. So far there had been no opposition, and Prince Frederick Henry, younger son of William the Silent, was securely in power. An alliance with the English royal family, however, would strengthen his position.

This was the proposition that Marie de Medici put to the King and Queen of England; and she brought with her the Sieur Johan Heenvliet, a Dutch nobleman in the confidence of Frederick Henry, to press the suit. King Charles, however, was less enthusiastic than the proposed bridegroom's father. The match in his view was unworthy of his daughter's rank. For the moment the proposal was dropped.

Two years later the position had changed. Charles had embarked on his ill-judged and ill-fated hostilities against the Scots; he was faced with growing opposition from a substantial proportion of his subjects; he had been forced to summon Parliament, and his tottering authority was upheld only by the force of character of the highly unpopular Lord Wentworth. In the circumstances an alliance with a family which, though not royal, was rich and powerful, with a Protestant record that might go far towards appeasing his anti-Catholic subjects, was not to be despised.

Diplomatic hints were dropped to the Prince of Orange, who lost no time in sending over another mission, consisting this time of three of the principal nobles of Holland, named Brederode, Aersen and Sommerdyke. They were received with open arms by the King and Queen and entertained in state in the Banqueting House at Whitehall. And it soon transpired that the proposed bride was no longer the little Princess Elizabeth but her elder sister Mary, now approaching her ninth birthday and known as the Princess Royal, though it does not appear that she was ever formally invested with that title.

At the beginning of 1641, with King Charles's fortunes sinking to their lowest ebb, the marriage contract was drawn up. Prince William was to come over himself for the marriage ceremony, but the bride was to stay in England till her twelfth year. Her dowry was to be £40,000, an attractive proposition to the impoverished English crown. The princess was to be allowed a suitable household, with English servants chosen by her father, and free exercise of her religion according to the Anglican rite, which differed considerably from the more extreme Protestantism of the Dutch reformed church.[38]

On 12 February 1641 the King announced the betrothal to Parliament, and for a brief moment the royal family enjoyed a renewal of popularity. But the Strafford trial was pending, and the marriage arrangements were overshadowed.

Plans for the wedding were pushed on with all possible speed. On 20 April Prince William left Holland with a fleet of twenty ships, commanded by the illustrious Dutch Admiral Marten van Tromp; they ran into a storm at sea, but William landed safely at Gravesend four days later. He was conducted in state to Whitehall, but the final stage of the Strafford drama was approaching and the streets were lined by all the guards available; not, as a contemporary observed, as a mere mark of respect to the Prince, 'but because the rabble, discontented and ferocious, threatened to disturb the proceedings'.[39]

William, a fine-looking, earnest and well-read boy of fifteen, was met at Whitehall by the Prince of Wales and the Duke of York. After the ceremonial reception he proceeded to Somerset House, where the King and Queen were waiting to present him to his betrothed. Later he made his respects to Queen Marie at St James's Palace. Everywhere his dignified bearing and cultured manners made an excellent impression.

The wedding took place in Whitehall chapel on 2 May. The Strafford affair was now boiling up towards its tremendous climax, and with this and the other troubles threatening the peace of the country it was thought advisable to make the ceremony as private as possible. The King, however, was glad to take time off from more depressing matters, and a festive air was given to the nuptials. Prince William, attended by Count Brederode and wearing a suit of rich crimson velvet, was led by Lord Arundel and Lord Strange to the private gallery of the palace, where he was received by the King and his two eldest sons. The royal ladies and peers and peeresses were also present, and a procession was performed to the chapel. The Princes Charles and James then fetched their sister, who entered the chapel dressed simply in a robe of silver tissue, with a necklace and chain of pendant pearls. Her train was borne by sixteen young ladies of noble family.

Archbishop Laud, persecuted with his colleague Strafford by the Pym faction, was like him in the Tower, and the wedding ceremony was performed by Dr Matthew Wren, Bishop of Ely and Dean of the Chapel Royal. Queen Henrietta, who still had qualms about attending Protestant services, was with her mother and her daughter Elizabeth in a small gallery 'where they could privately view the proceedings'.[40]

Prince William dined with the whole royal family, and further functions were held during the afternoon. Then the bride and bridegroom supped together, and finally, according to the custom of the time, they were ceremonially bedded. A contemporary described the scene:

. . . the young princess, exchanging her robes for a dishabille, was laid in a state-bed of blue velvet in her mother's chamber, which was brilliantly illuminated, in presence of her parents, brothers, the Dutch ambassadors, and the ladies of the court: the king then fetched in the Prince of Orange, attired in a loose robe of embroidered blue and green satin, lined with cloth of silver, and led him to a place in the bed occupied by the princess, but at a respectful distance from her. He kissed her several times on entering the bed, and again on leaving it, about a quarter of an hour afterwards: and this ceremony concluded the marriage.[41]

These decorous proceedings were deemed sufficient to constitute consummation of the marriage. Yet in view of the tender age of the bride the Stuart parents took no chances. Mary's nightdress was sewn up under her feet to obviate any possibility of a sudden move to assert a husband's rights. At the same time the horseplay customary on such occasions was provided by the Queen's dwarf, Jeffrey Hudson, who produced a pair of shears and made a move to cut the garment.[42]

Sir Anthony Van Dyck celebrated the marriage with one of his most charming pictures, showing the young bride and bridegroom holding hands in their wedding finery. If the painter's impression can be accepted, they made a singularly handsome couple.

The mood of euphoria engendered did not last long. William returned to Holland as agreed, and Mary remained with the rest of the family at St James's. She was there when the London mob were howling for the blood of Strafford and the Queen.

In August King Charles visited Scotland, in peace this time, officially to open the Scots Parliament and unofficially to sound out the extent of Scottish support in the coming struggle. He returned in November, having achieved nothing, to a surprisingly warm welcome from the City of London, which gave him a resounding civic reception. But opposition in the English Parliament was as implacable as ever, and from now on the situation went from bad to worse.

The climax came in the new year when Charles, alarmed by a report that the Commons intended to impeach Queen Henrietta, went to the House in person in an abortive attempt to arrest five of the members, headed by that John Pym who had hounded Strafford to his death. Warned of what was to happen, the five slipped out of the chamber, and the King suffered another humiliation.

There was now no hope of avoiding an appeal to arms. Whitehall was no longer safe for the royal family. The rabble were again being stirred up to demonstrations against the Queen. Marie de Medici had already left for the continent—a sure sign that the ship was sinking.

On the night of 10 January 1642 King Charles left his capital, never to return except as the prisoner of his enemies. He took his family on a hurried flight to Hampton Court, which was totally unprepared for their reception; so much so that that night they all had to share one bedroom. Two days later they went on to Windsor, to make what plans they could for a bleak future.

The parliamentary leaders were now in undisputed control of London. This meant that they had in their hands two priceless assets—the financial resources of the City and the weapons to wage a war; for the Tower of London was the country's principal arsenal. If Charles was to have any chance in the coming struggle, he must repair his deficiencies in these two respects.

This was the principal consideration which led to the decision that Henrietta Maria should leave England. She had valuable jewels, some of them the property of the crown since the days of Elizabeth I, which might raise a substantial sum on the Continent; and she might by personal appeal procure arms and military support among the princes of Europe.

There was also of course the question of the hatred that had been stirred up against the papist consort. As long as she remained in England the danger of assassination or lynching was acute, and she was more a liability than an asset to her family. Her courage was always at its highest when affairs were at their worst, but much as she hated leaving her husband she decided that she could serve him best elsewhere.

The trouble was that her flight to raise arms and money would hardly commend itself to those who now controlled most of the ports and could prevent her leaving the country. So the decision was made to advance the date of Princess Mary's departure for Holland. To this the parliamentary leaders could hardly object; nor could they in reason stop her mother accompanying her.

In the event no obstacle was placed in the way of mother and daughter. On 7 February the King sent a message to Parliament announcing the plan, and the Commons, presumably only too glad to get rid of their *bête noire*, agreed. Through the agency of the Dutch Ambassador, Johan Heenvliet, the Prince of Orange was asked to request Mary's immediate departure, and he promptly sent an escort fleet once more commanded by van Tromp.

The King and the Prince of Wales accompanied the ladies to Dover. There they met the soldier Prince Rupert, son of the exiled 'Winter Queen' Elizabeth of Bohemia, who had come to England to offer his services to his uncle. Charles was not yet ready to employ him, and he was asked to go back to Holland as personal escort to the Queen and the Princess Royal.

Henrietta and Mary embarked in the *Lion* on 23 February. King Charles was in tears when he bade them farewell, and when the ship sailed he rode along the cliff to keep it in sight as long as he could.

It was the first real separation in the family. Princess Mary of Orange was destined never to see her father again; nor did she have another sight of England till the last few months of her life. But in the years following her marriage she and her husband were to prove a tower of strength to the Stuart family in their darkest hour, an anchor in the sea of troubles that overwhelmed them.

3

Separated by War, 1642–6

The Princess Royal and her mother reached the Dutch port of
Hellevoetsluis on 1 March 1642, after an adventurous voyage.
Sea travel in the seventeenth century presented hazards difficult
to visualize today. Small sailing vessels, at the mercy of wind and
wave, were tossed about in the heavy seas for which the English
Channel and the North Sea have always been notorious in a
manner that made loss of life frequent and panic among
passengers more so. Queen Henrietta Maria was particularly
unlucky. She made a number of these short but dangerous
voyages in her life, and every time met with unpleasant
conditions. Her ill-fortune became a family joke in later years.

In this case the voyage began propitiously. The weather was
good for the time of year, and the fleet reached Flushing in
fifteen hours. But then in the northward journey severe winds
blew up, and the navigation of the Dutch coast, with its
numerous inlets, became increasingly difficult. At the entrance
to Hellevoetsluis harbour one of the baggage vessels capsized,
and Queen Henrietta lost a substantial quantity of her plate and
furniture. The royal ladies landed intact but shaken.

They were met by Prince William, who had hastened to
Hellevoetsluis as soon as news came of their impending landing.
His instructions from his father were to take them on by boat to
Rotterdam, but the Queen and Princess had had enough of the
water for the time being, and an overland journey was
substituted. At Brill they were met by the Prince of Orange, and
at Hounslerdike by other members of the court and family,
including Elizabeth of Bohemia, King Charles's sister, who now
met her sister-in-law and niece for the first time.

From Hounslerdike they proceeded in stately procession to
The Hague. In the principal state coach were a party of four; the

bride and bridegroom sat side by side, facing the two queens, Henrietta Maria and Elizabeth. These two great ladies, perhaps the most striking princesses of the age, provided a strong contrast: the 'Winter Queen' of Bohemia, staunch and redoubtable Protestant, beautiful and commanding, witty and vivacious, always gallant and self-confident in the misfortunes of her life; Henrietta Maria, the passionate Catholic, small, eager, volatile, with all her French charm and her mercurial temperament. They were alike at least in their vitality.

United in adversity, they got on admirably, chattering together during the drive to The Hague. 'The Queen of Bohemia is very frequently with the Queen,' wrote a correspondent a few days later, 'and most kind they are to one another.' [1] 'The Queen came hither to-morrow it will be a seven-night,' wrote the Winter Queen herself from The Hague to her great friend Sir Thomas Roe. 'She was received as well as the short warning they had could permit. She used me and my children extremely well, both for civility and her kindness.' [2]

Queen Elizabeth, whose home was now in Holland, was also delighted to meet her niece; henceforth she regarded Mary almost as a daughter, though in all conscience she had enough of her own. She was the mother of eight boys and five girls, though not all were alive at this time; in addition to which she maintained a menagerie of pet animals whom some said she preferred to her vigorous and turbulent children.

There was a splendid reception in the capital, with bells and fireworks and a salute from eighty pieces of cannon. Mary was escorted to the New Palace, and that night a banquet was held in her honour. Here, however, there appeared the first signs of the discord which was to bedevil her relations with the people of the Netherlands. They were perennially jealous of their republican status, and when the health of the Prince of Orange was drunk before the toast to the States-General the Burgomaster of The Hague objected. The result was an unseemly wrangle which lasted some days and affected the popularity of Princess Mary. She for her part imbibed from this incident a distaste for her husband's compatriots which was to serve her ill in the years to come.

Mary's heart was always centred in her own family, and she was doubtless glad to receive, soon after her arrival in Holland, her first letter from her eldest brother, the Prince of Wales. Whoever may have guided his hand on this occasion, the stilted tone of the epistle contrasted with the easy manner in which he corresponded with members of his family in later times:

To the hands of the Lady Marie, princess of Auriana, these present:
Most Royal Sister,
  Methinks, although I cannot enjoy that former happiness that I was wont, in the fruition of your society, being barred those joys by the parting waves, yet I cannot so forget the kindness I owe unto so dear a sister, as not to write, also expecting the like salutation from you, that thereby (although a while dissevered) we may reciprocally understand of each other's welfare. I could heartily, and with a fervent devotion, wish your return, were it not to lessen your delights in your loyal spouse, the Prince of Orange, who, as I conceived by his last letter, was as joyful for your presence as we are sad and mourning for your absence.
  My father is very much disconsolate and troubled, partly for my royal mother's and your absence, and partly from the disturbances of this kingdom.
  Dear sister, we are, as much as we may, merry; and more than we would, sad, in respect we cannot alter the present distempers of these troublesome times. My father's resolution is now for York, where he intends to reside, to see the event or sequel to these bad unpropitious beginnings; whither you direct your letter. Thus much desiring your comfortable answer to these my sad lines, I rest,
              Your loving brother,
Royston, March 9, 1642.   Carol. Princeps.[3]

Whether Prince Charles ever received the like salutation from his sister, the desired comfortable answer to his sad lines, does not appear. Mary was never a good correspondent, unlike a younger sister, as yet unborn, who was to become the beloved correspondent of her eldest brother.
  Queen Henrietta embarked at once on the business which was her real purpose in crossing the North Sea. She was only partially successful. Prince Frederick Henry did what he could

to help, and before long 'arms and money were beginning to pass quietly out of the mouth of the Maas, across the North Sea, to anchor in the Humber'.[4] But the Dutch and Jewish merchants to whom she tried to sell her jewels, and those that were doubtfully hers, were a tougher proposition, and the Queen found herself involved in some hard bargaining.

Mary for her part was striving to become accustomed to her new way of life. She had a doting young husband and an affectionate father-in-law, but the antagonism of the republican burghers of the Netherlands continued to distress her. They had little respect for royalty, and ostentatiously kept their hats on in her presence. The presence of her mother made them suspect her of Catholic sympathies, and 'no popery' demonstrations took place in The Hague.

Even in her married life there were frictions; for Mary, like many another bride throughout history, had to endure an aggressive and dominating mother-in-law. Amelia von Solms had been a maid of honour to Elizabeth of Bohemia. She was a noted beauty, and her marriage to Prince Frederick Henry was a love match; but with increasing age and ill-health she had become soured and petulant. Angered by her husband's deference to English royalty, she apparently took an instant dislike to her daughter-in-law.

In England, meanwhile, events pursued their inexorable course. Having seen his wife and elder daughter off to Holland, King Charles, as indicated in his son's letter to his sister, set off for York, taking Prince Charles with him. At the same time he sent his three younger children back to St James's Palace. With hindsight this action would appear inexplicable, savouring even of callousness; in all the circumstances of the time it is difficult to understand. True, King Charles did not foresee that he would be cut off indefinitely from his capital; but his very act in making for York showed the way his mind was working. At York he would be within distance of Hull, his northern arsenal, which not only itself contained munitions but was the port to which such supplies as Henrietta could raise would be sent. Obviously he was preparing actively for hostilities against his mutinous subjects. Yet at this moment he chose to send his children to a place where they would be at the mercy of those same subjects.

Such folly can be explained only by the muddled state of mind in which the King found himself at this juncture.

One of the children, the eldest, was soon extracted from their precarious refuge. The Earl of Newcastle had given up his charge of the Prince of Wales and had gone north to look after his extensive estates. The Marquess of Hertford was now governor to both the elder boys, and at this point the King had second thoughts about his second son, James Duke of York, whom he decided he must have with him in the boy's own titular city. He sent Hertford to St James's to fetch him, and the way things were going was shown by the fact that the Parliament promptly objected. There was as yet, however, a limit to the extent of their defiance. In the words of the future James II's official biographer, 'the Parliament having notice, sent a message to the Marquess forbidding him to do it: notwithstanding which he obeyd the King, and upon Easter Munday, setting forth from London, he conducted the Duke to York, where his Royall Highnes being arrived, he was made Knight of the Garter'.[5] Princess Elizabeth and the little Duke of Gloucester, who was less than two years old, were left at St James's.

The King soon found important work for the new Knight of the Garter. It was urgent that he should establish control of Hull, where the Governor, Sir John Hotham, was uncertain in his allegiance. Hotham was a member of parliament and was being pressed by his masters at Westminster to declare against the King. Charles therefore planned to force his hand by sending the young Duke of York on a social visit, 'as if it were only out of curiosity to see the place',[6] and then following it up by arriving himself and taking possession.

The result was failure and humiliation. On 22 April 1642 James rode to Hull, accompanied by his cousin the Elector Palatine of the Rhine (Charles Louis, the eldest son of Queen Elizabeth of Bohemia) and a few lords and gentleman. He was courteously received by Hotham, who invited him to stay the night. But when next morning Sir Lewis Dyves arrived to tell the Duke's host that the King was on his way, and would be pleased to dine with him that day, Hotham 'suddenly turn'd very pale, struck himself on the breast, and return'd no answer to him, but immediately desir'd the Duke with his company to retire to his lodging'.[7] Then, fearing for his own safety and urged on by some parliamentary colleagues who were with him, he ordered that the expected royal visitor should be denied entry. This was the situation when King Charles appeared, to find the gates shut in his face. He remonstrated with Hotham, who told him that he was acting under the orders of Parliament and refused to listen to any argument. The King had no choice but to make his way forlornly back to York, followed by his eight-year-old son and his retinue.

Such was Prince James's introduction to the public affairs of his father's kingdom. Like his elder brother's mission to Parliament at the time of the Strafford trial it was disastrous and degrading, and it made a lasting impression on his youthful mind. His attitude to his father was one of adoration, but in after years he became convinced that King Charles had contributed to his own tragedy by indecision and weakness. This was the first time that this was well and truly brought home to him. In the memoirs long afterwards written in his name his feelings were revealed:

. . . For had the King, instead of sending Sir Lewis Dyves, surpriz'd the governour by an unexpected visite, and without warning of his coming, in all probability he had been master of the place, for the inhabitants at that time were very affectionat to his service. . . .

Another great errour in this conduct was, that the King did not instruct some one bold and vigourous man of their number who were sent before with the Duke, with a commission to secur the person of Sir John Hotham, in case he should prove refractory, and with a positive order for the rest to obey the person so intrusted upon his producing the commission. . . .[8]

It is permissible to surmise that thus early in his experience James Duke of York determined to follow the course of resolution and firmness of purpose which was to become his guiding principle. Yet at the supreme crisis of his life he was to succumb to those very weaknesses that he had condemned in his father.

King Charles's failure to secure the port and the arsenal of Hull ensured that he would embark on hostilities at a serious disadvantage, further increased by the fact that the Earl of Northumberland, Lord High Admiral, declared for Parliament at this time with most of the Royal Navy. But war was now inevitable, and he spent the next few months making what preparations he could. Meanwhile a paper war continued, King and Parliament justifying their actions with words while spinning out time before the first blood should be spilt. In July Charles led his far from adequate forces south into the Midlands, and on 22 August he ceremonially raised the Royal Banner at Nottingham. By his side were his two sons Charles and James, as well as his nephew Rupert, who had come once more from the Continent to serve under his uncle, and Rupert's younger brother Maurice. The Great Civil War had begun.

The news quickly reached The Hague, and Henrietta Maria redoubled her efforts to raise money and arms. The Prince of Orange provided her with experienced Dutch officers to take with her to England, as well as cash and materials for war, hampered though he was by the Dutch leaders who were anxious that the republic should not be involved. At first it seemed that everything was in hand. 'Send me word where I must land,' wrote the Queen to her husband a week after the raising of the standard. 'I shall have eighteen ships to go with me to England.'[9] But hitches occurred, including heavy seas that delayed the journey again and again. It was to be several months before Henrietta could set out.

To her daughter Mary the outbreak of war made little immediate difference. She knew it was bound to happen, and her father-in-law was doing all that could be done to help her parents. The young princess, moreover, was fully occupied in feeling her way about court life in The Hague, and in particular trying to establish some sort of amicable relationship with her formidable mother-in-law.

The King's two youngest children felt the change acutely. They were now cut off from their father, and the nursery in St James's Palace was without question a prison. Most of King Charles's trusted servants were removed and replaced by stern Parliamentarian guards, while Parliament itself cut down the funds allotted to the welfare of Elizabeth and Henry. Lady Roxburgh, now an ailing woman, had been allowed to remain, and she sent an appeal to the Commons urging that a suitable allowance for the necessities of her royal pupils should be accorded by Parliament; they were in want of everything. But although the Speaker drew the House's attention to the unhappy condition of its captives, nothing for the moment was done.

The Prince of Wales and the Duke of York remained with their father, and just two months after the raising of the standard had their first taste of active warfare. The King's object was to march on London, and the Earl of Essex, son of Queen Elizabeth I's favourite, led the Parliamentary forces into the Midlands to obstruct his passage. The two armies met at Edgehill, near Kineton in Warwickshire, in the first important battle of the war on 23 October 1642.

The boys marched with the King behind the infantry, but when hostilities began they were sent to the rear. Accounts of what then occurred differ slightly, but the essentials are clear. The great physician William Harvey was with the King's forces, and according to John Aubrey, not always the most reliable chronicler, it was he who was put in charge of the princes. Bored with the military action that was taking place in front, Harvey took a book out of his pocket and began to read. He was suddenly aroused by the fall of a cannon ball close by, whereupon he hustled his royal charges away and under cover.[10]

Whether or not Harvey was a member of the party detailed to look after the princes, another physician, Sir John Hinton, certainly was. He was not, however, in command of it; this post was filled by Sir William Howard, as James II's biographer makes clear. 'Judging it not fit to expose the Prince and the Duke of York to same danger', runs his narrative, 'he (King Charles) order'd the Duke of Richmond to carry them out of the battell, and conduct them to the top of the hill; who excusing himself from that imployment, the King layd the same command on the Earle of Dorset, who answer'd him with an oath, That he would not be thought a Coward for the sake of any King's Sons in Christendom, and therefor humbly desir'd his Majesty to committ that charge to some other man: Therupon the King layd an absolute command on Sr Will Howard, with his pensioners, who were about fifty, to go off with them.'[11]

All reports agree on how close the princes came to death or

capture, and on the brave conduct of the elder of the two. The most authoritative is that of Sir John Hinton; in an account drawn up later and addressed to King Charles II he wrote:

> . . . the kings foot quitting the field, retreated towards that side of the hill, from whence his Majestie first marched downe to engage; upon which retreat your Majestie was unhappily left behind in a large feild, att which time I had the honour to attend your person, and seeing the sudden and quick march of the Enemie towards you, I did with all earnestnesse, most humbly, but at last somewhat rudely, importune your Highnesse to avoid this present and apparent danger of being killed or taken prisoner, for their horse was by this time come up within half muskett shott in full body, att which your Highnesse was pleased to tell mee, You feared them not, and drawing a pistoll out of one of your holsters, and spanning itt, resolved to charge them, but I did prevaile with your Highnesse to quitt the place, and ride from them, in som hast, but one of their troopers being excellently mounted, broke his rank, and coming full careere towards your Highnesse, I received his charge, and having spent a pistoll or two on each other, I dismounted him in the closeing, but being armed cap-a-pe, I could doe noe execution upon him with my sword, att which instant, one Mr Mathewes, a Gentleman Pensioner, rides in, and with a pole-axe immediately decides the businesse, and then overtaking your Highnesse, you gott safe to the Royall Army, and without this Providence you had undoubtedly miscarried at that time. . . . [12]

The battle continued for a good part of the day, and it is possible that Harvey and Hinton were both involved in somewhat similar incidents at different times. Be this as it may, Edgehill was a thrilling experience for the two boys, now aged twelve and nine. Prince Charles's gallant cry, 'I fear them not', was remembered for the rest of his life.

Edgehill was a fierce but indecisive engagement. At the end of it Essex withdrew to Warwick, having failed to bar his adversaries' road to London. The Royalists, however, did not follow up their advantage. Prince Rupert, who had commanded the cavalry, wanted to push on at once to the capital, but King

Charles decided that his army was too exhausted. Taking his two sons with him, he withdrew to Oxford, which was to be his capital city for the remainder of the war. Winter was setting in, and there was little fighting of importance during the remainder of 1642.

During the largely indecisive warfare, with the Royalists mainly in the ascendant, that took up the following year, the young princes spent most of their time in Oxford. Charles as heir to the throne was much at his father's side, inhaling the atmosphere of war and studying affairs of state. James was intended to be at his books, but there was little supervision by his tutors and in practice he too was caught up in more active pursuits.

Halfway through the year they were joined by their mother. Henrietta Maria now decided that, whatever the weather, she must delay no longer. On 19 January she embarked in the *Princess Royal* at Scheveningen; her quest for men and arms had been crowned with considerable success, and her ship was followed by eleven transports carrying her supplies, the convoy being once more commanded by van Tromp. She was seen off by her sister-in-law, the Winter Queen, and by her daughter Mary, after whom her vessel had been named and who, emotional child that she was, shed a torrent of tears in saying good-bye to her mother. But the full parting was not yet.

Henrietta lived up to her reputation for ill fortune at sea. A furious north-east gale blew up a little way from the Dutch coast, and the *Princess Royal* was in imminent danger of sinking. Henrietta was always at her best in adversity, and she rallied her panic-stricken ladies who, to her no little amusement, took to confessing their sins at the top of their voices to her priests. 'Comfort yourselves,' she gallantly proclaimed. 'Queens of England are never drowned.'[13] But the voyage could not be completed. The fleet was almost within sight of Newcastle-on-Tyne when van Tromp decided they must turn back. Nine days after setting out the Queen was back at Scheveningen, while her attendant ships made harbour one by one.

Promptly she prepared for a second voyage, and within a fortnight she was at sea again, seen off once more by her daughter as well as Prince William and his father and the Queen of Bohemia. This time the weather was better, and the ships crossed the North Sea in good time; but once more there was difficulty off Newcastle. The wind changed, and on 22 February the fleet was forced to drop anchor in Bridlington Bay.

Henrietta's adventures were not yet over. She landed safely, but the Parliament's naval forces had got wind of her voyage. Early next morning four vessels under Captain William Batten arrived in the bay and opened fire on the transports that contained her martial treasure. Her own lodgings were close to the shore, and she awoke to find herself under fire. The indomitable queen thereupon announced that she would lead the defence herself, and she emerged half-dressed from the house, followed by her frightened attendants. The bombardment increased, and they had to take refuge in a ditch, but on the way to it Henrietta suddenly turned back. She had left her dog Mitte behind, and it was not till she had rescued her that she consented to take cover. There she and her ladies lay for two hours until Batten, under a threat from van Tromp that the Dutch would break their neutrality by firing back, drew off.

Henrietta made for York, which was now under the control of Lord Newcastle. Meanwhile Prince Rupert had set out from Oxford to clear a way for her through such enemy forces as were on her route. He captured Birmingham and Lichfield, but was then ordered to turn southward in aid of the King who was in action in Berkshire. It was not till midsummer that he was able to resume his mission to the Queen, who was now, with forces provided by Newcastle, making her own way south-westward into the Midlands. On 11 July he met her at Stratford-on-Avon, and two days later the 'Generalissima', as she had taken to calling herself, was reunited with her husband and sons on the site of the battle of Edgehill. With the much-needed supply of men and munitions the family party proceeded happily to Oxford.

While the two princes were enjoying life in what was now the royal capital, the condition of their juniors, in the custody of the Parliament, was worsening. In May 1643 Lady Roxburgh died, and her place as governess of Elizabeth and Henry was taken by Mary Sackville, Countess of Dorset. Lady Dorset did what she could for her royal charges, and at her insistence an improvement was made in their diet. But in other ways they were treated with increasing harshness. The Commons ordered an inspection of the establishment at St James's Palace, with the purpose of rooting out any personnel who might still be suspected of sympathy with the royalist cause. Any 'superstitious' pictures found were to be defaced, and orders were given that 'all persons employed about the brother and sister should be compelled to take the Covenant, and whoever rejected it should be dismissed without delay'.[14]

Such rigid supervision of the inoffensive royal children was presumably inspired by something more than pure religious zeal. There was at this time no overt intention on the part of the Parliament to depose, much less kill, Charles I. But the future had to be considered, and if it proved impossible to reach an agreement with the King, and he was loyally supported by his two eldest sons, it might be useful to have an alternative puppet sovereign at hand. If Henry Duke of Gloucester, now in his third year, should prove useful in this respect, it would be as well to see that he was indoctrinated with impeccable principles of Puritanism and Parliamentary supremacy.

To the elder of the children the dismissal of such of her loved attendants as still remained was a matter of the deepest anguish, and the seven-year-old Princess Elizabeth appealed from the House of Commons to the House of Lords in a letter which as its simplicity indicates was almost certainly penned by herself:

> My Lords,
>   I count myself very miserable that I must have my servants taken from me, and strangers put to me. You promised me that you would have a care of me, and I hope you will shew it, in preventing so great a grief as this would be to me. I pray, my Lords, consider of it, and give me cause to thank you, and to rest,
>   Your loving friend,
>   Elizabeth.
> To the right honourable the lords and peers in parliament.[15]

This letter Princess Elizabeth handed to the Earl of Pembroke, who was Parliament's custodian at St James's, and by him it was delivered to the Lords. It was not without effect, for the always latent jealousy between the two Houses was stirred into life. The Lords had not been consulted on the changes at the palace, and they demanded to know whether the facts alleged by the princess were correct. The Commons admitted that they were, and gave as their justification an alleged conspiracy to remove Elizabeth and Henry to Oxford. The Lords were not satisfied; they voted the removal of the servants of the King's children without their consent to be a breach of privilege, and appointed a committee of peers to visit St James's and report on the state of the household. The upshot of it all was that the Lords became primarily responsible for the welfare of the children. Further reductions were made in the establishment, since the Commons insisted that it was costing too much; but more latitude was allowed in its composition. The Covenant was no longer imposed; those in charge of the children had only to promise to advance their education 'in the true Protestant religion, piety and holiness of life'.[16]

The King meanwhile was increasingly anxious about the children he had so thoughtlessly allowed to fall into the hands of his enemies. When he heard of the changes in their establishment he sent a message of protest, but was told by the Parliamentary leaders that they 'hoped that they should take as good care, both of the souls and bodies of his majesty's children, as those at Oxford could have done'. King Charles then endeavoured to effect an exchange of the children for some Parliamentary prisoners of war. This was refused on the ground that the children were not prisoners at all.

For the remainder of the Great Civil War there was little change in the conditions endured by Elizabeth and Henry. In the autumn of 1643 Elizabeth, while running across a room, fell and broke a leg. The injury healed well, but the little princess was never in good health. Frail in body and deprived of the companionship of any other children except her brother, who was little more than a baby, she was at least able to develop her mind; study became the one solace of her dreary existence.

In her captivity she had the good fortune to come under the tuition of a formidable lady with the strange name of Bathsua Makin, daughter of a Sussex clergyman and sister of John Pell, a noted linguist and mathematician. Mrs Makin had the reputation of being 'the most learned Englishwoman of her time';[17] in her later years she kept a school at Tottenham and

wrote a book on female education. To Princess Elizabeth she
imparted knowledge of Latin, Greek, Hebrew, French, Italian
and Spanish; among less academic subjects she taught singing,
dancing, writing and needlework.

Princess Elizabeth was an avid pupil, and by the age of nine,
so Mrs Makin later affirmed, she could read and write all the
languages in which she instructed her. She was particularly
inclined towards Greek and Hebrew, which helped her towards
the study of Scripture; at this same age she was able to discourse
on the doctrines and precepts of the Christian faith. 'Had she
lived,' wrote her tutoress, 'what a Miracle she would have been
of her sex'.[18]

Early in 1645, when Elizabeth was nine years old and Henry
four, an improvement came in their circumstances. Ironically
enough it was brought about by the disappearance from the
scene of their governess, the Countess of Dorset, who had won
their love by her devotion. They had been by this time removed
to Whitehall, and perhaps the two Westminster palaces were
not the most salubrious of habitations; or perhaps the strain of
looking after the royal children was greater than might appear.
At any rate Lady Dorset, after less than two years in her post,
followed her predecessor, Lady Roxburgh, to the grave. When
she was taken ill it was decided to place the prince and princess
in the care of the Earl and Countess of Northumberland as
governor and governess.

Algernon Percy, tenth Earl of Northumberland, though he
had adhered to the Parliamentary cause, was a punctilious
aristocrat who had never ceased to display respect to the person
of his sovereign; and before he would consent to look after that
sovereign's offspring he asked the permission of the House of
Lords to treat them as befitted their rank and 'in all respects as
was agreeable to their quality and his duty.'[19] Northumberland
was too important and influential a personage to be brushed
aside, and the permission, however reluctantly, was given. The
children once more found themselves in the atmosphere of a
royal court, treated with ceremonial courtesy, and when Lord
Northumberland that summer moved for his health into the
country he was allowed to take them with him. It was the first
time they had left London since the beginning of the war.

This was, by comparison at least, a happy time for them.

Northumberland possessed a number of mansions and it is not certain to which he took them, but it was probably Syon House in Middlesex, an elegant and spacious home, in the grounds of which Henry would have been able to play contentedly and where his sister could read undisturbed. She was also able to write to her sister Mary in Holland and to send her presents. One letter has survived:

> Dear Sister,
>   I am so glad of so fit an opportunity to present my love to you. I intended to have sent you some venison, but being prevented at this time, I hope I shall have it ready to entertain you at the Hague when you return. Pray believe me to be,
>   Your most affectionate sister,
> To my dear sister, Princess Mary.   Elizabeth.[20]

Whether the venison ever reached The Hague, or whether the elder sister replied to the letter, is not known. Mary, whatever her deficiencies as a correspondent, was deeply attached to her little sister.

Mary had been growing up in a court becoming increasingly alien to her views and temperament. It seemed to compare badly with the stately ceremony of that of her father, which she remembered with increasing nostalgia as childhood receded. Relations with her mother-in-law, moreover, did not improve, and were exacerbated by political differences. The Thirty Years War in its closing stages had developed to a great extent into a struggle between France and Spain, centred in the Spanish Netherlands. The independent Dutch provinces, bordering on this territory, became of diplomatic importance, and their government was courted by both contestants. Mary, who though still in her early teens was not without influence on her young husband, favoured her mother's country. Princess Amelia was inclined towards an agreement with Spain. Bickering in the princely family was aggravated by the fact that Prince Frederick Henry was at this time afflicted with a serious illness which affected his brain. He became moody and capricious, and was dominated by his strong-minded wife. The result was estrangement between the Prince of Orange and not only his daughter-in-law but his son. Things were not easy for Mary, and she looked with unhappy longing towards England, from which country the news was more and more alarming.

The tide had turned against King Charles. When, on that joyous day at Edgehill, he was reunited with his queen, his affairs looked more rosy than they had done since the outbreak of war. On that very day his nephew Prince Maurice and Sir Henry Wilmot routed the Parliamentary army of Sir William Waller on Roundway Down in Wiltshire; it was as complete a victory as any in the war. The Cavalier cause (the terms *Cavalier* and *Roundhead* were coming into general use at this time) was in the ascendant, and now Queen Henrietta Maria had arrived with a substantial train of artillery and reinforcements of soldiery.

But by the end of 1643 prospects no longer seemed so good. The King's greatest worry, now as always, was shortage of money; without it his forces could not be maintained in their present high state of morale and efficiency. His one real chance was to gain control of London and win the support of the City merchants. He had failed in this objective after Edgehill, and he had one more chance in the autumn of this year. The two main armies, those of the King and of Essex, were both moving, after operations in the west, in the direction of the capital, and they met south-west of Newbury. The First Battle of Newbury, as it came to be called, was in some respects Edgehill in reverse. It was fierce and bloody, but the result of the fighting, like so many engagements of the Civil War, was indecisive. Strategically, however, its effect was anything but indecisive. The King failed to bar his opponent's road towards London, and Essex, unlike Charles in the previous year, took advantage of the opportunity given him.

Thereafter, though this was not apparent at the time, King Charles's fortunes could only decline.

To make matters worse, there were bickerings in Oxford. Henrietta was at her best when affairs were going badly; at her worst when she was getting her own way. She now set herself up as the Generalissima she claimed to be, exerting her influence over her uxorious and weak-willed husband and squabbling with his wisest counsellors such as Sir Edward Hyde. Above all she opposed Prince Rupert, once her protégé and now by far the

King's most capable general. Her principal ally was George Lord Digby, a mercurial character who had now become Secretary of State in place of the distinguished Lord Falkland who had perished at Newbury. Digby, an incorrigible intriguer with an inflated idea of his own capacity, was totally unreliable; he was, moreover, perennially jealous of Prince Rupert.

Queen Henrietta headed what might be called a war party in that it advocated uncompromising hostility to the Roundheads, even to the extent of cold-shouldering rebel renegades who offered to defect to the King. But it was a war party without political or military judgement.

The outcome of the Civil War was virtually decided in 1644. With the King's advisers at odds, and Prince Rupert hampered in working out a strategy by the intrigues of the Queen and Digby, it became increasingly difficult to counter the tactics of the Roundhead commanders, Essex and Waller. Each of these commanded a substantial army, and had they not been thoroughly distrustful of one another they would probably have achieved a total victory in this year. As it was, by the spring they were both active in the west and a threat to Oxford was developing: thereupon the King decided on two important moves.

The first was a second parting from his queen. The reunion of husband and wife had had at least one happy result, and Henrietta was pregnant once again. On 17 April she left Oxford. It was not intended to be more than a temporary separation; it had been decided that the baby should be born in Bath, from which if necessary she could escape from the country through Bristol. In the event King Charles and Queen Henrietta were never to meet again.

She spent only a few days at Bath. Her journey had been a difficult one, and she was in the lowest spirits. Waller's army was in the west country, and she was terrified of capture. She insisted on pushing on to Exeter, and from there she got a note through to London imploring the assistance of her old physician Sir Theodore Mayerne, now in his seventies and sheltering in retirement from the storms of the time. She wrote also of her sufferings to her husband, who was moved to second her appeal. 'Mayerne, pour l'amour de moy, allé trouver ma Femme', he wrote succinctly to the old doctor.[21]

Somehow these letters reached their destination, and

Mayerne did not hesitate. He set out with a colleague, Sir Matthew Lister, and the pair reached Exeter in time. On 16 June Queen Henrietta, after one of the worst confinements she had had, was delivered of her ninth child, a daughter.

Meanwhile the King had taken the second of his decisions. Essex and Waller were converging towards Oxford, though without co-ordination or co-operation. To avoid a siege of his capital, and in the hope of joining his wife in the west, King Charles executed a brilliant tactical move. On the night of 3 June, taking the Prince of Wales with him but leaving the Duke of York behind, he marched out of Oxford with a small body of troops and slipped through between the forces of his two enemies into the Cotswolds. Essex and Waller predictably turned to pursue him, but equally predictably quarrelled on the question of tactics. Instead of joining forces with Waller, as the situation demanded and indeed as orders from Parliament required, Essex after a brief conference with his officially subordinate general abandoned the campaign and marched south-west to the relief of Lyme, which was being besieged by Prince Maurice. The King, having now only one foe to deal with, after some manoeuvring closed with Waller at Cropredy Bridge, near Banbury. There on 29 June, with his son Charles at his side, he won a victory which, for the time being at least, saved Oxford from capture. He then turned south-west in the direction of Exeter.

Henrietta had no intelligence of her husband's military success. All she knew was that Essex was approaching Exeter on his march towards Lyme. She sent a message to him asking for safe conduct to Bath or Bristol, but Essex, whose behaviour showed curiously alternating moods of generosity and brutality, replied that he was not concerned with her safety and would consent only to take her to London. Desperately ill and beset by something approaching nervous hysteria, fearing also that her husband might fall into a trap by marching to her rescue, Queen Henrietta decided on flight from the country.

Mayerne tried to interpose, warning her that her life was in danger. But Henrietta was determined. A fortnight after the birth of her daughter, whom she now left in the charge of the Countess of Dalkeith, she set off from Exeter in disguise with three attendants. Outside the town she was met by her faithful servant Lord Jermyn, and her dwarf Jeffrey Hudson, and when enemy troops were found to be in the neighbourhood the small party were obliged to hide for two days in a hut. Six days later, after further adventures, Henrietta reached Pendennis Castle in Cornwall and was carried in a litter, more dead than alive, to Falmouth. There she embarked in a Dutch vessel, and after a typically hazardous voyage, during which her craft was fired on by Parliamentary ships, Henrietta landed in Brittany and was able to make her way to safety at the French court.[22]

King Charles was on his way south when he heard of his daughter's birth, and he sent orders that she should be christened in Exeter Cathedral, apparently apprehensive that his wife might forestall him with a Catholic baptism. The baby was named Henrietta after her mother, and later the name Anne was added in honour of Anne of Austria, since the death of Louis XIII Queen-Regent of France. To posterity Henrietta Anne was to become best known as 'Minette', the pet name her eldest brother conferred on her, though in fact nobody but he ever called her that.

Essex had been threatening Exeter with a siege, though rather half-heartedly; after the Queen's flight he left it undisturbed and moved off in the direction of Cornwall. The King for his part continued in his march towards the city, where he arrived on 26 July. He found his baby daughter at Bedford House in the capable hands of Lady Dalkeith, and after one night he continued on his march in pursuit of Essex.

In the following month he achieved the greatest military triumph of his life. Having proved at Cropredy Bridge that when he took matters into his own hands he could act both efficiently and decisively, he entered on a Cornish campaign with vigorous confidence. In a series of skilful manoeuvres he outwitted Essex and then routed him at Beacon Hill and Castle Dore, forcing the Roundhead commander into ignominious flight by means of a fishing boat to Plymouth.

As regards his personal prestige, King Charles was on the crest of a wave. But his Cornish triumph was on a comparatively small scale, and elsewhere there was disaster. On his westward march the King had received the shattering news of the total defeat on 2 July of Prince Rupert and the Marquess of Newcastle, Prince Charles's old governor, at Marston Moor in

Yorkshire. Marston Moor was the biggest battle of the Civil War. The Scots had come in on the side of the Parliament, and it was a joint Anglo-Scottish force that demolished Rupert and Newcastle. It was a muddled affair which reflected little credit on the higher command, though much on two subordinate officers, Sir Thomas Fairfax and Oliver Cromwell. But its results were decisive. The war was far from over yet, but from now on the King was on the defensive. The news from Yorkshire quite overshadowed the Cornish campaign.

With the certainty that the northern Roundhead armies would move south, King Charles was concerned now to protect at least his capital city of Oxford. He therefore moved back in that direction, on the way re-entering Exeter on 17 September. There he saw once again his baby daughter Henrietta, as it turned out for the last time. During the week that he spent in the city he made what arrangements he could for her welfare, assigning for her maintenance the bulk of the excise revenues of Exeter and appointing as her chaplain Dr Thomas Fuller, who was to achieve fame as the author of *The Worthies of England*. For the rest he was content to leave her in the care of the courageous and resourceful Lady Dalkeith.

In October he had another encounter with Waller in the Second Battle of Newbury, holding his own in what was yet again an inconclusive engagement. By his side once more was Charles Prince of Wales, who at fourteen was becoming an experienced soldier.

The campaign of 1644 did little good to Charles I, in spite of his personal successes. For the Parliament they had a significant result. The weakest point in Roundhead strategy was divided command, and this was brought home to the London administration with redoubled force in that year. Essex and Waller were continuously at loggerheads. Lord Fairfax and the Earl of Manchester, two of the Parliamentary commanders at Marston Moor (the third was the Scottish Earl of Leven), were equally unable to co-operate. The Parliament had had enough of this. At the end of the year the decision was taken to combine its military resources in a new unified force which would be capable of finishing off the war.

The result was the establishment of the New Model Army, which began to form at Windsor in April, 1645. The supreme command was given to Sir Thomas Fairfax, Lord Fairfax's son, who with Oliver Cromwell had been the chief architect of victory at Marston Moor. In due course Cromwell became his lieutenant-general of horse and right-hand man.

It was the beginning of the end. There were to be no more Cavalier victories, and at this point King Charles decided it was time to part company with his heir. If it came to the worst they must not be killed or captured together.

The King's purpose was to hold Oxford. In the west country was Prince Rupert, who had rallied his troops after defeat in the north and was now in general command of the King's forces with his headquarters at Bristol. The King now appointed his eldest son nominal General of the Western Association and Generalissimo of all his forces, with a council which included Sir Edward Hyde as the principal member. Rupert remained in practice chief military commander, but in the west was subject to the council.

It was hoped that the new arrangement would strengthen the royalist position in the west, but it was hardly calculated to do anything of the sort. Rupert was not on the best of terms with Hyde, and the warlike prince did not find it easy to take orders from a council over which presided, if only nominally, a boy not yet fifteen. Prince Charles, however, was delighted. It was an exciting responsibility for him; his cousin Rupert was his hero, and he was only too glad to place himself under his tuition as a soldier.

On 5 March 1645 the Prince of Wales left Oxford for Bristol, saying good-bye for the last time to his father, who kept his second son James with him in the capital. Young Charles had high hopes, but they were hardly fulfilled. Bristol soon became a hornets' nest. The Prince of course had no personal power, but misfortunes were laid at his door, and his very presence led to bickerings among his political and military advisers.

It is not surprising that he indulged in what diversions he could find. He felt himself an adult now, with a fine appearance and a soldierly record. He was ready to take an interest in the opposite sex.

He had opportunities to move about his western command, and at Bridgwater he renewed his acquaintance with Christa-belle Wyndham, whose husband was governor of the town and who in Prince Charles's earliest days had been one of his nurses. She was now a mature and dashing lady, wanton and indiscreet, and she made no secret of the hold she soon gained over the young prince, even caressing him in public. How far their affair went is uncertain, but the latest biographer of Charles II is of the opinion that 'to Mrs Wyndham, in Bridgwater, should probably be accorded the honour of having seduced her former nurseling'.[23] If this was indeed the case she was the first of a long line of charming ladies who have enriched the fame of Charles Stuart.

In 1645 there were two major disasters, the defeat of King Charles's army at Naseby and the surrender of Bristol by Prince Rupert to Sir Thomas Fairfax. They put an end to effective Cavalier resistance.

Naseby, fought on 14 June in that central area of England (the village is in Northamptonshire) which saw so much of the action in the Civil War, marked the triumph of the New Model Army. Fairfax, with Cromwell at his side, inflicted total defeat on King Charles and Rupert, though had the royal command been better organized, and but for some muddled tactics in the closing stages, the result might have been reversed.

Naseby was so complete a repulse that even the indomitable Prince Rupert, the foremost fighting man on the Royalist side, advised King Charles to come to terms with his enemies. This he advocated on purely military grounds, being convinced that the cause was lost and that the only choice open to the King was between sacrificing part of his power and losing all. But Charles would have none of it. To give in on any vital point to the Roundheads would mean abandoning the supremacy of the Church of England, which was now anathema to the Parliamentarians; and this he would never do.

During the next few months the King wandered rather aimlessly around Herefordshire and the Cotswolds, vainly trying to recruit new forces. Rupert withdrew to organize the defence of Bristol and hold it for his sovereign. But Fairfax besieged the town with a powerful army, and Rupert, judging the military position hopeless, surrendered England's second port on terms on 11 September.

It was the biggest blow yet to fall on the King. Historians mainly agree that Rupert's decision was militarily correct;

Bristol was in the circumstances untenable, and to prolong the siege would have achieved nothing but useless bloodshed. The fact remains that he had told the King that he could hold the town for four months, and he had not, as Charles angrily told him, held it four days. In the circumstances the King's fury is understandable; but the hysteria with which he reacted shows the strain that these years of desperate war had imposed on him. He wrote his nephew a letter of bitter reproach, stripped him of all his offices, and ordered him to leave the country.

Undoubtedly King Charles was influenced by the advice Rupert had given him after Naseby; he suspected his nephew, quite unjustly, of treachery and of trying to make peace with Parliament for his own purposes. But that he could even think such a thing of one who had always enjoyed his complete trust was a sign of the mental deterioration that had overcome him at this time. In the event happier counsels prevailed; after Rupert had angrily demanded a military inquiry his honour was vindicated, and he did not in fact leave England till the war was over. For the moment, however, King Charles had deprived himself of his ablest general; but neither Rupert's services nor anybody else's could do much for him now.

These calamitous events had their effect on the members of his family. The Prince of Wales was the most deeply affected. He had been enjoying life in the west country, but at the time of the Naseby campaign he began to tire of being a figurehead and to endeavour to take things into his own hands. The King's affairs elsewhere were going badly; Prince Rupert was absent; it was time, the Prince felt, to assert himself.

Trouble was caused by the jealousies and intrigues of the two main local commanders, George Lord Goring and Sir Richard Grenville. Goring had fought gallantly at Marston Moor, but he was unreliable, usually drunk, and habitually insubordinate. Grenville was self-seeking and doubtful in his loyalty. These two, sometimes in alliance and sometimes in rivalry, wrought havoc in the western command. Prince Charles himself tried to take the matter in hand, and in doing so found himself more than once defying his father's orders. But he was on the spot, and he refused to give way. He ended by depriving Grenville of his command.

These transactions led to some acrimony between father and

son. Young Charles, however, though asserting his own initiative, was acting in concert with Hyde. In any case King Charles
was now hardly in control of his own affairs. His world was
falling about his ears, and his spirits were at their lowest ebb.
One of his greatest fears was that his eldest son might fall into the
hands of his enemies, as it was becoming more and more
probable that he himself would do. With both the King and his
heir in their power the Roundheads would be able to man-
ipulate things as they wished.

'Charles,' he wrote to his son on 5 August 1645, 'it is very fit
for me now to prepare for the worst. . . . Wherefore know that
my pleasure is, whensoever you find yourself in apparent danger
of falling into the rebels' hands, that you convey yourself into
France, and there to be under your mother's care; who is to have
the absolute full power of your education in all things except
religion, and in that not to meddle at all, but leave it entirely to
the care of your tutor, the bishop of Salisbury, or to whom he
shall appoint to supply his place, in time of his necessitated
absence.' [24]

The Bishop of Salisbury was the Prince's old mentor, Brian
Duppa, who was now in Oxford but was possibly earmarked to
go with him to France. The King commanded unquestioning
obedience to his orders from Charles and the council, and the
letter must have been a severe reminder to the young generalissimo that, in spite of his responsible position, he was still only
fifteen years old.

For the moment, however, there was no imminent danger of
his falling into the enemy's hands; so there was no immediate
necessity to leave England. During the autumn of 1645 and the
ensuing winter the Prince remained in the west country,
withdrawing by degrees towards the Cornish coast from which
he could sail when the situation seemed desperate. At one point
he fixed his headquarters in Exeter. There were many things on
his mind, and it does not appear that he took particular interest
in the presence at Bedford House of the one-year-old girl who
was his youngest sister.

From now on, however, events moved swiftly and fatally.
King Charles had given up the struggle, and although he was
not prepared to follow Rupert's advice and come to terms with
his English enemies (Rupert was now restored to favour though

not to his command) he made the strange decision to entrust his personal safety to the Scottish army, still in arms on English soil. In the words written in his name, 'Necessity is now my counsellour, and commands me to study my safety by a disguised withdrawing from my chiefest strength, and adventuring upon their loyalty, who first began my Troubles'.[25]

On 27 April, 1646, he slipped out of Oxford with the minimum of attendants, made his way northwards through the Roundhead-infested Midlands, and surrendered to the Scots. He had contemplated taking the Duke of York with him, but in the event left him behind. Thus once again he allowed one of his children to fall into the hands of his enemies, though in this case it made little difference. James would have been no better off as a prisoner of the Scots.

When King Charles left Oxford his eldest son had already begun to put his orders into effect. The Prince was under the guidance of Hyde, and he and the council decided at the beginning of March that it was time to carry out the King's instructions, even if his heir could not get immediately to France as enjoined. On the 10th of that month Prince Charles left Penzance for the Scilly Isles.

The Scillies, where conditions were primitive and food scarce, were only a temporary refuge. In the following month the Prince and his companions moved on to Jersey. This was a more congenial habitation, and Charles enjoyed himself. He was welcome and popular, and was able to keep up something at least resembling a court. There was little to be done in the realm of public affairs, and he amused himself by learning to sail, laying the foundations of that love of the sea which was to prove one of his favourite interests in years to come. Here too he continued his education on the lines so pleasantly laid down for him by Christabella Wyndham. There were some attractive ladies in Jersey who were only too glad to play their part in making the young royal exile's stay in their island more tolerable. It was said that in the following year a baby boy was born to a well-placed Jersey damsel, and that this first of his offspring was later privately acknowledged by him. The story is suspect, but there is little doubt that Prince Charles in Jersey took early steps towards becoming, as was said of him later, if not literally the father of his people, at least the father of a good many of them.

Jersey, however, was within the British dominions of which King Charles I was no longer master. At almost any moment the island might fall to the rebels. The King, moreover, had ordered his son to repair to France, and his consort was urging him to do so. She sent Lord Jermyn, her most trusted and most intimate adviser, to the Channel Islands to urge her case, and Charles was a sympathetic listener. Hyde, anti-French in sentiment and dreading the romanizing influence of Henrietta Maria, was opposed to a move; but the Prince asserted himself. After seven weeks in Jersey he embarked in the yacht provided for him by Jermyn, and on 26 June arrived at St Malo. From there he proceeded to Saint-Germain to join his mother. Hyde had refused to accompany him.

Thus the eldest of Charles I's six surviving children left British territory for exile abroad. Almost simultaneously, though hardly of her own volition, the youngest did the same.

Henrietta Maria, in the extremity of her distress after the birth of her daughter, had felt compelled to leave her in Exeter under the charge of Lady Dalkeith. Now she was desperate with anxiety to have the child with her. From her distant viewpoint in France it seemed to her that Henrietta's governess was making no effort to comply with her orders, which were to get the child out of Exeter, now in the early months of 1646 being besieged by Sir Thomas Fairfax, an altogether more formidable adversary than the vacillating Essex. She gave vent to bitter reproaches against Lady Dalkeith. In this she was grossly unjust, as was pointed out by Sir Edward Hyde in a dignified letter to Jermyn. To remove the princess at this juncture, Hyde protested, was quite impracticable. There was better security for her in Exeter, still holding out under the governor, Sir John Berkeley, than could be hoped for in any place to which she could be taken, while any attempt to get her out might jeopardize the prospects of the Prince of Wales, now himself planning to leave the country. Lady Dalkeith, concluded Sir Edward, 'could as easily have beaten Fairfax, as prevented being shut up in Exeter, from whence I hope she will yet get safely with her charge, to whom I am confident she hath omitted no part of her duty.'[26]

Lady Dalkeith was in fact both courageous and devoted, and her resourcefulness was to be abundantly proved during the ensuing months. The probability that the young Henrietta would soon be in the hands of the Roundheads was clear to her, but she was determined that, whatever the circumstances, she would herself be faithful to her mission and would not be separated from her charge except by brute force.

Berkeley resisted till April, but on the 13th of that month he surrendered to Fairfax. The terms were honourable, and as regards Princess Henrietta it was agreed that she and her household should go to any place the King should choose, that her future maintenance should be the responsibility of Parliament, and that a messenger should be given a pass to go to the King at Oxford to learn his pleasure on the matter. This was duly done, and Lady Dalkeith was able to inform Fairfax that King Charles had decided on Richmond as his daughter's residence.

It was one thing, however, to come to terms with Fairfax, and another to induce the Parliament to honour these terms. Parliament chose to ignore the King's wishes, and the little princess was sent not to Richmond but to Oatlands, near Weybridge in Surrey; the promised funds, moreover, were not forthcoming, and Lady Dalkeith was forced to maintain the household out of her own resources. She addressed repeated requests for redress to Westminster, but her letters were ignored until, at the end of May, she received orders to deliver the princess to the care of Lady Northumberland at St James's Palace, where she was to be incarcerated with her sister and brother, Elizabeth and Henry, and all her attendants dismissed.

The intrepid governess refused to be intimidated. She kept the princess with her at Oatlands, and on 28 June sent a spirited protest to the Speaker of the House of Lords:

My Lord,—Presently upon the surrender of Exeter, while the Princess Henrietta, under my care, was on her way towards these parts, I presented your Lordship my humble desires to Parliament, concerning the settlement of Her Highness with such allowance as to them should seem expedient, since which time, there having been nothing therein determined, I have been necessitated to renew those desires. I am not now so hopeful as I was, yet once more entreat that the honourable Houses would be pleased to consider that I received this trust from his Majesty; that I have his injunction . . . not to leave the Princess, and that, by the article of Exeter which concerns Her Highness, you may also perceive she is to be disposed of according to His Majesty's directions; that I have preserved Her Highness, not without many cares and fears, from a weak to a very hopeful condition of health, that I am best acquainted with her condition and constitution, that my coming into these parts was voluntary, that I have disbursed a great sum of money for the support of Her Highness and her family, since the treaty at Exeter, that I have, because the time is very precious in the condition I am in, endeavoured to anticipate all possible obstructions, which, I humbly conceive, did either arise from the charge or inconvenience of dividing the King's children into two families, or that they had not full confidence in me, or that there is some other exception to my person. . . .[27]

Lady Dalkeith proceeded to request that her attendance on Princess Henrietta should continue. 'But if this be not satisfactory, I have only these requests, that I may be reimbursed the money I have laid out during my attendance and expectation of the Parliament's pleasure, and that I may have a pass to send one to his Majesty to know his pleasure, without which, in honour and honesty, I cannot deliver up this child.'[28]

This letter had no more result than earlier protests; Parliament maintained its sullen silence. Lady Dalkeith, with the flight of the child's mother from Exeter doubtless in mind, decided on similar action. On the morning of 25 July princess and governess were found to be missing; after a few hours the following letter was brought to Oatlands:

Gentlewomen,

You are witness with what patience I have expected the pleasure of the parliament; I have found it impossible to obtain any justice to her highness, or favour to myself, or any of you. I was no longer able to keep her, which was the cause I have been forced to take this upon me. Be pleased to repair to his majesty, all of you, or as many of you as think fit; I then am sure you will enjoy the blessing of serving her highness, which, believe me, is heartily wished by me. It will be a great mark of your faithfulness and kindness to your mistress to conceal her being gone as long as you can, and it will make your past service more considered, and that to come more acceptable. And, trust me, your divulging it will be of no advantage to you. Thus you may do it, seeming to expect her the day following after the receipt of this letter, and then cause to deliver this other to Mr Marshall, after having read it, and tell him—which is truth—that I have removed her highness to a better air, whither you may, if you will, follow her.

All her wearing clothes, woollen or linen, you may distribute amongst you; the little plate she hath, Mrs Case will have a care of; her other things are to be continued with Mr Marshall. I am so confident you will behave yourselves kindly and faithfully to your mistress, that you will yet more oblige me to be, what you will always find me, which is to you all,

A very hearty, kind, friend,
A. Dalkeith.

For her Highness the Princess, Henrietta, her gentlewomen.[29]

It was hardly to be expected that the secret could be kept for long, and within three days the news had reached Parliament. It was received with equanimity. Members pointed out that now there would be no question of forking out money for the infant princess's maintenance, and no order was made for a search or pursuit.

Meanwhile Lady Dalkeith had lost no time. Disguising herself in a shabby cloak, and the princess in boy's clothes, she walked to Dover; she had only one attendant, who took turns with her in carrying the two-year-old child. What route she took is not known, but the journey cannot have been less than a hundred miles. It was not made easier by the outcries of the little girl, who kept complaining of the clothes she was forced to wear and protesting that she was a royal princess. At Dover the party boarded the packet boat for Calais, and a few days later young Henrietta was in her mother's arms.

'Intelligence of the whole affair,' wrote Père Cyprien de

Gamache, 'was despatched to the queen, who quickly sent her carriages; and the gouvernante, with all her train, reached Paris in safety, and respectfully placed in the hands of her majesty the precious deposit, which she had so happily preserved amidst so many awful dangers.'[30]

James Duke of York, now in his fourteenth year, was less lucky. Fairfax began the siege of Oxford on 1 May 1646, a few days after the King's escape. On 24 June the city surrendered; 'no other Article being made for the Duke than that he was to be deliver'd into the hands of the Parliament, to be disposed of according to their pleasure. And this particular was the more observable, because so exact a care was taken in relation to all others besides the Duke.'[31] This comment, recorded in the memoirs compiled many years later from his notes, shows how bitterly the young prince felt about his treatment.

His father had left him in the care of Sir George Radcliffe, whose chief claim to fame was his close friendship with the Earl of Strafford. Fairfax ordered Radcliffe to keep the Duke at Oxford till Parliament's pleasure was known; in the meantime letters arrived from the Queen urging that James should either be taken to Ireland or brought to her in France. 'But Sir George,' to quote the memoirs again, 'absolutely refused to comply with either of those commands; alledging for his excuse that he durst not convey any of the King's sons out of the kingdom, without an express order from his Majesty; which nicety, or I may rather call it indiscretion of his, might have cost his R: Highness dear, as being the occasion of his being put into the Rebell's hands.'[32] This seems hardly fair to Radcliffe. His real reason was surely that he had no choice but to obey Fairfax's orders.

Soon after this orders were received from Parliament that James should be brought to London, where he arrived on 28 July. Some four miles out of the city he and his attendants were met by the Earl of Northumberland, who promptly dismissed Radcliffe and the rest of the Duke's servants. James was then taken to join Elizabeth and Henry at St James's Palace, where Lord and Lady Northumberland, with their customary courtesy, 'treated the King's three children with the same respect and care, as if they had been intrusted with them immediately from his Majesty'.[33]

King Charles's trust in the Scots was entirely misplaced. At the beginning of the following year, in one of the most squalid bargains of the Civil War, they handed him over to the English Parliament in return for a cash payment.

The King and three of his children, half the royal family, were captives of the all-conquering Roundheads. The Queen, her eldest son and her youngest daughter were safe on the Continent but with no resources of their own, dependent for their maintenance on the charity of a foreign court.

Mary of Orange, the Princess Royal, the only member of her house enjoying prosperity, watched in helpless dismay from The Hague.

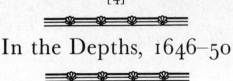

4

In the Depths, 1646–50

The next few years saw the total eclipse of the Stuart monarchy in Great Britain—an eclipse which, although the royal family never lost hope of a restoration, showed every sign of being permanent. By the end of 1646 the Roundheads were everywhere triumphant, and the all-powerful Parliament, holding the King in its hands, had, for the time being at any rate, the whole-hearted backing of the highly efficient, well-organized and well-paid New Model Army.

There was little hope of foreign aid. France was the native country of Queen Henrietta Maria, and she and two of her children found hospitality there. But that was as far as help could be expected to go. Louis XIII and Cardinal Richelieu were dead. The King, Louis XIV, was a boy of eight, and the country was rent by the internal dissensions normally attendant on a royal minority; Cardinal Mazarin, Richelieu's successor, was hated and not yet in firm authority. The other great Continental power, the Spain of Philip IV, weakened by war and by the decline of its imperial pretensions, had neither the will nor the strength to assist a cause which had nothing to offer in return. France and Spain, moreover, as well as the Empire, were locked in an exhausting struggle marking the closing stages of the Thirty Years War.

Only in the Netherlands could a gleam of hope be discerned; and it was nothing more than a gleam. The United Provinces were at this time advancing in commercial prosperity, in colonial expansion and in naval strength; but they were by no means the equals of France or Spain. Moreover their federal administration was republican in temper, and their leaders in natural sympathy with the Commonwealth of England which had renounced its monarchical constitution. The Stadtholder

Frederick Henry, titular commander of the States' armed forces and himself a whole-hearted royalist, was a dying man, and what political power he had wielded had virtually vanished. His vigorous son, with his young Stuart wife by his side, stood alone in his support for the fallen dynasty.

Having been handed over by the Scots to the English Parliamentarians, King Charles was taken early in 1647 to Holmby House in Northamptonshire. He was at first treated with the deference that was his due, but he was very much a prisoner and under constant guard. From then on he proceeded to indulge in somewhat devious and increasingly futile negotiations with his captors, seeking to find a way out from his miseries by playing off the Army and the Parliament against each other.

He was at least able to correspond with his wife, who was leading a far from happy existence in France. She lived mainly in the old palace of Saint-Germain which the French royal family had put at her disposal. She received from them a pension of 1,200 francs a day, far from sufficient for her needs. Most of it went on vain schemes for helping her husband, and she now had to support her son the Prince of Wales, who was given no pension. These two and the baby Princess Henrietta Anne lived in penury, sometimes unable to heat their rooms and often wondering where the next meal was to come from.

Queen Henrietta put her most ardent hopes in a rich marriage for her son. The intended bride was none other than the greatest heiress in France, Princess Anne-Marie, Duchesse de Montpensier. This imposing lady, known in her own time and to later generations as 'La Grande Mademoiselle', was the daughter of Gaston Duc d'Orléans, younger brother of Louis XIII. Her wealth, however, and her principal title came from her mother, Marie de Bourbon, Duchesse de Montpensier, heiress of the Guises, who had died when she was a few days old. Anne-Marie was three years older than her cousin Charles; she was tall, commanding and arrogant, full of her own importance and conscious of her proud position.

From the time of Prince Charles's arrival in the summer of 1646 Queen Henrietta contrived to throw these two young people together with all the determination of a born matchmaker, but there was never much chance of consummation.

Neither of them wanted it. Charles, though dutifully pursuing the courtship, found his cousin overpowering; while Mademoiselle hoped for a more rewarding alliance than one with a penniless prince in exile. The Emperor Ferdinand III, who was Anne of Austria's brother-in-law, had been recently widowed, and her eyes were turned towards Vienna.

In her memoirs written much later Anne-Marie spoke kindly but patronizingly of the sixteen-year-old prince who had come to court her. He was, she said, 'tall for his age—a beautiful head, black hair, a brown complexion, and of a tolerable figure'.[1] But he could not speak French, and even with the help of the linguist Prince Rupert as interpreter his courtship was halting and awkward. Describing a ball at which she was given a throne to sit on, she wrote complacently:

> . . . None of those present, indeed, omitted to tell me, that I had never appeared less constrained than when upon the throne; and that, as I was of a race to occupy it, I should fill it with an equal grace when in possession of it for a longer time than at the ball. Whilst thus enthroned, and the Prince of Wales at my feet, my heart viewed him *de haut en bas*, as well as my eyes. It was my wish to marry the Emperor, and, apparently, I had the consent of the court; indeed, it had been said by some of the ministers, that the Queen had the means of affording consolation to her widowed brother. Whilst dressing me that evening, she had talked of nothing but this marriage; saying that she wished it exceedingly, and that, for the happiness of her house, she should do all she could to bring it about. Thus, the idea of an empire so much occupied my mind, that I only looked on the Prince of Wales as an object of pity. . . .[2]

Faced with competition such as this, Prince Charles had no hope of winning a lady of the stature of Anne-Marie de Montpensier; the wonder is that even Henrietta Maria should have thought it possible. The Prince turned with relief to more entertaining if less exalted company. His boon companions the Duke of Buckingham and his brother Lord Francis Villiers appeared in Paris in the autumn of 1646, and the three of them joined in the pursuit of more accommodating ladies.

However depressing might be the circumstances and conditions surrounding him, Prince Charles usually contrived to enjoy himself. His brother James was of a harder, and perhaps more sensitive, temperament. He had resented keenly the way in which he had been delivered into the enemy's hands, and although at St James's, where he was treated honourably, he was better off physically than he had been in the siege conditions of Oxford, he was from the first determined to escape if it were humanly possible. In this aim he had the fervent support of his sister Elizabeth. This intense, introspective child was as high-spirited as she was physically frail; she was delighted to have her brother's company after her many months of virtual solitude, but she felt that it was his duty to their father to make every effort to break free from durance vile and fight the good fight in the world outside. '"Were I a boy," she told him when he joined her in the summer of 1646, "I would not long remain a captive, however light and glittering might be the fetters that bound me."'[3]

James was in correspondence with his father, and towards the end of the year he wrote to him about his intentions. King Charles, who was then still with the Scots, replied urging him to make his escape if he could do so without serious danger and join him in Newcastle, or else get to his mother in France. The King's letter was intercepted and its contents laid before Parliament, and the result was greater vigilance at Westminster. Northumberland protested that, as there were clearly plots on foot for the rescue of the Duke of York, he could not be any longer responsible for his safe-keeping; he was overruled, however, and ordered to see that no unauthorized persons were admitted to the prince's presence. Hopes of escape had been thwarted, and James could only bide his time.

In March 1647 Northumberland was given leave to take the royal children away from Westminster for the summer, and they were moved to Hampton Court. In the same month an event occurred across the sea which was of great importance to them—the death at The Hague of Prince Frederick Henry of Orange. His son William and his daughter-in-law Mary were with him when he died, and before the day was out William was elected by the States to all his father's offices. He was now Stadtholder of the United Provinces, and he and his wife, the

Princess Royal, were free to devote their attention to the object
nearest to Mary's heart—the welfare of her Stuart relations.

For the moment there was little enough that they could do.
Mary kept in touch with her family so far as she was able. But she
was not a good correspondent, and doubtless she felt that at this
stage it was best to keep her letters innocuous. One to the Prince
of Wales read:

Dear Brother,

Though I am afraid to be troublesome, yet that cannot
hinder me from writing to you, hoping by this means to keep
me still in your memory, since there is nothing I should
esteem myself more happy in than to have the happiness to
assure you, by word of mouth, how much I am, and ever will
be, dear brother,

Your most affectionate sister and friend,
Mary.

This letter was endorsed on receipt: 'Received the 27th of June,
1647, by Sir John Berkeley, from the young Princess of
Orange.'[4]

In the meantime Mary had other things to think about, for
she was now pregnant. The hope of perpetuating the Orange
dynasty was, however, for the moment frustrated. On 12
October Mary had a miscarriage.

In the meantime vital changes were taking place in the
fortunes of her father. The rivalry between Parliament and the
Army which was to play so important a part in English history
was now developing, and in this struggle possession of the person
of the King was of paramount importance. Fairfax was still in
command of the Army, but he had no political ambitions and it
was Oliver Cromwell and his son-in-law Henry Ireton who took
the initiative in the moves that followed. It was almost certainly
at their orders that on 3 June 1647, a certain Cornet Joyce,
otherwise unknown to fame, appeared at Holmby House with a
band of soldiers and demanded that King Charles should
accompany them. When he asked what warrant Joyce had for
his action, the cornet simply pointed to his troops; the King,
with dignified resignation, replied that the warrant was written
in a fair and legible hand.

The news was received with something akin to panic in Parliamentary circles in the capital. It was feared that the royal children too would be kidnapped by the Army, and Northumberland was ordered to bring them back immediately to St James's Palace. There they were placed under close guard.

The King meanwhile was being taken under strong military escort towards London. A stop was made at Windsor, and from there he sent a request to Parliament to be allowed to see his children. In Parliament's present mood it was hardly surprising that the request was peremptorily refused; but when the King was moved to Lord Craven's house at Caversham he laid his case before Sir Thomas Fairfax. The Captain-General of the New Model Army, though he was gradually being pushed out of the limelight, was still too important a person to be ignored, and on his intercession consent to the meeting was reluctantly given. The King wrote to his second son:

Casam, July 4, 1647.

James,

I am in hope that you may be permitted, with your brother and sister, to come to some place betwixt this and London, where I may see you.

To this end, therefore, I command you to ask leave of the two Houses to make a journey (if it may be) for a night or two.

But rather than not see you, I will be content that you come to some convenient place to dine, and go back again at night.

And foreseeing the fear of your being brought within the power of the Army as I am, may be objected, to hinder this my desire, I have full assurance from Sir Thomas Fairfax, and the chief officers that there will be no interruption or impediment made by them for your return how and when you please. So God bless you,

Your loving father,

Charles R.

Send me word as soon as you can of the time and place where I shall have the contentment of seeing you, your brother and sister.[5]

Fairfax duly used his influence, personally guaranteeing the safe return of the children if they could spend two days with their father. The Commons, after some hesitation, agreed to the visit, provided Lord Northumberland accompanied his charges.

The day selected was 16 July. The three children (James, the eldest, was not yet fourteen) left St James's at seven in the morning, travelling by coach and attended by a strong guard of the City of London militia. At ten they reached Maidenhead, where it had been arranged that the King should meet them. They arrived before him, to find the streets strewn with flowers, herbs and green boughs, and a cheering crowd to greet them. There was no doubt where the sympathies of the country people lay.

The meeting with their father was, inevitably, highly emotional, though conducted with due dignity. It was more than five years since he had seen the younger two; Elizabeth had then been a child of six, Henry a baby not two years old. They were now eleven and seven.

The reunion took place at the Greyhound inn; the little Duke of Gloucester made no pretence of recognizing his father. '"Do you know me, child?" said Charles. "No", was the boy's reply. The king, in a mournful tone, rejoined: "I am your father, child; and it is not one of the least of my misfortunes that I have brought you and your brothers and sisters into the world to share my miseries."'[6]

Elizabeth, though she burst into tears at her father's words, behaved with the gravity and decorum that she always displayed. When Fairfax, who had discreetly stayed out of sight when father and children met, entered the room in which they were talking, she asked who he was, and, on being told that he was the general, 'courteously addressed him and thanked him for the happiness she and her brother now enjoyed in the sight of their dear father, which she knew was procured by his goodness, and assured him she should always be grateful to him, and, should it ever be in her power, she should be only too happy to requite the favour.'[7] Fairfax, not to be outdone in politeness, thanked her, said that he had only performed his duty to his sovereign's children, and humbly craved permission to kiss her hand, a request that was gracefully granted.

The family dined at Maidenhead with Fairfax and Northumberland, and then drove off to Caversham, where the permitted two days were spent. The children were then taken back to Westminster.

This was not the last of such occasions. About a week later there was an outbreak of plague in Westminster, and Northumberland asked to be allowed to take the children to Syon House. Permission was given, but almost immediately revoked on the pretext that a plot was afoot to rescue them from the control of Parliament. Instead of going to Syon House they were taken into the City of London and incarcerated in the house of the Lord Mayor.

This, however, proved to be only a temporary arrangement. In August the Army took possession of London, and the Army leaders once more showed themselves more sympathetic to the King and his family than was Parliament. The move to Syon House now took place, while at the end of August the King himself was moved to Hampton Court. The two residences were within easy distance of each other, and Northumberland was allowed to arrange frequent family meetings. The children, says Clarendon, 'were all three at the earl of Northumberland's house at Syon, from the time the King came to Hampton Court, and had liberty to attend his majesty when he pleased; so that sometimes he sent for them to come to him at Hampton Court, and sometimes he went to them to Syon; which gave him great divertisement.'[8]

For the four of them it was the happiest time since the King's surrender to his enemies. On 13 September the *Weekly Intelligencer* recorded: 'His majesty's children came yesterday in the afternoon to Hampton Court, to ask blessing of him; they were a long time in the garden, running and playing before the king. His majesty expressed much joy to see them with him, and his faithful subjects that were there expressed as much joy to see them all together.'[9] The Hampton Court correspondent of another newspaper, *Perfect Occurrences*, wrote: 'The king dined here yesterday; the Duke of York sat on his majesty's right hand; his majesty is very fond of him, and loving to all the children; he bears the young lady often in his arms.'[10]

Oliver Cromwell, now rapidly becoming the most important man in England, was present at some of these interviews. At this time he treated the royal family with as much respect as did Fairfax, and he expressed himself as deeply touched at the devotion shown between them.[11] He was presumably not there when King Charles reiterated his urgings to the Duke of York to make his escape and get out of England. 'The place he recommended to him was Holland; where he presumed his sister would receive him very kindly, and that the Prince of Aurange her husband would be well pleased with it.'¹²

In October the children were moved back to their winter quarters in St James's Palace, but the King again petitioned Fairfax, asking that the visits to Hampton Court should continue. The request was granted, and it was even arranged that the three should spend a week-end with their father. In the meantime it appears that he had been in touch with James but not with Elizabeth, and that she was getting restive. On 20 October King Charles wrote to her from Hampton Court:

Dear daughter,
   This is to assure you that it is not through forgetfulness that I have not all this time sent for you; the reasons of which, and when you shall come, shall be told you by your brother James this evening, and so God bless you.
                    Your loving father,
                         Charles R.
Kiss your brother Harry and my Lady Northumberland for me.¹³

A week later he wrote again with more positive news:

                    Hampton Court, October 27, 1647.
Dear Daughter,
   This is to assure you that it is not through forgetfulness nor any want of kindness, that I have not, all this time, sent for you; but for such reasons as is fitter for you to imagine (which you may easily do) than me to write. But now I hope to see you upon Friday or Saturday next, as your brother James can more particularly tell you, to whom referring you, I rest
                    Your loving father,
                         Charles R.¹⁴

The reasons which it was fitter for Princess Elizabeth to imagine than for King Charles to write were doubtless concerned with his resolution to take a new and drastic step. His attempts to drive a wedge between the Army and the Parliament were bearing little fruit. These two powers were indeed far from being in agreement, but neither had any thought of restoring the King to his authority. The Army, which was firmly in control of the royal prisoner, was assuming an increasingly political role, and Cromwell was its political leader. At the same time the treatment of the King became noticeably less respectful.

In these circumstances King Charles decided that he must escape from military custody. If he could get out of the country, so much the better; if not, he might be able to negotiate with the Parliament. He had no hesitation in confiding his plans to his fourteen-year-old son, and to his even younger daughter when opportunity presented itself. The week-end visit duly took place. The children arrived at Hampton Court on the first Saturday in November, and remained there till Monday, happy in the presence of their father except that Elizabeth, who was evidently suffering from nervous tension as well as physical weakness, complained repeatedly that she could not sleep owing to the tramp of the guards outside her bedroom. Some days after the return of the children to St James's they heard, probably without surprise, that their father had made his ill-advised flight from Hampton Court.

It took place on the night of 10 November. Sir John Berkeley and two other attendants on the King were in the secret, and horses had been obtained. Security at Hampton Court seems to have been singularly lax; it is at least possible that the Army leaders connived at the escape for their own purposes. Be that as it may, the King with his three companions got away easily enough. They made for the Hampshire coast, where a ship was supposed to be waiting; but there was no ship to be found. The whole affair was mishandled, as was so often the case in the fortunes of Charles I. 'There is reason to believe that he did resolve to transport himself beyond the seas,' wrote Clarendon later, 'which had been no hard matter to have brought to pass; but with whom he consulted for the way of doing it is not to this day discovered, they who were instrumental in his remove pretending to know nothing of the resolution or counsel.' [15]

In the event the King took refuge in the Isle of Wight, where he thought the Governor, Colonel Robert Hammond, would be sympathetic to his cause. In fact he was shut up in Carisbrooke Castle and more closely guarded than before; while from this time on the Army and the Parliament were united in determination to destroy him.

James now turned his thoughts seriously towards the possibility of escape. The King's orders to him had been to endeavour to get away if the situation deteriorated, and there was no doubt in his or Elizabeth's mind that the time had come. They discussed the matter together, and one of Elizabeth's attendants, Mrs Kilvert, and James's barber, named Hill, were recruited to help. Unfortunately James, who seems to have been unintelligent in his epistolatory designs, under pretext of writing to his sister Mary drafted a letter in cipher intended for the King. Hill, to whom it was entrusted, was caught, and the letter intercepted. The barber was clapped into prison, but the Duke managed to slip the key to the cipher to Mrs Kilvert, who was not under suspicion, and himself denied all knowledge of the letter. His captors failed to prove anything against him, but they had little doubt of the truth and he was in danger of being removed to the greater security of the Tower of London. This proposal was overruled in the House of Commons, but Northumberland was ordered to keep a closer watch on his senior prisoner and the prospects seemed blacker than ever. 'But nothing they cou'd do or say to him was capable of hindering him from endeavouring his escape.'[16]

The Duke of York might be lacking in intelligence, but never in determination; and he had his sister, brighter and more resourceful than himself, to egg him on. The final attempt came in the spring of 1648, and this time no unnecessary letters were written, though of course some accomplices had to be employed—in particular a certain Colonel Joseph Bamfeild.

At any rate the plan was now well worked out. The three children took to playing hide and seek. They were allowed to use most of the palace, and as they played every evening, and no suspicious circumstances were detected, the guards relaxed their vigilance. The Duke in particular gained the reputation of finding ingenious hiding places, and it was sometimes half an hour or more before he was found.

At about eight o'clock on the evening of 20 April Lord Northumberland, who had been away from the palace during the day, paid his usual visit to his charges, and then retired to his own apartments. The children turned to their game of hide and seek, and James said that he would hide. Henry, who was not in the secret, was ready to search for him, but James, instead of hiding, went to his sister's room and locked up a small dog that normally followed him; then slipped out to the servants' hall and asked the gardener for his keys into the garden and his lodge, saying he wanted to hide there. The trusting gardener gave them to him, and the Duke quickly got from the garden into the park, where Bamfeild was waiting for him.

The search in the palace went on, but eventually the little Duke of Gloucester got tired. Then one of the servants whispered to him that his brother was hidden in the gardener's lodge. They went there, and it was not till this was found to be still locked that there was any suspicion. Northumberland was aroused, and a thorough search was made of the palace. The only person inside the building who knew what had happened was Princess Elizabeth, and it seems that no suspicion fell on her.

James was well away. He and Bamfeild went by coach into the City of London, and thence to the river. In a house by the quayside Bamfeild's mistress, Anne Murray, was waiting with women's clothes which she had had specially made, and thus disguised the Duke of York got into a barge hired by Bamfeild.

There were still hazards ahead. Bamfeild had said he was bringing a friend with him on his trip to Gravesend to take ship, but the bargemaster, whose name was John Owen, was suspicious of the appearance of the Duke of York and began to make difficulties. It would be impossible, he said, to pass the blockhouse at Gravesend without discovery, and equally impossible to get hold of a boat to take them to the ship. Then, while he and Bamfeild were arguing, 'the master of the barge became fully satisfied concerning those suspicions which he had, that this woman was some disguised person of considerable quality; for peeping through a cranny of the door into the barge room, where there was a candle burning befor the Duke, he perceiv'd his Royall Highnes laying his leg upon the table, and plucking up his stocking in so unwomanish a manner, that he concluded his former surmizes of him were undoubted truths, as he afterwards acknowledg'd to them.'[17]

In this ticklish situation James and Bamfeild decided that the best thing to do was to tell the bargemaster the truth and confide in his fidelity. 'Thereupon the Duke told him who he was, and with all assured him he would not be unmindfull of this action, but take care of his fortune, and provide for him; And that if he thought it hazardous to return to London, he would carry him over with him into Holland.'[18]

Their trust in Owen was justified. The bargemaster agreed to guide his vessel past the blockhouse with lights extinguished, and to take them to the 70-ton Dutch pink in which it had been arranged that they would sail to Holland. He also took advantage of James's offer to take him with them.

All went well. Aboard the pink three friends of Bamfeild—Sir Nicholas Armorer, Colonel Mayard and Richard Johnson—were waiting, and at daybreak the ship sailed for Middleburgh in the Netherlands. They came to anchor at Flushing, but here there was a scare. Owen, whose nerves were evidently a little on edge, came running into the Duke's cabin with the news that an English Parliamentary frigate was approaching. He was sure, he said, that it had been sent in pursuit of them, and they must set sail at once for Middleburgh. The ship's master agreed, and the voyage continued; but the 'frigate' turned out to be a harmless merchantman. There were further adventures, the pink narrowly escaping wreck on the Middleburgh sandbanks; but eventually the port was reached.

James was still in his feminine garments, having left his own clothes in London. From Middleburgh he wrote to his sister Mary, and there was great rejoicing at The Hague. Tailors were put to work to prepare costly apparel for the Duke, and Prince William sent his own yacht to bring him to Hounslerdike. There the Prince and Princess awaited him. William went out in another yacht to meet him, and when they landed 'so great was Mary's impatience that she ran down to the street door of her palace, and regardless of the presence of bystanders, embraced her brother with passionate tenderness.'[19] James was escorted in triumph to The Hague, where the States, hostile though they were to the Stuarts, after some deliberation sent a delegation to offer him their compliments.

In London the escape of James brought less of an outcry than might have been expected. Northumberland gave official notice of the occurrence to Parliament, and was exonerated from blame. It was clear that he was wearying of the charge entrusted to him, and the Parliament leaders humoured him so far as they could. He emphasized that he had previously refused to hold himself responsible for the security of the Duke; only by making him an absolute prisoner could every avenue of escape have been barred. The earl was thanked for his services, and given leave to take the two remaining royal children to Syon House.

Princess Mary was overjoyed at the way things were going. Hers was a mercurial temperament, and the coming of her brother James seemed to her to herald the dawn of better days for her family. And there was more good news to come. In the summer of 1648 came the Second Civil War. Some military garrisons in various parts of England declared for King Charles, and Royalist risings took place on a scale sufficient to cause serious concern to Fairfax and Cromwell; the New Model Army was once more on the march. A more important development, and one which concerned William and Mary directly, was that a substantial portion of the Roundhead fleet renounced its masters; five large naval vessels and three frigates declared for the King and sailed for Holland.

It was the captains' design to put ships at the disposal of the Prince of Wales. Hearing, however, that the Duke of York was at The Hague, they made for Hellevoetsluis, where they arrived at the end of May. There they invited the Duke to take command of the fleet pending instructions from the Prince on behalf of their father the King.

James was delighted. In his early years he had been designated by his father as future Lord High Admiral, though the appointment had been given to Lord Northumberland at the King's pleasure, with the understanding that the young Duke should take over when he was of an age to do so.

Mary was less sure. She had her brother with her and wanted to keep him there; and she feared that the whole thing might be a plot to get him back into the power of his enemies. There were also complications in the shape of the peculiar behaviour of Colonel Bamfeild, who after his help in James's escape developed an exaggerated idea of his personal importance and tried to exploit what influence he had gained with his young master for his own purposes. The details are obscure, but according to Clarendon Bamfeild intrigued against Sir John

Berkeley, who had come to The Hague to be the Duke's
governor but 'had not been acceptable to his royal highness'.[20]

> . . . Then, taking the opportunity of the fleet's being come to
> Helvorde Sluce, he [Bamfeild] went thither, and having, as is
> said before, a wonderful address to the disposing men to
> mutiny, and to work upon common men, which the fleet
> consisted of, the greatest officer among them being not above
> the quality of a boatswain or master's mate, he persuaded
> them to declare for the duke of York, without any respect to
> the King or Prince; and when his highness should be on board
> they should not meddle in the quarrel between the King and
> the Parliament, but entirely join with the Presbyterian party
> and the city of London, which by this means would bring the
> Parliament to reason: and he prepared his friends the seamen
> when the duke should come to them, that they would except
> against sir John Berkely, and cause him to be dismissed; and
> then he believed he should be able to govern both his highness
> and the fleet.[21]

Bamfeild clearly was a dangerous man, who was acting in the
Presbyterian interest (now predominant in the English Parliament but not in the Army) rather than in that of the Royalists.
Lord Willoughby of Parham, a noted Presbyterian who had
recently defected from the Parliament, had arrived in Holland,
and Bamfeild proposed that James should make him his vice-
admiral. James, whose gratitude to Bamfeild was great, allowed
himself to be persuaded.

Mary was still uneasy, but she and her husband were eager to
do anything they could to further the Royalist cause. William
authorized his brother-in-law to raise troops in the Netherlands,
and the Prince and Princess escorted him, with a train of two
hundred coaches, to Hellevoetsluis, where James boarded the
principal ship and the assembled captains saluted him as their
Admiral. When this had been done, however, William and
Mary prevailed on the newly appointed Admiral to accompany
them back to The Hague before committing himself further. It
would be for the Prince of Wales to decide what was to be done.

The news of what was happening brought Prince Charles
hotfoot to Holland. Arriving at Hellevoetsluis, he promptly took

over himself as Admiral of the revolted fleet, directing James to remain with their sister at The Hague. Willoughby's loyalty was not in doubt, and according to Clarendon the Prince kept him in office. Clarendon, however, who wrote many years later, is obviously wrong; for it is well established that Charles immediately sent for his cousin Prince Rupert, whom Clarendon does not mention at this stage, to act as his Vice-Admiral. At the same time Captain William Batten, who had for a time been in command of the Parliamentary fleet, defected in his turn and arrived in a frigate to offer his services to the Royalists. Prince Charles knighted him and made him Rear-Admiral.

These new developments naturally disappointed the Duke of York, baulked of his hope of commanding the fleet in action. However, he accepted his brother's authority and did as he was told. At Charles's instance he dismissed Bamfeild from his employment, though in view of his past services he continued to support him financially. The money was presumably provided by Mary, for James had none of his own.

In the sorting out of the affairs of the fleet Prince Charles showed a decisiveness that boded well for the future. For her part Mary was overjoyed to have two of her brothers with her, and she celebrated the reunion by giving a magnificent banquet for them at The Hague. Many English Royalist exiles were present, as well as Prince Rupert and his brothers Maurice and Philip.

On 22 July the Prince's fleet sailed for the English coast. Despite the high hopes engendered the tactics to be employed were not clearly worked out, and were a subject of dispute. Prince Rupert had an audacious plan to make for the Isle of Wight and rescue the King; but he was overruled. The loyalty of the seamen could not be taken for granted, and unless they could be assured of prize money there might be trouble. So it was decided to attempt a blockade of London and capture such ships as attempted to leave or enter the port.

That this decision was the best in the circumstances was indicated by the fact that a mutiny did in truth break out through the lack of prizes. It took place in the *Satisfaction*, the Admiral's flagship, and it was only Prince Charles's coolness and courage that saved the situation. The expedition accomplished nothing, and having taken few prizes and fought no

action the fleet returned to Holland. Prince Charles was back at
The Hague in September, and in the meantime the risings
dignified by the name of the Second Civil War had petered out
on English soil.

At The Hague the Prince of Wales was accorded a formal
reception by the States-General, to whom he appealed for
support in attempting the rescue of his father. Their reply was
cold and non-committal; they were not prepared to compromise
their neutrality. They assigned a house to him, but after a few
days' residence there he said that he preferred the hospitality of
his sister and moved into Mary's palace. In October he
contracted smallpox, that dreaded plague of the seventeenth
century; Prince William, fearing for Mary's safety, moved her
and the Duke of York to the palace of Teyling, near Haarlem.
But the Prince recovered, and the family were together again at
The Hague at Christmas.

In the meantime the Prince had found time to beget his most
famous bastard. The mother of the boy who was to cause so
much trouble in the future was Lucy Walter, a lady of good
family, considerable beauty, and the loosest of morals. The
latest writer on the subject aptly describes her as 'sexy, earthy,
arousing, the kind of woman who knows her assets and how best
to exploit them'.[22] Prince Charles may have known her at an
earlier date, but the affair developed in the summer of 1648,
between the Prince's arrival at The Hague and his taking his
fleet to sea. In the following April was born the baby who was to
grow up into the turbulent and irresponsible James Duke of
Monmouth.

The escape of the Duke of York from St James's Palace and the
revolt of the English ships against the Commonwealth were the
last heartening events for the Stuart family in the 1640s. For the
remainder of the decade all was gloom and despondency.

Queen Henrietta Maria was suffering privations in France.
The civil war known as the Fronde, which had been simmering
for some time, broke out in earnest in 1648. It was primarily a
revolt against the rule of the unpopular Cardinal Mazarin,
complicated by intervention on the part of the French princes,
unruly magnates adept at fishing in troubled waters; although
the issues were very different, it looked for a time as though the

French monarchy might go the same way as the English. Henrietta remained buoyant. Deprived of the company of her eldest son, she moved from Saint-Germain into Paris in the summer to show her sympathy with her sister-in-law, the Regent Anne of Austria, on whose support Mazarin depended for his power and position. With her went her little daughter, now four years old.

The Fronde, however, made Queen Henrietta's position more precarious than ever, and she was desperately poor. When some friends visited her in Paris, 'she turned to them with characteristic vivacity, and holding out a little gold cup from which she was accustomed to drink, asked them to believe that this represented all the gold that she possessed in the world.'[23]

The worst tribulation was that Henrietta was virtually cut off from communication with her husband. King Charles in these last months was a voluminous writer, but in the now chaotic conditions no letters were getting through. The last one she had received was of extreme despondency, to the effect that the King did not think he was destined to remain for much longer in the present world and was preparing himself for a better one.

In England the King's life was in fact moving towards its final, terrible crisis. The Second Civil War had done him no good. On the contrary it had driven the Army leaders towards the conclusion that there could be no security for their own rule except through the death of the monarch. And the Army was now supreme in the land.

King Charles, in the intervals of further futile attempts to escape from his captors, was still trying to negotiate for his freedom and some semblance of a return to kingly authority. But all was in vain. Prolonged disputations with Parliamentary commissioners in the Isle of Wight town of Newport were doomed from the outset. It was no longer Parliament that could settle terms.

When the talks had been finally broken off, he wrote a long letter of affection and advice to his eldest son. It was dated 29 November, 1648, from Newport:

Son,
By what hath been said, you may see how long we have laboured in search of peace. Do not you be discouraged to

tread those ways, to restore yourself to your right; but prefer the way of peace. Show the greatness of your mind, rather to conquer your enemies by pardoning than punishing. If you saw how unmanly and unchristianly this implacable disposition is in our evil willers, you would avoid that spirit. Censure us not, for having parted with too much of our own right; the price was great; the commodity was security to us, peace to our people. And we are confident another Parliament would remember how useful a King's power is to a people's liberty.

Of how much we have divested ourself, that we and they might meet again in a due Parliamentary way to agree the bounds for Prince and people! And in this, give belief to our experience, never to affect more greatness or prerogative than what is really and intrinsically for the good of our subjects (not satisfaction of favourites). And, if you thus use it, you will never want means to be a father to all, and a bountiful Prince to any you would be extraordinary gracious to. . . .

These considerations may make you a great Prince, as your father is now a low one; and your state may be so much the more established, as mine hath been shaken. For subjects have learnt (we dare say) that victories over their Princes are but triumphs over themselves; and so, will be more unwilling to hearken to changes hereafter. . . .

To conclude, if God give you success, use it humbly and far from revenge. If He restore you to your right upon hard conditions, whatever you promise, keep. Those men which have forced laws which they were bound to observe, will find their triumphs full of troubles. Do not think anything in this world worth obtaining by foul and unjust means. You are the son of our love; and, as we direct you to what we have recommended to you, so we assure you, we do not more affectionately pray for you (to whom we are a natural parent) than we do, that the ancient glory and renown of this nation be not buried in irreligion and fanatic humour: and that all our subjects (to whom we are a political parent) may have such sober thoughts as to seek their peace in the orthodox profession of the Christian religion, as it was established since the Reformation in this kingdom, and not in new revelation; and that the ancient laws, with the interpretation according to the known practices, may once again be a hedge about them; that you may in due time govern, and they be governed, as in the fear of the Lord.

C.R.

The Commissioners are gone; the corn is now in the ground; we expect the harvest. If the fruit be peace, we hope the God of peace will, in time, reduce all to truth and order again: which that He may do, is the prayer of

C.R.[24]

On 1 December the King was removed by a military guard from Carisbrooke Castle. He was taken first to Hurst Castle on the mainland, and while he was there the House of Commons declared that he had been transferred without its consent; it voted to resume negotiations with him. This was the last flicker of independence from Parliament. On 6 December Colonel Thomas Pride entered the House with his soldiers, turned out all members considered to be antagonistic to the Army, and put them under arrest. The dictatorship of General Oliver Cromwell was in being.

King Charles was next taken to Windsor Castle, where he was treated undisguisedly as a prisoner; all royal ceremonial was discarded. On 19 January 1649, he was brought to Westminster and lodged in St James's Palace. Next day he was taken by boat along the Thames to stand his trial in Westminster Hall before an improvised court assembled under the influence of Cromwell.

King Charles's dignified behaviour in this supreme crisis of his life has been described in virtually every book on the period. The charge of 'high treason' was of course even more absurd than in the case of Strafford, and Charles treated it with contempt. He refused to recognize the validity of the court, and would not compromise his regality by making any sort of plea. He simply asked by what authority he was being tried.

The result was a foregone conclusion. After four days of argument, during which the court repeatedly and vainly tried to bully the prisoner into pleading, the King of Great Britain was sentenced to 'be put to death by the severing of his head from his body'.

The Prince of Wales was still at The Hague. When the

horrifying news reached him that his father was to be put on trial by his subjects, he made frantic efforts to save him. On 13 January 1649 (Old Style), he sent a personal letter to Fairfax and the Army Council, in which he wrote:

> . . . We have reason to believe that, at the end of the time assigned for the treaty made with His Majesty in the Isle of Wight, His Majesty has been withdrawn from that island to Hurst Castle, and thence conducted to Windsor, with some intention of proceeding against him with more rigour, or of deposing him from the royal dignity given him by God alone, who invested his person with it by a succession undisputed, or even of taking his life; the mere thought of which seems so horrible and incredible that it has moved us to address these presents to you, who now have power, for the last time, either to test your fidelity, by reinstating your lawful King, and to restore peace to the kingdom—an honour never before given to so small a number as you—or to be the authors of misery unprecedented in this country, by contributing to an action which all Christians think repugnant to the principles of their religion, or any fashion of government whatever, and destructive of all security. I therefore conjure you to think seriously of the difference there is in the choice you make, and I doubt not you will choose what will be most honourable and most just, and preserve and defend the King, whereto you are by oath obliged. It is the only way in which any of you can promise himself peace of conscience, the favour and good will of His Majesty, the country, and all good men, and more particularly of your friend,
>
> Charles P.[25]

Brave words, but of course they had no effect. Fairfax, whether or not he had wanted to, could not alter the course of events at this stage. Charles then appealed to his brother-in-law, who was only too anxious to help but could do little. William agreed to send two Dutch envoys to England with Charles's own messenger, Sir Henry Seymour; but the mission reached England after the sentence of death had been passed. The King was allowed to receive Sir Henry, to whom he gave a farewell letter for Henrietta Maria.

There was nothing more Prince Charles could do. Doubt has recently been cast on the story, previously accepted by historians, that he sent a blank sheet of paper with his signature to the Parliament, inviting its leaders to inscribe thereon any terms they wished in return for his father's life.[26]

King Charles could now only prepare himself for death. He was visited by the Bishop of London, the gentle William Juxon, and after a long session of prayer he gave the Bishop another epistle for his son and heir. It reiterated at greater length the advice given in the letter from Newport; and it ended with the words:

> At worst, I trust I shall go before you to a better kingdom, which God hath prepared for me, and me for it, through my Saviour Jesus Christ, to whose mercy I commend you, and all mine.
>
> Farewell, till we meet, if not on earth, yet in Heaven.[27]

The final request that the King had to make to his gaolers was that he should have a farewell interview with his children Elizabeth and Henry. They were not now in St James's Palace, having been taken to Syon House by Lord Northumberland when Charles was brought to trial. He was instructed to bring them back to see their father.

The King was at this time attended by Thomas Herbert, who left his account of this final interview:

> . . . Next day Princess *Elizabeth*, and the Duke of *Gloucester*, her Brother, came to take their sad Farewel of the King their Father, and to ask his Blessing. This was the 29th of *Jan*. The Princess being the elder, was the most sensible of her Royal Father's Condition, as appear'd by her sorrowful Look and excessive weeping, and her little Brother seeing his Sister weep, he took the like Impression, though by reason of his tender age he could not have the like Apprehension. The King rais'd them both from off their Knees; he kiss'd them, gave them his Blessing, and setting them on his Knees, admonish'd them concerning their Duty and Loyal Observance to the Queen their Mother, the Prince that was his successor, Love to the Duke of *York*, and his other Relations.

The King then gave them all his Jewels, save the George he
wore, which was cut in an Onyx with great Curiosity, and set
about with 21 fair Diamonds, and the Reverse set with the
like Number; and again kissing his Children, had such pretty
and pertinent Answers from them both, as drew Tears of Joy
and Love from his Eyes; and then praying God Almighty to
bless 'em, he turned about expressing a tender and fatherly
Affection. Most sorrowful was this Parting, the young
Princess shedding Tears and crying lamentably, so as mov'd
others to Pity, that formerly were hard-hearted; and at
opening the Bed-Chamber Door, the King return'd hastily
from the Window and kiss'd 'em and bless'd 'em; so parted.[28]

A more precise, and a more immediate, recording of the
words uttered during this last harrowing scene was made by
Elizabeth herself. That night the thirteen-year-old princess sat
down and wrote her own version under the heading 'What the
King said to me on the 29th of January, 1648–9, the last time I
had the happiness to see him':

He told me he was glad I was come, and although he had not
time to say much, yet somewhat he had to say to me, which he
could not to another, or leave in writing, because he feared
their cruelty was such, as they would not have permitted him
to write to me. He wished me not to grieve and torment myself
for him, for that would be a glorious death that he should
die—it being for the laws and liberties of this land, and for
maintaining the true Protestant religion. He bade me read
Bishop Andrews's sermons, Hooker's Ecclesiastical Polity,
and Bishop Laud's book against Fisher, which would ground
me against Popery. He told me he had forgiven all his
enemies, and hoped God would forgive them also; and
commanded us, and all the rest of my brothers and sisters, to
forgive them. He bid me tell my mother that his thoughts
never strayed from her, and that his love should be the same
to the last. Withal, he commanded me and my brother to be
obedient to her, and bid me send his blessing to the rest of my
brothers and sisters, with commendation to all his friends. So,
after he had given me his blessing, I took my leave.
Farther, he commanded us all to forgive these people, but

never trust them; for they had been most false to him and to those that gave them power, and he feared also to their own souls; and he desired me not to grieve for him, for he should die a martyr, and that he doubted not but that the Lord would settle his throne upon his son, and that we should all be happier than we could have expected to have been if he had lived; with many other things, which at present I cannot remember.

Elizabeth.[29]

A little later, evidently after talking to her little brother, she added a further passage on what the King had said to his eight-year-old son:

Then, taking my brother Gloucester upon his knee, he said, 'Sweetheart, now they will cut off thy father's head.' Upon which the child looked very steadfastly upon him. 'Heed, my child, what I say; they will cut off my head, and perhaps make thee a king. But, mark what I say, you must not be a king so long as your brothers Charles and James do live. For they will cut off your brothers' heads, when they can catch them, and cut off thy head too at the last. And therefore, I charge you, do not be made a king by them.' At which the child, sighing deeply, replied, 'I will be torn in pieces first.' And these words, coming so unexpectedly from so young a child, rejoiced my father exceedingly. And His Majesty spoke to him of the welfare of his soul, and to keep his religion, commanding him to fear God, and He would provide for him. All which the young child earnestly promised.[30]

Had Princess Elizabeth lived to maturity, it can hardly be doubted that she would have written her memoirs. They would have been among the major sources for the history of her time.

The interview over, the children were hurried back to Syon House. Next day, 30 January 1649, King Charles I, after being callously kept waiting for more than three hours in Whitehall Palace, was beheaded on a scaffold erected outside the Banqueting House.

When the news spread over Europe, the shock it caused was not confined to the Stuart family. The concept of royalty itself

Execution of Charles I outside the Banqueting Hall, Whitehall

was shaken to its foundations. In preceding centuries kings had often been deposed by rival claimants; many had been assassinated. Such things were occupational hazards, a regrettable component of royal destiny. But that a monarch should be put on trial before a so-called court set up by his own subjects, and done to death with all the trappings of legal ceremonial, was something new and terrible. In France, in Spain, in Germany and the Empire, the occupants of thrones trembled in fascinated horror.

To those immediately concerned it seemed that the world had come to an end. Up to the last moment they had tried to convince themselves that the final tragedy would be averted. The impact of the fatal intelligence was so much the greater.

Mary, it would appear, was the first of the family, other than the two children at home, to know the worst. James had left to join his mother in Paris, but Charles was still at The Hague. News travelled slowly; it was not till 4 February that, in a strangely haphazard manner, William of Orange learned what had happened. He was sailing off the Dutch coast when his yacht was hailed by a fishing boat on its way home from English waters. Its captain boarded the Prince's yacht and told him of King Charles's death on the scaffold five days before. Having convinced himself of the truth of the man's narrative, William returned to The Hague and broke the news to his wife.

Mary was devastated. She was devoted to her father; she had corresponded with him during his imprisonment, and prayers for his preservation and deliverance had been constantly read in her chapel. The immediate problem, however, was how to break the news to her brother, who was now *de jure* King of England. Mary and William agreed that the best person to do so was Charles's chaplain, Dr Stephen Goffe. The chaplain entered the new sovereign's room, hesitated for a moment, and then began his message of condolence with the words 'Your Majesty'.

This told Charles all he needed to know. He was not an emotional young man, but the news of his father's murder affected him perhaps more deeply than anything else in his life. He burst into a fit of bitter tears, then ran out of the room and into his bedchamber, where he refused to see anybody. He remained alone with his grief for several hours.[31]

A few days later the news reached Paris, where Queen Henrietta was awaiting the arrival of her second son. The Fronde rebellion was at its height, and access was difficult; but while the Queen was at dinner she was told that a messenger had arrived with intelligence from England. Jermyn went to interview him, and on his return broke the news as gently as he could. Father Cyprien de Gamache, who was present, described the scene:

> The Queen, not expecting anything of the kind, was so deeply shocked that for the moment she was quite overwhelmed, without words, without action, without motion, like a statue. A great philosopher says that moderate afflictions permit the heart to sigh and the mouth to lament, but that very extraordinary, terrible, and fatal accidents, fill the soul with a stupor which renders the lips mute and prevents the action of the senses. *Curae leves loquuntur, graves stupent.* Such was the pitiable state to which the Queen was reduced. The words and the reasons that we employed to rouse her, found her deaf

and insensible. We were obliged to desist, and to remain about her all in profound silence, some weeping, others sighing, all with dejected countenance, sympathizing in her extreme grief.[32]

A few days later, feeling that she could not face the world, the Queen retired temporarily to the Carmelite convent in the Faubourg St Jacques. She left her four-year-old daughter Henrietta in the Louvre in the care of the Countess of Morton (the former Lady Dalkeith), with Father Cyprien de Gamache as her spiritual guide.

Meanwhile James Duke of York had reached Paris, 'where he heard of the most horrid murder of the King his Father; and what impression that made both upon the Queen and the Duke, may be more easily imagin'd, then express'd.'[33]

In the summer he was followed to Paris by his elder brother. Life had not been easy for Charles at The Hague. William and Mary had done all they could for him, paying his servants, providing him with ready money, and co-operating with him in plans which he was already devising for an expedition to Scotland as the first step towards gaining the throne that was now his by right. But the States-General viewed his presence with a jaundiced eye. They were meditating an alliance with republican England, and the English Commonwealth sent an agent named Dorislaus on a semi-official mission to The Hague. He was promptly murdered at supper by a gang of six masked English royalists.

Charles was in no way involved in the killing of Dorislaus, but William as Stadtholder and chief magistrate was obliged to denounce the murder and it was deemed advisable for the new King to leave the country. He travelled in style, accompanied to Breda by the Prince and Princess of Orange and the Queen of Bohemia. He was treated with all the distinctions due to a reigning monarch; at Breda a magnificent feast was given in his honour, at which his sister presided. On 29 June 1649, he left for France.

Within a few weeks of the death of Charles I there were printed the first copies of *E'ικών Βασιλική* [Royal Image]: *The Portraicture of His Sacred Majestie in His Solitudes and Sufferings*. It purported to have been written by the King during his captivity at Carisbrooke Castle, and it gave a full defence of his actions during the Civil War and after.

Nobody doubted at the time that the book was the King's own work, but after the Restoration Dr John Gauden claimed that he had himself written it. The authorship has never been proved either way, but anyone who reads the book is bound to be sceptical of Gauden's claim. Internal evidence cannot be conclusive, but *Eikon Basilike* throughout bespeaks not only the workings of Charles I's mind but the style of his writing, as known from the many letters, undoubtedly of his own composition, which survive. Gauden was a time-server whose main aim in life was ecclesiastical preferment. If he was indeed the author he possessed a literary expertise which it is hard to associate with him.

The sorrows of the House of Stuart at this time did not end with the tragedy of King Charles I. Two more deaths were to follow.

Back at Syon House the two children continued their unhappy existence. Elizabeth refused to wear any clothes other than those of deepest mourning, and her health steadily deteriorated. The faithful old family physician Sir Theodore Mayerne attended her, and he recorded that 'the Princess Elizabeth, who was aforetime sad and somewhat liable to complain of the spleen, and suffered a little from scurvy, from the death of her father, King Charles, beheaded 30th of January, 1648–9, fell into great sorrow, whereby all the other ailments from which she suffered were increased.'[34] A hard tumour had appeared in her body, while her stomach was so sickly that only small quantities of medicine could be swallowed.

The Earl of Northumberland had opposed the killing of the King, and after the event he wrote to Parliament saying that he could no longer be responsible for the custody of the children; he added the more practical consideration that he was badly out of pocket over his care of them. He was prevailed upon to carry on until other arrangements were made, during which time Elizabeth appealed to Parliament for her brother and herself to be sent to their sister in Holland. There was a debate on the subject, but the request was refused.

In the summer of 1649 Elizabeth and Henry were transferred to the care of the Earl and Countess of Leicester and taken to the

Sydney family home at Penshurst in Kent. Lady Leicester treated them as kindly as she was allowed to, but England had now been officially declared a republic and the Leicesters were instructed to dispense with all ceremonial that savoured of regality. They were even visited by William Lenthall, Speaker of the Commons, to make sure that no undue respect was shown to the prince and princess.

The final change came in the following summer. News arrived that King Charles II had landed in Scotland, and it was decided that the presence of the children so near to London could endanger the peace of the country. So the ailing girl and her small brother were taken to the Isle of Wight and lodged in Carisbrooke Castle, the grim fortress where their father had been incarcerated. There, on 8 September 1650, Elizabeth Stuart died. She was three months short of her fifteenth birthday.

Two days after her death permission from the Parliament for her and her brother to leave for the Continent reached Carisbrooke.

Elizabeth was not well known to the remaining members of the family. She had been a child of six when she parted from them before the outbreak of hostilities in England; since then only James had seen her. Nevertheless her death was yet one more cause for grief and mourning.

'The Queen, her mother', wrote Father Cyprien de Gamache, 'could not learn her melancholy death without shedding many tears. The King, her brother, the Duke of York, the Duke of Gloucester, and the Princess of Orange, manifested the greater sorrow, on account of the illustrious and extraordinary qualities with which Nature had enriched that beautiful princess. They looked upon her as an instrument that might contribute to the re-establishment of their royal house by means of some high marriage.'[35]

Mary, now once more in an advanced stage of pregnancy, felt particularly keenly the loss of the sister who had shared her childhood. Worse, so far as she was concerned, was to follow. Internal troubles in the Netherlands had forced her husband to leave her for a tour of Guelderland, but on hearing of her distress and her poor state of health he hurried back to The Hague. There he contracted smallpox.

It was first reported to be a mild attack; but it rapidly grew worse. On 6 November 1650, Prince William II of Orange, prop and stay of the Stuarts in exile, died at the age of twenty-four. He had been Stadtholder of the Netherlands for just three years.

For Mary, always the most emotional of her family, it was just too much. In less than two years she had lost her father, her sister, and now her husband. She had been kept away for fear of infection, but now she rushed into his room and threw herself on to his body with shrieks and lamentations; then had to be carried out in a dead faint. A fortnight later she was brought to bed of a son.

5

Haven in Holland, 1650–8

The death of William of Orange left his widow in a difficult, and largely an isolated, position. The marriage had been happy. There had been rifts caused by William's infidelities, the normal infidelities of a seventeenth-century prince which Mary had not learned to tolerate; but she had doted on her husband, and in matters of politics had shown unquestioning faith in his judgement. Now she was alone, a nineteen-year-old widow with an infant son, having no official position in her adopted country, at odds with its republican administrators and equally so with her mother-in-law, the dominant representative of the House of Orange.

These antagonisms were quickly in evidence. The first tussle with the Princess Dowager Amelia occurred over the name of the baby prince. Mary wanted it to be Charles after his grandfather and uncle; Amelia was determined that it should be William. The elder lady had her way.

More serious was the dispute over guardianship. Mary claimed this as Prince William's mother, but her mother-in-law objected that she was too young for the position. The States-General of the United Provinces decided in favour of Mary, but then revised their decision; a council of guardians was appointed, Mary having only a minority voice, outvoted by the Dowager and the Elector of Brandenburg who was Amelia's son-in-law. Once again she was forced to submit.

With the Netherlands officials she had no influence, and they lost little time in working for the eclipse of the House of Orange. William had not been popular with the Dutch, and in the years of his Stadtholdership he had been at loggerheads with the States-General and the States of Holland in matters of policy. They now decided that the time had come to break with his family.

There had been no difficulty in accepting William II as successor to his father; the prestige of William the Silent had extended to his grandson, who as a handsome and gallant youth seemed admirably qualified to carry out the duties of Admiral and Captain-General. But a new-born baby was a very different thing. Republican sentiment, moreover, had grown with the disputes of the past three years; and the burghers felt increasing affinity with the new régime across the sea, whose prime enemies were the family to which the mother of the new prince belonged.

In 1651 an assembly met in The Hague to devise a new constitution. The Stadtholdership was left vacant and the offices of Admiral and Captain-General abolished. In their place a Council of State was set up, with army and navy boards to be responsible for the defence of the federated republic. The effect was to put the chief official of Holland, the Grand Pensionary, into the position of prime minister of the United Provinces. This post was filled at the time, as it was to be for many years to come, by the extremely capable Johan de Witt.

The opposition now facing her on every side brought out all the wilful obstinacy of Mary's nature. Her dealings with her husband's countrymen had never been remarkable for tact. Now she seemed to set out to antagonize them with all the power at her command. Dutchmen were hardly received at her court, at which the chosen spoken language was French; she made no secret of the fact that she regarded the people of the Netherlands as uncouth barbarians. She used the title of Princess of Orange as little as possible, preferring to be known as the Princess Royal of England. Her closest confidante was her aunt, the exiled Queen Elizabeth of Bohemia, who had taken up permanent residence in The Hague.

Mary remained devoted to the memory of her husband, and she made it clear that she had no intention of remarrying. Her life was now dedicated to two objects. The first was the recognition of what she regarded as the hereditary rights of her son, violated in her view by the actions of the States-General. The second was the succouring of her Stuart relations in their exile. As regards the first object, her attitude towards those in power in the Netherlands was hardly calculated to advance Prince William's fortunes, though she never ceased to agitate for his advancement. To the second she devoted all the ardour of

Mary of Orange, by Hanneman

her fervent nature. She was not by royal standards a rich woman, but she was far better off than the rest of her family, all of whom found her a constant friend in time of trouble.

First in her affections came her brothers Charles and James. The Duke of York returned to The Hague for his brother-in-law's funeral, and Mary invited him to stay as long as he chose. He was yet without employment, and desperately short of money; his sister's court was his only refuge.

He was still there when it was made known that ambassadors from Cromwell's Commonwealth government were to be received by the States-General. James, 'thinking it no way proper for him to remain in a Town where they were to make their solemn entry, and to avoide the mortification of so disagreeable a sight, when the murderers of his Father were to be received in State,'[1] then left for Mary's dower residence at Breda. When the reception was over, however, he returned to The Hague, only to find that the English envoys were trying to persuade their Dutch hosts to require not only James, but Mary too, to keep away from the capital while discussions were being held. This demand was for the time being refused, but the ambassadors persevered, and in the summer of 1651 the States-General requested that the Duke of York should be sent to Hounslerdike, where his sister had another house. Mary complied, but to show her solidarity with her brother she insisted on going with him.

The movements of James were at this time of particular concern to the English Parliamentary authorities because of the activities of his elder brother. After the death of his father King Charles II had never rested from his efforts to gain the throne that was his by hereditary right. Invasion of either Scotland or Ireland was considered to be the necessary preliminary. Ireland was the first choice, and with a view to an expedition he went once more to Jersey in the summer of 1649, taking James with him. But in the meantime Cromwell landed in Ireland and subdued the country with ruthless efficiency. The royal brothers returned to the Continent, and Charles and his advisers turned their attention to Scotland. After lengthy negotiations, most of which took place at Breda with the co-operation of William II of Orange, it was decided that the King must throw in his lot with the Covenanters and agree to accept Presbyterianism. In doing so he abandoned to his fate his most loyal supporter, James Graham, Marquess of Montrose, who met an ignominious death at the hands of the Covenanters.

Charles landed in Scotland in July 1650. He was in that country when the news reached him of the deaths first of his sister Elizabeth and then of his brother-in-law William. Now, when James and Mary were together in Holland, he was preparing, after acceding to humiliating demands from the Covenanters, to invade England at the head of an Anglo-Scottish army.

In these circumstances it was hardly surprising that the English republicans should renew their efforts to drive the Duke of York, next heir to his father's throne, from his haven in the Netherlands. They unearthed a treaty which Henry VII had made with the Archduke Philip of the Netherlands, and which 'stipulated not only that neither of the contracting parties should give aid to the enemies of the other, but also that each should lend military aid to suppress them at the expense of its ally; and that neither should receive or support rebels or fugitives of the other, but that each should expel them if they had already found a refuge on its soil'.[2] Insisting on the literal interpretation of the terms of this pact, the ambassadors demanded that James should be immediately expelled and that Mary's property should be confiscated if she continued to harbour him. The Dutch were not prepared to go as far as this, and they replied: 'We cannot banish from our soil all persons who are banished out of England. Our country is a refuge for the exiles of all nations.'[3] Shortly after this the negotiations between the Commonwealth and the Netherlands broke down.

James's presence, however, was clearly exacerbating Mary's relations with the Netherlanders, particularly as she herself characteristically showed no sign of conciliation. She brought James back to The Hague, and 'every day her Royal Highness and her brother, the Duke of York, rode slowly past the [English] ambassador's residence, with ostentatious pomp and an imposing suite, staring at the house from top to bottom, in a manner to encourage the rabble, which her procession gathered up in its way, to commit an insult.'[4] It was perhaps providential that at this time instructions should arrive from King Charles in Scotland for his brother to return to France.

James's sojourn in Holland had been against the wishes of his mother. Henrietta Maria, who had emerged from her convent, was becoming increasingly possessive and domineering towards her children, and the young Duke of York chafed at the restraints she put on him. He felt more at liberty in his sister's company. To King Charles, however, it was important that his brother should be close to the court of the French King. He was hoping for a successful campaign in England, and French help might be forthcoming in time of need. Early in June 1651 James 'received a letter from his Majesty then in Scotland, by which he commanded him to return to Paris, and withall Signifyd his displeasure for his removall from thence; And by the same letter he was order'd . . . to submitt himself, and be intirely govern'd by the directions of the Queen his Mother; all which commands were immediately obeyd by his Royall Highness, who accordingly left the Hague, and went for France and arriv'd at Paris towards the end of June.'[5]

His attempt to escape from his mother's apron-strings had failed, and he went back meekly enough. Queen Henrietta received him graciously, and for a time at least there was peace, in spite of poverty, among those members of the royal family dependent on the charity of the French court. The Queen's Catholic fervour had not diminished with the years, and she had the happiness to know that at any rate one of her children was growing up in her own faith. Henrietta Anne was now seven years old, and under the spiritual direction of Father Cyprien de Gamache she was exemplary in her piety. The decision to bring her up as a Catholic met with considerable opposition, particularly from Sir Edward Hyde; but the Queen insisted that she had her husband's permission for the course she took. It was impossible to confirm her claim, but it is possible that King Charles I, so adamant in his instructions to his elder children to refuse to follow their mother in the matter of religion, may have allowed her to have her way in the upbringing of the youngest.

The Queen now had hopes that her second son might also enter the fold. The ground on which she tried to sow her seed was not infertile, and if Gilbert Burnet's testimony is to be accepted the beginnings of James's change of faith, which did not in fact occur till much later, were present in his mind at this time. Bishop Burnet claimed in later years to have been much in the Duke of York's confidence, and he wrote:

> . . . He gave me this account of his changing his religion:
> when he escaped out of the hands of the earl of Northumber-
> land, who had the charge of his education trusted to him by
> the parliament, and had used him with much respect, all due
> care was taken, as soon as he got beyond sea, to form him to a
> strict adherence to the church of England: among other
> things, much was said of the authority of the church, and of
> the tradition from the apostles, in support of episcopacy: so
> that, when he came to observe that there was more reason to
> submit to the catholic church than to one particular church,
> and that other traditions might be taken on her word, as well
> as episcopacy was received among us, he thought that the step
> was not great, but that it was very reasonable to go over to the
> church of Rome: and doctor Steward having taught him to
> believe a real but inconceivable presence of Christ in the
> sacrament, he thought this went more than half way to
> transubstantiation. He said, that a nun's advice to him to
> pray every day, that, if he was not in the right way, God
> would set him right, did make a great impression on
> him. . . .[6]

James Duke of York was eventually to prove the most
convinced Catholic of all his family, and this was to lose him his
throne not long after he had succeeded to it. It is certain that he
was attracted to Rome quite early in his life, and perhaps, as
Burnet suggested, soon after his escape to the Continent. It is
equally certain, however, that he had even before this developed
those traits of obduracy and determination to pursue his own
course in his own way which were to mark his progress through
life. If he contemplated conversion, it would not be at the
urgings of his mother. He was deaf to any plea she may have
made.

In October 1651 all religious intrigues, all spiritual considerations, were put into the shade by the news that reached Paris of
the return of Charles II to the Continent. The young king had
duly led his army into England in August, hoping to circumvent
Cromwell who had been conducting a victorious campaign in

Scotland against Charles's new allies and now himself moved south in pursuit of the King. The rival armies marched on parallel lines through the north of England, and met at Worcester on 3 September. The battle that followed lasted three hours and resulted in total defeat for the Royalists. Charles fought with great gallantry, and it was not till all was lost that he made his escape from the city.

Since then no news of him had reached the exiles on the Continent. His mother had almost made up her mind that he was dead, and the Duke of York was ready to take up the cares of sovereignty. He had been preparing to follow the court of France on one of its progresses, but in the changed circumstances the Queen decided that he must stay in Paris. Then, on 19 October, came the news that his brother had landed at Fécamp, on the coast of Normandy, unattended except by his faithful follower Lord Wilmot. The Duke hastened from Paris to meet him and bring him to the capital, where he was 'not only wellcom'd by the Queen his Mother, but received by all the persons of quality then in Town, with all the demonstrations of joy which could possibly be expected'.[7]

His adventures had been extraordinary, the most remarkable that were ever to befall him in a life that for the head of a royal house was singularly full and varied. A hunted man after the defeat at Worcester, he had made his way in various disguises for seven weeks through an England swarming with Roundhead troops on the look-out for him, till at last he found a ship's captain willing to transport him from the Sussex coast to Normandy. During his wanderings he had hidden in hovels, in cellars, in priest-holes, and at least once in a tree, the 'Boscobel oak' which was to become part of English folk-lore. Through it all he never lost his natural gaiety, showing courage and resource that earned the admiration of the few companions who shared his flight and of those English men and women to whom his identity became known. Among all who recognized him— and it was estimated that more than a hundred did so—not one betrayed him.

When he landed in France he was ragged and unshaven, without money and without a change of clothing. The latter was quickly provided, but there was little money available to the band of exiles and King Charles entered on a period of penury even worse than that before he had embarked for Scotland. But his experiences had rendered him fitter for his destiny. His expedition had been a disastrous failure. He had humiliated himself in his northern kingdom to no purpose; his military venture had been eclipsed in total rout, and he had fled his country as a hunted fugitive. But he was a different man now from the somewhat *gauche* youth who had earned the scorn of Mademoiselle de Montpensier. He had commanded an army, had dealt with friends and foes in matters of state, and in his wanderings had acquired a knowledge of ordinary men and women such as had come the way of few if any of his ancestors. Never again would he allow his mother or anybody else to dominate him. He could speak and act with an authority that was acknowledged by all.

Mademoiselle herself recognized the change. She was still unmarried; none of the grand matches envisaged for her had materialized. She looked with new favour on the gallant young prince who had acquired better looks, with a poise and grace that had previously been lacking, and whose French had improved, though how this had come about while he was away from France was far from clear.

The matrimony project was revived, and this time both parties were more inclined to pursue it. But again it came to nothing. Mademoiselle, albeit attracted to King Charles, had her eye on another cousin, the young Louis XIV, now thirteen and growing up fast, and Mazarin, in firm charge of the young monarch, was not prepared to see the greatest fortune in France go out of the country. Soon afterwards, however, Anne-Marie de Montpensier herself threw away her chance of realizing any of her ambitions by taking an active and spirited part in the civil war of the Fronde, fighting in person for yet another cousin, that proud rebel prince 'the Great Condé,' in his revolt against the crown. Louis XIV never forgave her, and it was long before she would even be received at court again.

Times were bad for the English exiles. Money was short, and war conditions in France meant that even the pension awarded to Henrietta Maria was only intermittently paid. The rest of the family lived from hand to mouth. The English prospect was hopeless. Any form of restoration appeared further off than ever.

La Grande Mademoiselle, by Bourguignon

Best off among the exiles was the Duke of York. At the age of
eighteen James at least could earn his own living, and he was
eager for a martial career. Like Charles he had been the subject
of a matrimonial project. The lady suggested was the daughter
of the Duc de Longueville, a lady of royal blood and, next to *la
Grande Mademoiselle*, the greatest heiress in France. Charles,
James and their mother were all in favour of the match, but
Mazarin again interposed his veto. Disappointed of the prospect
of a wealthy marriage, the Duke was ready to seek a more
modest fortune in arms.

Here there was no lack of opportunity. The Thirty Years
War, which had devastated Europe more terribly than any
conflict before 1914, had officially ended with the Peace of
Westphalia in 1648, but in the north-west corner of the
continent hostilities dragged on between France and Spain;
these were now complicated by France's civil war, the 'Fronde
of the Princes' as it had now become. There were at this time two
French generals who rank among the pre-eminent commanders
of modern European history. One was 'the Great Condé', the
Prince Rupert of France; the brilliant, dashing cousin of King
Louis who had blazed into military glory in his early twenties.
The other was the more mature Henri Vicomte de Turenne, a
strategist and tactician of the first order, a man whose probity
and judgement commanded universal respect.

These two were now ranged against each other. Condé,
unruly and ambitious, leader of the rebels of the Fronde, had
thrown in his lot with the Spaniards who were threatening
France's frontiers in Flanders. He justified his treason by the
fiction that he was fighting not against his sovereign but against
the King's evil advisers; in other words, Cardinal Mazarin. Such
a plea had been familiar enough to the English in the Great Civil
War. The forces of King Louis and Mazarin were commanded
by Turenne.

James was prepared to fight frankly as a mercenary; money
and military experience were his objects. But there could be no
question as to which side he must join. His family existed on the
charity of the French King's court, and he applied to serve as a
volunteer in Turenne's army. This meant seeking the approval
of Mazarin, who gave it on condition that King Charles did not
object. After a certain amount of argument on terms, and some

difficulty in finding the money to purchase his necessary equipment, the Duke set out to join Turenne towards the end of April 1652.

Here he found himself. James was no military genius, but he proved himself a splendid soldier—brave, conscientious and painstaking; he took naturally to army discipline. He set himself to master the art of war with all the earnestness of his nature, and he won the complete confidence of Turenne, on whose staff he served and who in 1654 made him lieutenant-general. He was with the French forces for four years; they may well have been the happiest years of his life, and they were certainly among the most successful.

The campaigns in which he served were described in detail in his own memoirs. Doubts have been cast on the reliability of *The Life of James the Second*, accepted as being written by William Dicconson and 'collected out of memoirs writ of his [James's] own hand', and published in 1816. How completely such memoirs were actually written is uncertain; probably they consisted largely of notes, certainly voluminous since all his life he was a compulsive, though not an inspired, writer. But it is known that he did compile a continuous narrative of his years of military service, and some twenty years ago a French translation of these memoirs was discovered. There can be no doubt of the authenticity of this portion of his autobiography, which differs little from the relevant passages of the *Life*.

It cannot be said that it makes lively reading. James had none of the sparkling humour that makes his elder brother's letters a constant delight; nor had he the literary gifts of his grandfather or the cultured feeling for English prose which, in spite of a certain tortuousness of style, made some of his father's effusions memorable. What he had was a soldierly gift for straightforward narrative, laconic and always to the point. His memoirs, singularly free from self-glorification, may be described as a series of military dispatches characterized by sense and clarity.

King Charles was leading an aimless existence, without employment and without money. In the summer of 1652 he was given a ticklish task. The Duke of Lorraine, a slippery customer with an army of his own, had joined Condé and the Spaniards, and Charles was invited to bring him to terms with the French court, now at Melun, south-east of Paris. Glad to have something to do, the King accepted and made his way to the Duke's headquarters at Villeneuve Saint-Georges. Here he met his brother, who was empowered by Turenne to approach Lorraine with terms. The latter prevaricated, and, 'imagining that this young Prince's [James's] hands were itching and that he felt more inclination for a battle than for an agreement, he asked the King to send Lord Jermyn with him in order to try and obtain from Monsieur de Turenne terms that were more endurable'.[8] King Charles returned to Paris with no concrete achievement to his credit. There he found himself at the mercy of Condé who, outmanoeuvred by Turenne, temporarily captured the French capital. It was at this point that *la Grande Mademoiselle* performed her most spectacular exploit, donning soldier's costume and fighting for Condé at the barricades. Her erstwhile suitor found himself ignominiously ordered out of the city by the victorious prince; he retired meekly to Saint-Germain.

The King's existence became increasingly aimless. His Scottish enterprise had failed, and there was no immediate prospect of any further attempt to re-establish the monarchy. Mary as always was a stand-by, helping him with advice, with hospitality when it could be arranged, and with money. Early in 1652 she had helped him to fit out a one-ship expedition to rescue the Scottish regalia from the coastal castle of Dunottar, the one fortress in the northern kingdom which held out for its sovereign. But there were delays. The English authorities got wind of the plan; Dunottar was blockaded, and the venture had to be abandoned.

The devotion of Charles, James and Mary to each other at this time is well attested. One contemporary wrote of the King's 'beloved sister, the Princesse Royal Mary Princesse of Orange, whose tender love and zeal to him in his affliction deserves to be written in brasse, and graven with the point of a Diamond'.[9]

Charles and Mary were planning to meet in the summer of 1652, either at Spa or at Breda. The plan was dropped, however, after a temporary rift in their relations with each other. The King's advisers, principally Hyde and Nicholas, kept a close watch on the Orange court at The Hague, recognizing its importance to the royal cause. They now became convinced that Mary was too much under the influence of her former governess, Lady Stanhope, who had married the superintendent of her household, Johan van Heenvliet, and that this influence was inimical to the Stuarts. Heenvliet had long ago been involved in the negotiations leading up to the marriage of the Prince and Princess of Orange, and so far as is known he and his wife were always devoted to the Princess's best interests. But suspicions were aroused, and were fed by the antagonistic Princess Dowager Amelia. Charles was reluctantly persuaded to write a letter of protest to Mary.

Mary, hot-headed and passionate, was furious. When it came to her choice of attendants and advisers she would not be dictated to by her brother or anybody else, and she replied with a vigorous defence of her friend, blaming the Duke of Buckingham and others for poisoning the King's mind against her. King Charles, who had never felt strongly in the matter, and was personally friendly with Lady Stanhope, replied in mild and conciliatory terms, but for a time there was a coldness between him and his sister.

It was a storm in a teacup, which before long blew over. When her anger had cooled the Princess Royal was anxious to return to the old intimacy, and felt that a personal interview was the only way. This time she suggested that she should travel to France. The proposal, however, was not favoured by the King's council; partly because it was thought she could do more good in Holland, partly because of the unsettled condition of Paris.

No such visit could yet take place; events occurred which rendered the idea irrelevant. In the first place, in the summer of 1652 war broke out between the United Provinces and the English Commonwealth. It was concerned with trade and maritime rights, and hostilities were limited to sea warfare. King Charles naturally hoped to reap some advantage from the situation, but his expectations were doomed to disappointment. He asked for permission to go to Holland and give the Dutch his assistance, but he had nothing concrete to offer and the request was refused. He then asked the Provinces to provide him with ships so that he could oppose the Commonwealth in person; this impracticable proposal was likewise turned down.

The war went against the Dutch, and its main effect was to strengthen the hand of Oliver Cromwell, who in December 1653 was declared Lord Protector of England, Scotland and Ireland. In April 1654 a peace humiliating to the Netherlands was concluded; one of its provisions was that the House of Orange was 'secluded' from the government of the country. So far as Mary was concerned, the recognition of her son's rights was further off than ever.

A happier diversion was provided by the arrival on the Continent of the Duke of Gloucester. As long ago as September 1650 the English Council of State had decided to release both the captive children of Charles I, but the death of Princess Elizabeth led to second thoughts and the young Prince Henry was left a prisoner in Carisbrooke Castle. His title was banned, and he was known as 'Master Harry Stuart'; but he became an object of intrigue, and there was for a time an idea of placing him on the throne as a puppet monarch: an eventuality against which his father had expressly warned him. It was said that Cromwell himself was at one time partial to such a scheme, but as time went on, and Cromwell's own ambitions of supreme power became evident, it was decided that the presence of the Duke in England was an embarrassment rather than an asset to his captors.[10] On 15 December 1652, permission was once more given for his departure; a ship was hired, £500 was provided for his expenses, and on 12 February 1653 he sailed from Cowes.

He landed at Dunkirk and proceeded to Antwerp, where he was met by Sir Edward Hyde's wife and where Dr George Morley described him as having 'an high character for natural and acquisitive abilities, for understanding and learning much above his years'.[11] In the following month he went on to Delft, to be received with open arms by his sister Mary.

The Princess Royal was beside herself with joy. Here was another brother to take under her wing; one moreover whom she had last seen as a baby not two years old, and who was now a lively and handsome boy of twelve. She took him promptly to The Hague, dressed him in fine clothes, lavished every care on his welfare, and introduced him to his great-aunt, Elizabeth of Bohemia, who was equally delighted with him. The two royal ladies pampered him in a way that made the preceding years of captivity in England seem like a ghastly nightmare.

Henry stayed for two months at The Hague, greatly enjoying

the attentions that were lavished on him. He wanted to remain there indefinitely, and Mary, who loved his company as much as he did hers, asked her eldest brother for permission to keep him with her. The King was happy to agree; Mary could afford to maintain their young brother, but he could not. Provided the States-General would turn a blind eye to the prince's presence, he was welcome to stay; and no difficulty was experienced in this direction. King Charles sent Henry the insignia of the Order of the Garter, the only honour he was able to bestow on him; and on Easter Sunday, 14 April, a ceremony of investiture was performed by Sir Edward Walker, Garter King of Arms, in the presence of the Princess Royal and the Queen of Bohemia. The same honour was shortly afterwards conferred on Mary's young son, William III of Orange.

One achievement standing to the credit of the young prince was an at least partial reconciliation between Mary and her mother-in-law. The Princess Dowager was as much charmed with Henry's grace and manners as were the other women at The Hague, and his presence was made the pretext for a sumptuous entertainment provided by Princess Amelia for Mary and her aunt Elizabeth. Mary reciprocated with a country feast at her palace at Hounslerdike. The sun seemed to be shining once more on the House of Orange, and the hero of the hour was Henry Duke of Gloucester.

But these halcyon days were too good to last. King Charles might give his permission for his brother's permanent residence at The Hague; but there was another personage whose wishes could not be ignored. Queen Henrietta Maria wanted her youngest son with her, and clamoured vociferously for him to be sent to Paris.

Neither Charles nor Mary wanted to accede to her wishes. There was not only the question of expense; it was considered certain that the Queen would exercise her proselytizing zeal, and possible that at his impressionable age young Harry might be tempted to succumb. Henrietta however, who had parted from her son in his infancy, could hardly be denied the right to see him now. Charles ordered Mary to send the boy to Paris, promising at the same time that the separation would not be permanent and that Henry would return to Holland within a few months. Mary protested and appealed to Sir Edward

Nicholas, who was at this time at The Hague; but Nicholas could only reply that the King's command must be obeyed.

Towards the end of April Henry started his journey. Cromwell's agent John Thurloe reported that 'his sister and he conversed with as mutual love and joy, as I think ever such relations did; so as his parting from her was with great passion of sorrow in both, though with hopes of being together e'er this'.[12]

Henry, however, was soon consoled by the rapturous welcome he received in France. King Charles met him a few miles from Paris, and the Queen was waiting for him at the Palais Royal. Hyde wrote to Henry Wilmot, who had now been created Earl of Rochester:

> The sweete Duke of Gloucester arrived here on Wednesday last, and is in truth the fynest youth and of the most manly understanding that I have ever known, soe yt yow see they are now all three in one place, where I hope their stay will not be long, and when his Majesty removes his residence yt the Duke of Gloucester shall return to his sister, who is exceedingly fond of him.[13]

Hyde was at one with Charles and Mary in their anxieties concerning Henry's religion. Before consenting to the Paris trip the King had extracted from his mother a promise that she would not compel her youngest son to embrace her faith; but this, so far as he was concerned, did not mean much. Charles at twenty-three was already a cynic. He attached little importance to the keeping of promises, his own or those of others.

For the moment there was no friction. Henry had been accompanied to Paris by his tutor, Robert Lovell, and his education continued. For his own part he settled down happily. Money was scarce, and he did not live in the luxury he had known at The Hague. He went on foot through the city to his riding, fencing and dancing lessons. But it was all exciting experience to a boy who had spent most of his existence as a closely watched prisoner. Also he made the acquaintance, for the first time, of his little sister Henrietta Anne, now a fascinating nine-year-old. She was the closest to him in age of all the family, and the two children took to each other at once.

His mother doted on him, and kept him closely under her eye.

King Charles accepted the situation, and as the months passed there was no more talk of a return to Holland.

In the summer of 1653 Charles had a serious illness, diagnosed as a 'fever'. He soon shook it off, and in the following year he left Paris. This was not of his own free will. Mazarin and Cromwell, each now in undisputed control of the government in their respective countries, were negotiating an alliance, and it suited Mazarin to get rid of his embarrassing English guest. The promise of a pension from France had been long dangled in front of Charles's eyes, but hardly any money had actually been forthcoming. He was now offered full payment provided he left the country within ten days. He accepted the condition.

He decided to move to Germany, and before going he drew up private instructions for his brother James who, still with the French army, would be in closer touch with Paris, and possibly with developments in England, than himself. These instructions, dated 3 July 1654, contained a passage relating to the Duke of Gloucester:

> I have told you what the Queen hath promised me concerning my brother Harry in point of religion, and I have given him charge to inform you if any attempt shall be made upon him to the contrary; in which case you will take the best care you can to prevent his being wrought upon, since you cannot but know how much you and I are concerned in it.[14]

The Elector of Cologne had agreed to receive the King in his territory, and Charles decided to go first to Spa, where he had arranged to meet his sister. He was for once, comparatively speaking, in funds. Mazarin, eager to be rid of him, had not only seen that the arrears of his pension were paid, but had promised to settle his not inconsiderable debts in Paris. Contributions to his expenses were also received from sympathizers among the German princes, while the Earls of Southampton and Hertford, influential royalist agents in England, succeeded in raising £3,000 for him. He was therefore in high spirits when he set off from Paris with a small train on 18 July, 1654. Henry asked to be allowed to go with him, and Charles, who had become greatly attached to his young brother, was inclined to consent. But he allowed his mother to override him. His most important attendant was the Marquess of Ormonde.

At Spa the long planned meeting between King Charles and Princess Mary took place. All acrimony had disappeared, and they were enchanted with each other's company. In the words of the King's latest biographer, 'their mutual devotion was the subject of sentimental and approving comment'.[15] They occupied the two chief hotels in the town, and were constantly in and out of each other's quarters. The weather was bad, and they had to spend most of their time indoors; but there they put aside all care and devoted themselves to laughter and merriment.

After a few days they moved on to Cologne, where the round of gaiety continued. On 27 July the King wrote to Elizabeth of Bohemia:

> Madam,
>   I am just now beginning this letter in my sister's chamber, where there is such a noise that I never hope to end it, and much less write sense. For what concerns my sister's journey and the accidents that happened on the way, I leave her to give Your Majesty an account of. I shall only tell Your Majesty that we are now thinking how to pass our time; and in the first place of dancing, in which we find two difficulties, the one for want of the fiddlers, the other for somebody both to teach and assist at the dancing the new dances. And I have got my sister to send for Silvius as one that is able to perform both.[16]

This visit to Cologne was only a brief trip. Charles and Mary went back to Spa, but when smallpox broke out there they moved to the old imperial capital of Aachen, or Aix-la-Chapelle, where they were joined by Hyde. Their carefree existence continued unabated; they were fêted by the local authorities and invited to see and handle the relics—the skull and a hand—of Charlemagne in the Cathedral.

By now it was October, and time for Mary to return home, but Charles had been invited by the Archbishop-Elector to make a longer stay at Cologne, and his sister accompanied him there on her way. They were received with a triple salute by a band of three hundred musketeers and presented with two casks of Rhenish wine. Cologne was a staunchly Catholic centre, and the King and Princess were entertained in lavish style by the Jesuits at their refectory, where before the banquet 'seven young boys stood ready to receive them, each bearing a shield inscribed with one of the seven letters forming the word Carolus: after each child had sung a brief stanza of gratulation, all turned their shields simultaneously, and the letters of the word Colonia appeared; upon which they dropped on the knee before the royal pair, and chaunted Colonia's welcome.'[17] Mary, an uncompromising Protestant, seemingly enjoyed the feast as wholeheartedly as did her brother.

Other entertainments followed, and then the royal tourists sailed down the Rhine to Düsseldorf as guests of the Duke of Neuburg. They were attended by Ormonde and, it is interesting to note, by Lady Stanhope (she was still known by this name after her marriage to Heenvliet), whose presence evidently aroused no protest. Charles was received by the Duke as a reigning monarch, and a further three days of feasting ensued.

Here ended this idyllic episode. Mary left for The Hague, shedding a torrent of tears on parting with her brother; he for his part returned to Cologne, where he hired a house for the winter.

He was there when the storm broke. Henrietta Maria, freed from the watchful presence of her eldest son, decided in the face of all opposition on a determined effort to change the religious allegiance of her youngest. The result was the most furious breach within the royal family that occurred during the years of exile.

Queen Henrietta's conduct in the matter of the Duke of Gloucester's religion has been condemned by virtually all historians. Her point of view, however, must be appreciated. She was a convinced and a devout Catholic, and as such she believed that the only certain road to salvation was through the Church of Rome. Clearly she must do all she could to save the souls of her own children. If she did not make this her first priority she would be failing in her spiritual duty. Furthermore, she had been promised before her marriage to King Charles I that any children born should be subject to her supervision until the age of thirteen. The marriage treaty itself was ambiguously worded, but Henrietta interpreted it as implying that she would have at least an equal say in the choice of religion for her offspring. She had never ceased to resent what she considered to be a breach of agreement in the subsequent upbringing of her family.

The fact remains that she now deliberately and flagrantly disregarded the promise she had, only a few months before, made to her son who was now the titular King of England. And whatever may have been the merits of her motives, the way she set about achieving her aim was devoid alike of tact, of honesty, and of charity.

She laid her plans deliberately. The first step was to detach the Duke from his Protestant tutor, Robert Lovell. This was not difficult. Lovell was a mild man who exercised little authority over his charge. In September Henry was allowed to join his brother James with the army; there he was given a temporary commission, and served at the siege of Arras. He acquitted himself well, and earned the approval of Turenne. But when he returned to Paris the spoilt fourteen-year-old boy became insufferable. He was a soldier now, and military glory had gone to his head. He gave himself airs, refused to attend to his studies, and would listen to nobody. 'It is exceedingly to be feared,' wrote Lord Hatton, 'that the Duke of Gloucester will contract soe great a rudeness, besides other vices, as may be very troublesome and incorrigible another day, and believe me Mr Lovell signifies so little with him as it hath no effect but contempt on Mr Lovell himself. . . . Indeed the Duke of Gloucester's carriage to all persons is insupportable.'[18]

Henrietta Maria had every excuse for holding that a stronger hand than that of Lovell was needed, and she put him under the charge of her almoner, the Abbé Walter Montagu, an English royalist and a Catholic convert. Then Montagu, under her instructions, moved him from Paris to the seminary over which he presided at Pontoise.

Henry at first made no objection; but he soon found that the reason for his sojourn at Pontoise was that there he could be subjected to a wholehearted onslaught on his Protestant convictions. Montagu and his fellow priests subjected him to a barrage of argument, giving him no peace and dangling before him the prospect of a cardinal's hat, which he was told the Pope would certainly give him as a Catholic prince.

Henrietta and the Pontoise clergy had, however, mistaken the nature of the young duke. He had all the independence and determination characteristic of his family, and nothing would induce him to abandon the faith in which he had been brought up. Whether at his tender age he had any deep theological convictions may be doubted; what he certainly had, as had his brothers and sisters, was an almost mystical veneration for the memory of his martyred father. And his father, in those last interviews before his death, had again and again adjured him never to abandon the Church of England and never, in this one instance, to be influenced by his mother. He wrote at the first opportunity to his eldest brother imploring his intervention, and to his sister Mary asking for advice.

Reports of what was happening were now all over Paris, and others besides Henry wrote to Charles at Cologne. He received the news at the end of October, and from now on letters went back and forth in profusion. Meanwhile James obtained leave from Turenne and made with all speed for Paris.

Charles and James, unlike Mary and Henry, were sympathetic to the Roman faith. James, as has been indicated, probably had leanings himself in that direction; Charles was always in favour of toleration of all creeds, and during his wanderings after Worcester he had been imbued with deep gratitude for the loyalty shown him by humble English Catholics who had risked their lives to shelter him. But in this crisis both were inspired by purely political considerations. The existence of a Catholic brother would imperil, probably fatally, the chances of restoration. They were appalled at the possibility, and King Charles aroused himself from his life of ease at Cologne to send urgent letters to France. To his mother he said:

At the same time that I received Your Majesty's letter of the 23rd October, I received one from my brother Harry and another from Mr Lovell, in which they give me an account of what Your Majesty and Mr Montagu said to them concerning the change of my brother's religion. And likewise I have other informations that there are lodgings providing for him in the Jesuits College, which is quite contrary to the promise Your Majesty made me before I came from Paris, which was that Mr Lovell should continue his place about my brother, and that he should have the free exercise of his religion in his chamber which I am sure he can never have in the Jesuits College.

I must confess that this news does trouble me so much that I cannot say all that I could at another time, but upon the whole matter I must conclude that if Your Majesty does continue to proceed in the change of my brother's religion, I cannot expect Your Majesty does either believe or wish my return into England. . . . Therefore if Your Majesty has the least kindness for me I beg of you not to press him further in it. And remember the last words of my dead father (whose memory I doubt not will work upon you) which were to charge him upon his blessing never to change his religion, whatsoever mischief shall fall either upon me or my affairs, hereafter.[19]

This letter was dated 31 October 1654. On the same day Charles wrote to both his brothers. To James he said:

The news I have received from Paris of the endeavours that are used to change my brother Harry's religion does trouble me so much that if I have any things to answer to any of your letters, you must excuse me if I omit this post. All that I can say at this time is I do conjure you as you love the memory of your father, and if you have any care of yourself, or kindness to me, to hinder all that lies in your power any such practices, without any consideration of any person whatsoever.

I have written very home both to the Queen and my brother about it, and I expect that you should second what I have said to them both, with all the arguments you can, for neither you nor I were ever so much concerned in all respects as we are in this.[20]

The longest letter was to Henry. Acknowledging the letter— 'yours without a date'—the King wrote:

. . . I do not doubt that you remember very well the commands I left with you concerning that point, and so am confident you will observe them. Yet the letters that come from Paris say that it is the Queen's purpose to do all she can to change your religion, which if you hearken to her or anybody else in that matter you must never think to see England or me again. And whatsoever mischief shall fall to me or my affairs from this time I must lay all upon you as being the sole cause of it. Therefore consider what it is not only to be the cause of the ruin of a brother that loves you so well, but also of your King and country, and do not let them persuade you either by force or fair promises. . . .[21]

The urgency of Charles's tone suggests that, in spite of Harry's protestations, he thought the arguments of his oppressors might be too strong for his constancy. The letter went on to order the boy not to join in argument, 'for though you have the reason on your side, yet they, being prepared, will have the advantage of anybody that is not upon the same security as they are'. Harry was to depend on the counsel of the Marquess of Ormonde, who was deputed to take the letters to Paris.

Sir Edward Hyde, as the King's Lord Chancellor, wrote to the Princess Royal to tell her what was happening. 'I have never in my life', he said in his letter, 'seen the king, your brother, in so great trouble of mind'.[22] Mary already knew about it from Henry, and she replied:

Mr Chancellor,
I give you as many thanks for your letter as I wish myself ways to hinder this misfortune that is likely to fall upon our family by my brother Harry's being made a Papist. I received a letter from my brother this last week; all the counsel I was able to give him was to resolve to obey his majesty's orders, and not to let his tutor go from him without the king's leave. This last, I fear, he has not been able to perform; I pray he may the first, for certainly there could not have happened a more fatal thing to his majesty at this time; but I hope God will give us some means of preventing it; if there is likelihood of any, I entreat you to let me know it, for it would be a very great satisfaction to,
Mr Chancellor,
Your affectionate friend,
Marie.[23]
Teyling, this 16th of November, 1654.

James, on the spot in Paris, added his remonstrances, and Henry, when summoned to his mother's presence, protested against receiving instruction in the Catholic faith, pleading his father's and his brother's orders. Queen Henrietta thus found herself faced with the united opposition of her children, with the exception of her little daughter who was too young to take sides in a family row. Then Ormonde arrived with the King's letters. Confronted with his majestic presence, Henrietta prevaricated. She admitted her promise, but pleaded that it was only against the use of force. Ormonde was unimpressed. Armed with the authority of King Charles II and with the strength of his own personality, he insisted that the Duke of Gloucester should go with him to join his brother at Cologne. And Henrietta, though urged by Anne of Austria and Cardinal Mazarin to stand firm, submitted.

In the final scene she behaved with cruelty and petulance. His brother James took Henry to their mother at the Palais Royal to say goodbye and ask her blessing. She made one more appeal to him, and when he refused to capitulate she threw him out. 'I will not own you as my son,' she is recorded as saying. 'I will see your face no more. Leave me, leave my lodgings—you shall have nothing. My lord of Ormonde shall provide for you.'[24] When he tried to approach his little sister, she could only burst into tears, crying: 'Oh God, my brother! Oh me, my mother! I am undone for ever! What shall I do?'[25]

So ended this unhappy episode, which might well have created a permanent breach between the Queen and her eldest son. Charles, however, was too good-natured to bear enduring resentment against his mother. He merely, for the future, disregarded anything she might say in the way of advice or remonstrance.

On 18 December Ormonde set out with his youthful charge. Royalist funds had run out, and he had to sell his Garter insignia to pay for the journey. They decided to go through Flanders, and at Antwerp Henry fell ill. He soon recovered, but there was further anxiety about the expenses of the delay. Mary, however, was at hand to help, as she was always ready to do. At the same time she asked that the journey should again be broken so that her young brother could spend some more time with her, in spite of any objections the States-General might make. She was supported by her aunt Elizabeth, who wrote in a characteristic letter:

> I am sure our Hoghens Moghens [their 'High Mightinesses' the States-General] will take no notice of it, if they be not asked the question, as they were for the King's coming to Breda.[26]

Charles agreed to the visit, and it was decided to take the risk. So once more Henry found himself in his sister's company; she received him at Teyling in January, and the round of gaieties and amusements was resumed. Mary was in no hurry to send her brother on, and the visit seemed likely to be protracted. Gloucester's tutor Lovell was with him once more, while Ormonde returned to the King at Cologne.

In the early months of 1655 hopes arose of a rising in England in favour of the King. The Sealed Knot, the Royalist secret organization, was active, and Charles was advised to move to the coast so that he could sail quickly to England if things should go well. He was as usual short of money, and in February he wrote to his sister:

> I write to you now upon a business I think I never wrote to you before in my life, and I never was more unwilling to do it than now. It is of money, of which, I believe, you are not much better provided than myself; yet I cannot but tell you that I am like, within a few days, to have a good occasion offered me, upon which, if I can lay hold, I may lay a foundation to compass all my business, and truly, if I am not able, I may feel the inconvenience long. I know you are without money, and cannot very easily borrow it, at least upon so little warning; but, if you will send me any jewel that I may pawn for 1,500*l.* sterling, I do promise you, that you shall have the jewel in your hands again before Christmas, and I shall be able to make a journey that I think will do my business. This is only between you and me, and I do not desire it should be known to anybody else, and if you think I may pass through the States' dominions incognito, without giving them offence, I can take some such place in my way as I may

conveniently see you. Let me know your mind as soon as may be.[27]

Mary replied favourably to this persuasive appeal, though what she managed in the way of jewellery does not appear; clearly, as her brother suggested, she too was now feeling the pinch financially. Encouraged by the silence of the States regarding the Duke of Gloucester's visit, she further suggested that Charles might be able to come to Teyling without arousing protest.

Here she was over-optimistic. At the mere rumour that King Charles was in their territory their High Mightinesses sent a remonstrance to the Princess. In this, dated 8 March 1655, they said that they were 'privately informed that King Charles, your royal highness's lord and brother, hath made his repair into the parts under the obedience of this state, and particularly that his abode is at present in the house at Teiling'.[28] They pointed out that this was contrary to the treaty made in 1653 between Holland and the Commonwealth of England; they demanded to be told the truth of the matter, and called on Mary to 'help to hinder, and prevent that the afore-mentioned lord-king do not repair within the power of their high mightinesses'.[29]

King Charles was not at Teyling, and Mary replied to the States' 'uncivil letter' merely with a verbal message that they were mistaken. Charles did, however, at this time pay a secret visit to Middleburgh in Zeeland; the province of Zeeland was always less antagonistic to the Stuarts than was Holland. But the prospects of a rising in England faded, and the King in April returned to Cologne.

The episode led to the removal of the Duke of Gloucester. He continued at Teyling the arrogant behaviour he had displayed in Paris, drawing attention to his presence by assumptions of regal ceremonial, such as mounting his horse at the foot of the staircase instead of in the courtyard. The offences seemed trivial enough, but the States-General made them the pretext for demanding his dismissal. Mary was disposed to ignore them, but King Charles thought it best to send for his brother, who left for Cologne in May.

There followed a further period of frustration, so far as any hope of a restoration was concerned. Charles gave himself up to enjoyment, and his first thought was to arrange another meeting with Mary. He moved to Aix-la-Chapelle in July, and there his sister joined him. It was in the nature of a family reunion, for James, free for the moment from military duties, came to meet them at Meurs.

In September Charles and Mary went together to Cologne, and then with Henry to Frankfort, where the annual fair was in progress. Mary had not been well, and it was hoped that the festivities would do her good. They travelled incognito, but there was no secret about their identity. The tour was reported in the English press; the correspondent of *Mercurius Publicus* wrote:

> Having been lately at Frankfort Fair, I saw there the Scottish King, as they call him, with whom there was his sister, the Princess of Orange, and his youngest brother, Henry, who travelled all together from Cologne to Frankfort. . . .
>
> In the acting of this frolic they would needs pretend to pass incognito, yet carried the matter so notoriously that it was known all abroad, and therefore, in every Prince's country they passed through, they had the civility of a compliment by their chief officers and were saluted by the great ordnance of all their towns and castles.[30]

At Frankfort they were visited by the eccentric Queen Christina of Sweden, who had gone to Cologne to see them and now followed them. She had abdicated her throne the year before, had been received into the Catholic Church, and was now on her way to Rome. She wore strange clothes, and her conduct was unaccountable and unpredictable. She had once been suggested as a bride for Charles II, and now she was delighted to see him. She suggested taking young Henry to Rome with her, and later she was reported as saying: 'The people talk that I am going to Loretto, to offer up a sceptre and crown to the lady Mary there. I laid down these regalities in Sweden, and if I had another crown to dispose of I would rather bestow it on the good poor king of England.'[31]

Christina went on her way to Rome, and the royal party returned to Cologne. On 15 November the Princess Royal went home to Holland. She was still in poor health and she wrote to Charles:

> If I forgot to let you know of my receiving your letter written the Tuesday after you were returned to Cologne, you must not wonder at it; for in earnest I have not been well since I came home, and I know nothing so well able to cure me as to see you in Flanders, which I am sorry to find is not so near as you expected when we parted; 'tis so late now that I humbly beg your pardon if I do not say much at this time; for truly, writing troubles my head, and I must give a little relation to the doctor of my health; for now from the green sickness I begin to fancy I shall fall into a consumption, though none is of my opinion; which I believe they disguise, because they would put that fancy out of my head that can do me no good.[32]

Early in the following year Princess Mary visited Henrietta Maria in Paris. She went partly because she felt she could get the best medical advice in the French capital, but also in order to establish better relations with her mother. There had been a distinct coolness between them, and not only owing to the episode of the Duke of Gloucester. Further friction had come through Mary's insistence on selecting the Chancellor's daughter, Anne Hyde, as one of her maids of honour. Anne was a lively girl of eighteen, and had lived for some time in the house at Breda granted by Mary to her mother.

Mary was on excellent terms with Sir Edward Hyde, who spent much of his time in Holland. The Queen, on the other hand, disliked Hyde and always resented his influence over the royal family. She therefore opposed the appointment of Anne, and her objection was shared by Sir Edward himself, ostensibly on the ground that his only daughter ought to stay as companion to her mother but really because he feared the appointment would exacerbate friction between himself and the Queen.

Mary had a will of her own; Hyde yielded to her insistence and the appointment, which was to have unforeseen and momentous consequences, was made. Queen Henrietta was at first affronted, but at length she relented and sent kind messages to her daughter, who wrote to King Charles:

> I do now with great joy tell you that the queen has received
> my letter, and commanded my brother [James] to tell me,
> that she is so sick that she could not write; but that when she is
> well, I shall hear from her; and he withal assures me from
> himself, that I shall have a kind answer, which is an extreme
> satisfaction to me. I hope now there will be a good
> understanding amongst us all, in spite of all hot heads, which
> has studied nothing but how to make the queen angry both
> with you and me.[33]

Mary had a loving heart and was devoted to her mother, and
she wanted a personal reconciliation. Arrangements for a visit
were quickly made, and in the middle of January 1656 the
Princess Royal left The Hague for Paris. With her went Anne
Hyde.

In France the Princess was received with royal honours. She
was met at the frontier by representatives of the French
royal family, while adherents of the Stuarts flocked to meet her;
among them was the old Lord Rochford, Robert Carey, who so
long ago had watched over her father's childhood. On 28
January she was joined by her brother James, who now,
apparently for the first time, met the blooming young damsel
Anne Hyde. Whether he fell in love with her on this occasion is
not known, but he was a susceptible young man and it was not
long before a secret affair blossomed.

In Paris the two surviving Stuart sisters had their first
meeting. Henrietta Anne was now in her twelfth year, coming to
maturity as the seventeenth century reckoned age. She was a
sprightly child, inclined to be skinny and with shoulders of
uneven height; she lacked Mary's beauty but made up for it with
a vivacity of manner that was beginning to charm the courtiers
of France. She was thrilled to meet an unknown elder sister, and
Mary as always was delighted to extend her affection to another
member of the family.

Court life in France at this time was a stately round of balls,
masques and gorgeous fêtes. The Fronde troubles were at an
end. Politically Mazarin was still in supreme power, but in the
social sphere Louis XIV, now in his eighteenth year, was coming

into his own, single-minded in his aim to make his court the most splendid in Europe. Balls were given in honour of Mary, and Louis himself escorted her to a comedy and a classical ballet. Anne of Austria, still Regent of France, did not approve of widows dancing; so at the ball given for Mary by Philip Duke of Anjou, King Louis's young brother, the guest of honour had to be a spectator while the King opened the proceedings with her little sister; Henrietta, it was recorded in the court chronicle, 'looked like an angel upon earth . . . and danced so perfectly that a thousand blessings were showered upon her'.[34]

Queen Henrietta, who yet again had hopes of making a convert of one of her children, took her elder daughter to her favourite convent at Chaillot and introduced her once more to Catholic ceremonies, as she had done when she was a small child. Mary was not so receptive now. She unbent so far as to attend the taking of the veil by a young English lady, but further than that she would not go.

The French visit, however, was an unqualified success and was prolonged for most of the year. In September it was enlivened by the presence of Christina of Sweden, still on her capricious wanderings through Europe. In the words of Carola Oman, she 'arrived wearing a man's periwig and shoes, a chemise "sticking out all around her petticoat . . . ill-fastened and not over-straight", much powder on a countenance of strong features pitted with smallpox, quantities of pomatum and no gloves on hands which were remarkably dirty. She proceeded to swear, fall into spectacular brown studies, and dance at court balls with astonishing vigour and inelegance.'[35]

It was not till she heard that her young son, William of Orange, had developed a fit of measles that Mary was induced to leave for home. This was in November. When she departed the three remaining female members of the Stuart family were in delighted harmony.

For Mary's brothers there had been changes of diplomatic importance. Charles II had completed a treaty with Philip IV of Spain by which arms and money were promised and the Low Countries were to be used as the starting point for an expedition into England. Charles therefore moved his headquarters to Bruges in the Spanish Netherlands. There, without returning to

Holland, Mary joined him; she had heard that young William had recovered, and she decided he could do without her.

She was not unmindful of her son. She in fact felt that the best hope for his future lay in a restoration of Stuart fortunes; and her brother's crown came first in her estimation. But there was in fact no serious hope of an invasion of England at this time. On 2 February 1657, the Princess of Orange at last returned to The Hague.

It was to James that the new developments made the biggest difference. Campaigning in the Low Countries during the past few years had been of a desultory nature, though the young duke had been happy learning the military art. Now, however, when Spain was in alliance with his royal brother, it was impossible for him to go on fighting with French troops against Spaniards. Mazarin, moreover, had come to terms with Cromwell, and the agreement provided that James should quit French service.

The Duke was most reluctant to do so. Mazarin was complaisant, and the French authorities 'not only expressed the desire they had to retain him in the service, but assured him that, if Cromwell would not consent to the propositions they had made to him in this matter, his pension would still be paid him in what ever place he might retire to, provided that he did not serve against France'.[36]

James would have been happy to stay on as a pensioner of the French court, ready to take up arms again with his comrades if the circumstances should change. But this was not agreeable to his brother. 'The King, far from consenting to the Duke's request, immediately sent him an absolute order to come and join him in Flanders with all possible diligence. He at once obeyed, and the French Court consented.'[37]

The Duke of York was thus reminded of his status. His first duty was to his brother, and he must obey him in all circumstances. Subject to this consideration he was a mercenary soldier, who must not identify himself with any particular foreign country. In 1657 he joined the Spanish forces, fighting against his old mentor Turenne and his erstwhile French comrades.

The change-over was not effected without a dispute with his elder brother. James indeed obeyed the royal command, but on reporting to Bruges he found anything but a cordial reception.

As in the previous quarrel with Mary, Charles objected to his brother's choice of attendants. In particular Sir John Berkeley and his nephew Charles, who were in James's special confidence, were represented to the King as being pro-French and anti-Spanish. The Earl of Bristol, the former Lord Digby who was the most inveterate intriguer in the Royalist camp, made it his business to cause trouble between the brothers, and Charles ordered the dismissal of the Berkeleys. James, who considered he had done his duty sufficiently in agreeing to enter the Spanish service, for once showed himself mutinous. He flounced out of Bruges and threw himself on his sister's hospitality in Holland. The contretemps did not last long. James, presumably on Mary's advice, sent his brother a conciliatory letter, and Charles, one of whose assets, unusual in a Stuart, was an instinct for knowing when it was best to give in, consented that the Berkeleys should stay. James returned to Bruges and busied himself in helping the King to raise forces of English, Scottish and Irish exiles to serve with the Spanish. He then took the field under the Marqués de Caracena. His young brother Henry, who had been with Charles in Bruges, was already serving with the Spaniards as a volunteer.

In the campaigns that followed, which in general were as inconclusive as those which had gone before, James added to his military reputation. He was an experienced soldier now; he had served as lieutenant-general under Turenne, and with the Spaniards he commanded the substantial English contingent. The Flanders climate was unhealthy, and there was much sickness. James recorded in his memoirs:

> . . . The troops commanded by the Duke of York suffered the worst; he himself was almost the only person among the officers or volunteers of quality, or the members of his household, who was not attacked [by fever]. The Duke of Gloucester left the army, sick; and the Prince de Condé was holden with such a fever that the doctors feared for his life.[38]

In these unpropitious circumstances the Duke managed to maintain his forces in a state of order and discipline. In September 1657, when the troops were in the neighbourhood of Dunkirk, King Charles arrived to confer with Don Juan, King

James II, when Duke of York, by Lely

Philip's illegitimate son who was Governor of Flanders; and when he left, taking Don Juan and Caracena with him on a visit to Bruges, James was left in command of the whole Spanish army.

The years of exile, and the frustrations that always seemed to obviate any hope of restoration, were telling on King Charles, and his normally easy-going nature gave place to a tendency to seek quarrels within his own family circle. His altercation with James having been smoothed over, he now proceeded to squabble once more with Mary.

Mary during this time, as always during the years of exile, provided a haven of solace for her brothers. Her palace at Breda, being within the personal patrimony of the Prince of Orange, was free from the direct jurisdiction of the States-General; here she maintained a suite of rooms always available for members of her family when they needed refuge. It was here that the Duke of Gloucester stayed to recuperate after he had been taken ill on active service in Flanders.

During 1657 Mary moved between Breda and Bruges, and all was well until, in September, differences arose. The cause was the same as usual, and this time the people concerned were Lord and Lady Balcarres. Balcarres, a Scots Presbyterian and an ardent royalist, had been recommended to his sister's service by the King himself; but Charles now suspected him of intriguing against him with Mazarin. He wanted Lady Balcarres dismissed from her post as Lady of the Bedchamber to Mary, and some acrimonious correspondence ensued. Mary refused to comply, and Charles, as he so often did when confronted with opposition, gave way. But a more serious difference followed.

The Flanders campaign ceased for the winter, and the Duke of York went to stay with his sister at Breda, joining his younger brother there. With him he took his friend Harry Jermyn, nephew of Queen Henrietta's favourite counsellor. Young Jermyn, well supplied with money by his uncle, was a prepossessing youth, though not much trusted in royal circles. Mary was plainly attracted, and the intimacy she granted him, anxious as she was to hear details of her mother's court, soon gave rise to gossip. It was freely said that the Princess Royal would soon either marry the young man or become his mistress.

When Charles heard these rumours he was appalled. Once

again he reacted angrily, and demanded that Jermyn should be
sent to him at Bruges. Mary complied, but with a bad grace.
'Now that you see how exactly you are obeyed,' she wrote in a
letter from Breda on 2 February 1658, 'I hope you will give me
leave to desire you to consider what consequences your severity
will bring upon me; to justify any of my actions to you in this
occasion were, I think, to do as much wrong to both my brothers
as my own innocency, since they have been witnesses to what
some persons' insolency has declared to represent unto you as
faults.'[39] She asked for Jermyn to be sent back to her.

Charles at first angrily refused. It was not that he believed the
rumours, but once again it was a case of French influence, which
was becoming an obsession with him. At length, however, after
further correspondence, he agreed to submit the question to the
arbitration of the Duke of York. The result was a family
conference, after which Charles grudgingly allowed Jermyn to
return to Breda as the best means of avoiding scandal.

There was general desire for a reconciliation, and in March
Mary and all her three brothers gathered together at Antwerp,
where King Charles's old tutor, the Marquess of Newcastle, and
the Marchioness were staying. There were the usual festivities,
and it seemed that happy relations were restored. But before
they separated Charles was tactless enough to remark to Mary
that 'the Jermyns were destined to be his ruin'.[40] Mary replied
with bitterness. Next day she left in dudgeon for Breda, taking
James and Henry with her.

So the months of 1658 passed, with breaches within the royal
family and no apparent hope of a return to England. In May
Mary fell foul of the States of Holland through taking her
brothers to The Hague for the fair. She hoped the visit would not
be noticed, but the States demanded their expulsion. Mary left
with them, and the three went on to Brussels, where they were
the guests of the burghers. Then in the summer James and
Henry returned to the Spanish army, which was preparing to
defend Dunkirk against the French.

The battle when it came, as it did in June 1658, was on a much
bigger scale than any fighting that had preceded it. From the
English royalists' point of view it was a disaster. The French and
their allies from Cromwell's Commonwealth stormed through

the Spanish lines among the sandhills on the outskirts of Dunkirk; the English in particular fought with magnificent determination, as was generously admitted by the Duke of York when he came to write his memoirs. Condé was still with the Spanish forces, and after the Battle of the Dunes, as it was called, he and Caracena surrendered the town of Dunkirk to the French.

The royal brothers were well to the fore. King Charles had himself joined the Spanish army for a brief period, and had led a charge at Mardyke. He was not, however, at Dunkirk, where James and Henry did their full share. Before the fighting began Condé went to the Duke of Gloucester and asked him whether he had ever seen a battle, and when the boy said he had not, Condé, who had a low opinion of Caracena's tactical ability, told him that within half an hour he would see one lost. So it turned out; Henry, however, proved himself a true soldier. His conduct was thus described by his elder brother in his memoirs:

> The Duke of Glocester, who during the action of all that day had seconded me, and behav'd himself as bravely as any of his Ancestors had ever done, had his sword either struck out of his hand by one of the Enemy, or it flew out of his hand by a blow which he had given; but which of the two I remember not: It happen'd that a gentleman one Villeneuve, Ecuier to the Prince de Ligny, who was next him, saw this accident; whereupon he leap'd down immediately from his horse, took up the sword, and delivered it to my Brother, who with his pistoll in his hand, stood ready to secure him till he was remounted. But immediately after, the same gentleman was shott through the body; not withstanding which it was his fortune to gett off, and to recover of his wound.[41]

This action marked the end of the Stuart brothers' active military service on the Continent. Henry returned to Bruges, while James withdrew up the coast to Nieuport and awaited events. Meanwhile Mary, who had been for a time distressed by a rumour that James had been taken prisoner, heard that Charles, after hovering in the Dunkirk area, was on his way to Frankfort. She hastened to Breda to meet him; all enmity appeared to have vanished. Quarrels between King Charles and his sister never lasted long.

After this brief reunion Charles resumed his aimless wandering through the Spanish Netherlands. In September he was at Hoogstraeten, close to the Dutch border. There on the 10th of that month he was playing tennis, his favourite game, when Sir Stephen Fox entered the *dedans*, fell on his knees, and interrupted the game to give the King momentous news. Just a week before, on 3 September, the anniversary of the Roundhead victories of Dunbar and Worcester, Oliver Cromwell had died at Whitehall.

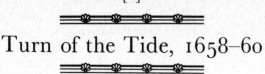

6

Turn of the Tide, 1658–60

The death of Cromwell meant diplomatic upheaval in Europe. The great Lord Protector had not been loved; but he had been both feared and respected. During his years of dominion England had been a power to be reckoned with, and European rulers had shown themselves reluctant to offend the island republic. Mazarin's France had sought an English alliance, and even the Spanish monarchy had been wary of pursuing an openly anti-English policy.

Now there was a different spirit abroad. With the exception of the Netherlands States-General no European government had any sympathy with republican principles or with regicide. It was only the personal reputation of the English dictator that influenced continental rulers, and once his iron hand was removed they were prepared to think again. It was taken for granted that the inheritors of his dominion would soon begin to squabble among themselves, and republican England would then cease to be a useful ally.

A mood of unreasoning euphoria seized the English exiles. Nothing, it was felt, could go wrong now. With Oliver Cromwell out of the way it was only a matter of time before royalist risings took place in England, and the King would return on the crest of a wave. The fact that Richard Cromwell, the Protector's elder son and his designated successor, had taken over quietly and without the least hint of disturbance was brushed aside as of no significance.

King Charles himself did not lose his head; he seldom did. But he put himself in readiness to leave for England at short notice; and he took a step which for a time alienated him from the rest of the family.

He decided it was time for him to take a wife. A married

monarch might be more acceptable to his subjects than a roving bachelor king, and a suitable diplomatic alliance would strengthen his position. The prospective bride on whom he cast his eye was Princess Henrietta Catherine, sister of his late brother-in-law William II of Orange. The Dutch would be valuable allies. The United Provinces were strong at sea and wealthy; they had recently been at war with the republican régime in England, and though they had little use for Prince William's widow they looked with favour on his mother, the still formidable Dowager Princess Amelia, who had identified herself with Dutch national interests in a way Mary had never tried to do, and therefore on her daughter.

The project, however, was not dictated by purely diplomatic considerations. The Princess Dowager had a palace at Turnhout, four miles from Hoogstraeten, where Charles had taken up residence. There she lived with her two unmarried daughters, and during the early autumn of 1658 the young king became friendly with the family. Henrietta, the elder of the daughters, was a lovely and vivacious girl of twenty, who had already shown her spirit by flatly rejecting the first suitor chosen by her forceful mother, simply because she did not like him: a most unjustifiable reason by seventeenth-century standards. She now quickly fell whole-heartedly in love with the handsome young exiled king; the feeling, as was demonstrated in letters which he wrote at this time, was fully reciprocated. If Charles II was ever genuinely in love in his life, it was with Princess Henrietta Catherine.[1]

In its initial stages the romance stopped short of any suggestion of matrimony. Charles was up against his perennial difficulty; a penniless exile was no acceptable match for an eligible princess. Now, however, with a restoration in prospect, the situation was changed. He made a formal offer of marriage, and the Princess Dowager, sharing the mood of the moment and rejoicing in the vision of her daughter on a throne, invited King Charles to come to Turnhout immediately. As for the prospective bride, she promptly fell ill with emotion.

The rejoicing was premature. King Charles was royally received and entertained at Turnhout. But no betrothal was announced. The Princess Dowager, when she had time to consider the matter, came to the conclusion that little was changed. There was no sign that England was turning back towards royalty, and the claimant to the throne was no richer and no more powerful than he had been in previous months. Charles left Turnhout with no promises made, and conscious of increasing coolness in the hospitality shown by Princess Amelia. Before the year was out the betrothal was announced of Princess Henrietta Catherine to Prince John George of Anhalt-Dessau. The Princess, for all the ardour she had shown in her brief love affair with the English King, this time submitted with docility to her mother's wishes.

It was an episode of surprising brevity. But so far as family relations were concerned the damage was done. Charles had made his advances towards the Orange alliance without informing his sister, and Mary, as soon as she heard the news, reacted with a fury that was characteristic of her emotional temperament. The reconciliation with her mother-in-law that had followed the arrival of the Duke of Gloucester in Holland five years earlier had not lasted. Relations between the two princesses were in 1658 as bad as ever, aggravated as they were by their opposing attitudes towards the Dutch authorities. Mary had subordinated everything to her eldest brother's interests; she had given him shelter, provided him with money, and worked with all the passion of her nature to help him towards the regaining of his father's throne. And now this same brother had gone behind her back and intrigued for an alliance with her enemy. Moreover, if this alliance came to pass, her despised sister-in-law, the daughter of the hated Amelia, would be Queen of England and take precedence of the King's loyal and devoted sister. To Mary such questions of etiquette were of the highest importance.

The Duke of York had laid down his commission in the Spanish army as soon as he heard the news of Cromwell's death. 'I sent immediately to Don John', he wrote in his memoirs, 'at the same time desiring him to send Some other who might take upon him my command; it being of absolute necessity for me to go to Bruxelles, and attend the King my Brother upon this new alteration of affaires in England.'[2]

At Brussels he found there was nothing he could do to help. So, picking up his young brother Henry on his way, he made for The Hague. The two princes, who still had no right to be there, arrived at their sister's palace at ten o'clock on the night of Sunday 22 September, just as Mary was going to bed. She went down to receive them, and the three stayed up till dawn talking. Then, at her urgent representation, her brothers left for neutral territory. There were further comings and goings, and then Mary made a secret journey to join them at Breda.

There she worked on their feelings, with the result that all three were estranged from their eldest brother and sovereign. Pouring out her heart to Lady Stanhope, the Princess Royal declared that King Charles 'had ruined her fame; that if he were in his kingdom he could not make her satisfaction; that hereafter she would never have anything to do with him, what change soever should be in his or her fortune'.[3] Alone of the family, the head of it was denied hospitality at Breda.

After the bright hopes of September King Charles's fortunes seemed to be at their lowest ebb. His matrimonial prospects had evaporated in humiliation, there was no good news from England, he was without influence on events, and now he was no longer on speaking terms with his own family. Despairing and indigent, he retired once more to Bruges, where the bickerings and clamourings of his poverty-stricken courtiers made life miserable for him.

Yet in fact the tide was turning. All might seem to be going smoothly in England, but it was only on the surface. Unseen by the royalists on the Continent, forces were being set in motion which would in due course undermine the republican régime. The predominant feeling on the death of Oliver Cromwell was relief. John Evelyn, who watched the imposing procession when the Protector's body was taken to Westminster Abbey, recorded that 'it was the joyfullest funerall that ever I saw, for there was none that Cried, but dogs, which the souldiers hooted away with a barbarous noise; drinking, & taking *Tabacco* in the streets as they went'.[4] A few months later the same diarist reported 'a wonderfull & suddaine change in the face of the publique: The new *Protector Richard* slighted, severall pretenders, & parties strive for the Government, all *Anarchy* and confusion; Lord have mercy on us.'[5]

Evelyn was a royalist, though not of a type whose loyalty would ever find vent in dangerous action. But his diary comments were not merely an expression of wishful thinking. Richard Cromwell was hopelessly inadequate as a national dictator in unsettled times. A pleasant, easy-going man, he was not of the stuff of which his father was made. Under his weak rule the men who had been Oliver's main supporters—Generals Charles Fleetwood, John Desborough and John Lambert, and the parliamentarians Sir Arthur Haslerig and Sir Henry Vane the younger—soon began manoeuvring for power. In Scotland General George Monk, supreme in that country as Commander-in-Chief, watched carefully with a critical eye, but for the moment made no move.

Rivalries came into the open in April 1659. Richard Cromwell, in need of money, had called a new parliament, and this body, under the influence of Vane and Haslerig, attacked the army leaders by passing a resolution that while Parliament was sitting no councils or meetings of officers should be held without the consent of the Protector and both Houses. The Army under General Fleetwood defied the order, holding a meeting at which he and Desborough demanded the dissolution of Parliament. The Protector gave in, and his parliament met for the last time on 22 April. His own authority had evaporated, and a few weeks later he unobtrusively retired into private life.

In the power vacuum that ensued Fleetwood and Desborough, vacillating and jealous of each other, failed to provide effective leadership, and on 7 May the Rump of the Long Parliament, which constitutionally had never ceased to exist, reassembled at Westminster. Vane and Haslerig, with Edmund Ludlow, staunchest of republicans, were in power again; but their rule was precarious.

In the Army Fleetwood was appointed Commander-in-Chief, a post which had been held nominally by Protector Richard. Desborough was next in seniority, but the most significant military figure was John Lambert. He had been Oliver Cromwell's right-hand man, but at the close of the dictator's life had broken with him and been deprived of his commission. Now he was restored to his commands. He was by far the most capable and the most forceful of the army leaders.

Clearly a new struggle for power was imminent; and when the news of these events reached the Continent the hopes of the Royalists rose once more. King Charles, moving uneasily between Bruges and Brussels, saw his prospects rising; those who had prophesied that chaos would follow the Lord Protector's death were not so far wrong after all. But what to do about it all was not easy to decide. Probably the best course would have been masterly inactivity: let the Commonwealth leaders fight it out among themselves, and then perhaps the King could step in to restore order. But Charles and his advisers chafed at the thought of inaction, and plans for new royalist risings in England were quickly set on foot. At the same time the wisest heads among the King's counsellors spotted the true man of destiny. Early in 1659 Royalist agents were making tentative approaches to General Monk.

By midsummer the plans were ready. Risings were to take place in various parts of England, co-ordinated by Viscount Mordaunt, most ardent of royalist agents. The great day was to be 1 August, and as soon as success was achieved King Charles was to sail from Calais to Deal.

Any ill-feeling that still existed between the King and his brothers was quickly dissipated by the prospect of effective action at last. The Dukes of York and Gloucester hastened to respond to the King's orders, which were that James should make for Boulogne and arrange for a vessel to take him to England when Charles sailed from Calais; Henry was to go to Brussels and await further orders.

Charles actually got to Calais, and James to Boulogne, only to learn that everything had gone wrong. The Sealed Knot, as always, was to play a key part in the risings; but one of its members, Sir Richard Willis, unsuspected by anybody, had long been betraying loyalist plans to the Commonwealth government. The military leaders knew all about what was happening, and the Army was alerted. Learning of the treachery, though not of the identity of the traitor, Mordaunt called off the risings. His orders failed to reach one Cavalier leader, Sir George Booth, who rose in arms in Cheshire on 31 July—which was in any case one day early. Lambert was sent north, defeated Booth without difficulty, and took him captive to London.

While waiting for news from England, Charles and James hung about the Channel ports. There appears to have been a strange lack of liaison between them. Perhaps some feelings of acrimony still lingered; at any rate the King left his brother guessing concerning his own movements, which were somewhat erratic and mysterious. Negotiations had started to end the seemingly endless hostilities between France and Spain; the French court was moving south for discussions on the Spanish border, and Charles had developed the idea of moving uninvited in that direction in the hope of gaining advantage for himself. He knew now that his stay at Calais could lead to nothing, but omitted to tell James of his intentions.

In this bewildering situation the Duke of York received a truly remarkable offer from his old commander and more recent adversary, the Vicomte de Turenne, which throws a clear light on the excellent impression he had made on that experienced and level-headed soldier. The episode is thus recorded in James's memoirs:

> . . . Captain Thomas Cook came thither (to Boulogne) from Paris, with letters to the Duke from the Queen his mother, and commands to find out his Maty. These letters likewise inform'd him, that Monsr. de Turenne who was then about Amiens desir'd to speak with the King in reference to his affaires in England. Upon which the Duke went immediately to Abbeville, hoping there to have found the King; but his Maty was departed from thence, and all his R. H. could hear of him was that he was gone towards Dieppe, and thither he sent Captain Cook after him; who missing of him there also, went in quest of him as farr as Rouen, but his Maty was gone from thence also on his way to St Malo: Whereupon Cook return'd to the Duke, and gave him an account of his fruitless diligence.
>
> The business was of too great importance to be neglected, and therefore his R. H. resolv'd on going himself privately to Monsr. de Turenne; when he was come to him at Amiens, Monsr. de Turenne told him, He had desired to speak to the King his brother, but since his Maty was not to be found, he would do him the same service in the Duke's person: Therupon he offer'd him his own Regiment of foot, which he would make up twelve hundred men, and the Scots-Gendarmes, to carry over into England with him: That besides this, he would furnish him with three or four thousand spare armes, six feild pieces with ammunition propor-

tionable, and tooles, and as much meale as would serve for the
Sustenance of five thousand men for the space of six weeks, or
two months; and farther, would furnish him with Vessels for
the conveyance of all this into England, and permitt the
Troopes that his Maty had in Flanders, to march to Boulogne
and there imbarke, with orders to follow the Duke as fast as
Vessells could be provided for them; advising his R. H. to
send directions to them, that they should march immediately
to St. Omers where a pass should meet them.

And that all these preparations might be compass'd with
more ease and certainty, he offer'd the Duke to pawne his
plate and make use besides of all his interest and credit, to
make up such a sum of mony as should be thought necessary
for the carrying on of the business: Concluding all with this
expression, That his R. H. might easily beleeve he had no
orders from the Cardinal, who was then at the Conference, to
perform all this; but what he did was freely of himself, out of
no other motive than kindness to the Duke, and to his family.[6]

James was overjoyed at this extraordinary mark of confidence. Turenne's offer, made on his own responsibility without
reference to the King of France or his chief minister, was
officially to King Charles as commander of the proposed
expedition; but it was plainly intended as personal to himself.
What would have been the result to Turenne if it had been
implemented can only be conjectured; his prestige in France was
so immense that he could probably have overridden any
opposition from official quarters. But when James returned to
Boulogne, eager to prepare an immediate invasion of England,
he heard of Booth's defeat and the abandonment of the
expedition.

He was reluctant to give up so splendid an opportunity. He
returned to Turenne, represented that the missing Charles
might well be actually in England, and urged that an invasion of
his own could save his brother by creating a diversion. But
Turenne, the old soldier, thought differently. His offer had been
made on the understanding that the Royalists would have risen
in England. He was not prepared to risk his forces in a venture
that had only a remote chance of success. He counselled
patience, and consoled his protégé by lending him 300 pistoles.

Once again royalist plans for a restoration were at a standstill. There was nothing for James to do but return to Brussels, there to await news of his errant brother.

Charles was in fact travelling in a somewhat leisurely manner towards Spain. With the failure of the English risings he had fallen into one of those sauntering, lackadaisical moods that were characteristic of him. There was nothing to be hoped for in England, there was still some coolness between him and other members of his family, and he knew nothing of the magnificent offer made by Turenne to the Duke of York. In these unpropitious circumstances he decided just to enjoy himself, and he evidently did so on his journey southward. Hyde, who favoured the seeking of international help, was kept in the dark on his sovereign's movements and was irritated by his dilatoriness. Even after entering Spanish territory Charles made little attempt to hurry. On 5 October he wrote to Hyde from Saragossa:

> You will wonder to find me no farther advanced in my journey than this place where I arrived last night. For the truth is our greediness of getting into Spain with all haste, hath made us lose this time. . . .
>
> Our journey hath been very lucky, having met with many pleasant accidents and not one ill one to any of our company, hardly as much as the fall of a horse. But I am very much deceived in the travelling in Spain, for by all reports I did expect ill cheer and worse lying, and hitherto we have found both the beds and especially the meat very good. The only thing I find troublesome is the dust, and particularly in this town, there having fallen no rain on this side the Perineans [Pyrenees] these four months. God keep you, and send you to eat as good mutton as we have every meal.[7]

The King did not specify the nature of the many pleasant accidents, nor enlarge on what company he enjoyed in the good Spanish beds; but clearly the journey was giving him pleasure. And in this light-hearted spirit he went on to Fuenterrabia, where the peace conference was being held. He had been joined on his travels by Ormonde and Bristol.

At Fuenterrabia, where he arrived on 18 October, he was

treated with elaborate courtesy; the Spaniards received him with royal honours, and the French were equally polite. Neither, however, showed any inclination to do anything practical to help him, and when he offered to marry Hortense Mancini, one of Mazarin's glamorous nieces, the Cardinal refused on the ground that this would be unsuitable while the first unmarried lady of France (La Grande Mademoiselle) remained in that state.

The Franco-Spanish peace was duly achieved, with the betrothal of Louis XIV to the Infanta Maria Teresa, daughter of the ageing King Philip IV. The prospects of the exiled King of England were politely ignored in the peace treaty, and Charles left Fuenterrabia on 8 November.

He had decided to visit his mother on his way back to Brussels. They had not met since the dark days of 1654, and Henrietta Maria was still resentful of the part he had played in the affair of Henry Duke of Gloucester. Now it was felt that a full reconciliation was desirable for all concerned; Hyde, much as he and the Queen disliked each other, was especially in favour of it. Charles wrote to his mother in respectfully affectionate terms, and she replied: '*Monsieur mon Fils*, although you show me no confidence, I continue to serve you.'[8]

So King Charles broke his journey at Colombes, reaching his mother's home there on 5 December. Queen Henrietta received him in a flood of happy tears, but the visit was momentous for Charles for another reason. At Colombes he renewed his acquaintance with his little sister Henrietta Anne, and the reunion marked the development of what became, without question, the deepest love of his life.

He had apparently already been writing to her, for the earliest of her letters to survive, the first in a celebrated correspondence which was to extend over the next decade, was clearly sent before the meeting at Colombes. Princess Henrietta wrote (in French, for her English was rudimentary):

I would not let my Lord Inchiquin leave without assuring Your Majesty of the respect I have for you. You do me too much honour in writing to me so often. I fear it must give you trouble and I should be grieved that Your Majesty should take so much for a little sister who is not worthy of it, but who can realize this honour and rejoice in it. I hope that the Peace will give you all the happiness you can desire and I shall rejoice in it because of the love and respect I have for Your Majesty. This is a great joy to me since it gives me the hope of seeing Your Majesty, which is a thing passionately desired by your very humble servant.[9]

Henrietta, now fifteen years old, was growing into a young woman of quite exceptional charm. She was warm-blooded and warm-hearted, in temperament more like her eldest brother than any other member of the family. She resembled him too in possessing a keener intelligence than any of her brothers and sisters other than the dead Elizabeth whom she had never known. Attractive rather than beautiful, she already had the courtiers of France, of both sexes, at her feet. A fashionable young lady, Madame de Brégis, wrote of her at this time in ecstatic terms:

To begin with her height, I must tell you that this young Princess is still growing, and that she will soon attain a perfect stature. Her air is as noble as her birth, her hair is of a bright chestnut hue, and her complexion rivals that of the gayest flowers. The snowy whiteness of her skin betrays the lilies from which she sprang. Her eyes are blue and brilliant, her lips ruddy, her throat beautiful, her arms and hands well made. Her charms show that she was born on a throne, and is destined to return there. Her wit is lively and agreeable. She is admired in her serious moments and beloved in her most ordinary ones; she is gentle and obliging, and her kindness of heart will not allow her to laugh at others, as cleverly as she could, if she chose. She spends most of her time in learning all that can make a princess perfect, and devotes her spare moments to the most varied accomplishments. She dances with incomparable grace, she sings like an angel, and the spinet is never so well played as by her fair hands. All this makes the young Cleopatra the most amiable Princess in the world, and if Fortune once unties the fold that wraps her eyes, to gaze upon her, she will not refuse to give her the greatest of earth's glories, for she deserves them well. I wish them for her, more passionately than I can say.[10]

English observers, as well as French, were attracted by her natural gaiety, which was quite unaffected by the adulation she received. 'The young Princess, then about fifteen years,' wrote the Yorkshire squire Sir John Reresby, who visited Paris in this same year, 'used me with all the civil freedom that might be, made me dance with her, played on the harpsichord to me in Her Highness's chamber, suffered me to attend upon her, when she walked in the garden with the rest of her retinue, and sometimes to toss her in a swing made of a cable which she sat upon, tied between two trees, and in fine suffered me to be present at most of her innocent diversions.'[11]

When Charles had last seen her she was ten. She had developed out of all recognition, so much so that when he came into her presence in her mother's drawing room he was about to kiss the wrong young lady when the mistake was pointed out to him. He was immediately enchanted with her, and bestowed on her the nickname 'Minette', or 'Little Puss', by which she has become best known to posterity. She for her part regarded him with adoring admiration.

King Charles spent only two days at Colombes. On 7 December he went on his way with a lighter heart, to meet James and Henry in Brussels. The news from England was more hopeful, and Mary, generous and forgiving as always, sent him money. Family concord was restored, and the year 1659 closed more harmoniously than it had opened.

In England the republican régime was sliding into anarchy. The Rump had been expelled by Lambert, who in October assumed almost Cromwellian authority. He was, however, distrusted by his fellow generals who were now busy cutting each others' throats. The Royalists were in touch with Monk, who was preparing to invade England with his seasoned, well-disciplined and well-paid army.

On the first day of the new year Monk began his momentous march. His vanguard crossed the border on 1 January 1660, and he himself with the main body of his troops followed next day. His most important ally in England was Lord Fairfax, the former Captain-General of the New Model Army. Fairfax, who had broken with Cromwell over the putting to death of King Charles I and had retired into private life, was now almost openly royalist. He was a wealthy man with great possessions in Yorkshire; and his prestige was immense.

A few weeks earlier Lambert had gone north to meet Monk— ostensibly for negotiation but really to oppose him in arms should he advance into England. In Lambert's absence Fleetwood recalled the Rump, but it had little to do except wait and see what line Monk would take.

Monk had not as yet declared for the King. His proclaimed objects were the restoration of order in England and the calling of a 'full and free parliament'. But the exiles were filled with renewed hope. For the first time the prospect loomed of a restoration of monarchy brought about not by armed rebellion in England, nor by foreign intervention, but by the spontaneous will of King Charles II's most influential subjects, with the concurrence of the mass of the populace.[12]

As the advance of the northern army continued, Lambert's forces disintegrated and there was no more opposition. Monk made personal contact with Fairfax in York and then continued his march. On 3 February he arrived in London, and from then on he was in control of the situation.

The bright dawn of the fateful year 1660 had come, and the sun shone on the watching Stuarts. For the moment there was nothing for King Charles, kicking his heels in Brussels, to do except wait for the longed-for summons to England. Hyde, Ormonde and Nicholas were in charge of his affairs, and these experienced counsellors saw that, so long as no false step was made, the tide would carry them home.

The King and his sister 'Minette' had been corresponding, but not many of the letters of this period have survived. Henrietta had perhaps reproached her brother for writing in English, for at the beginning of February he wrote to her from Brussels:

I begin this letter in French by assuring you that I do not mind your scolding me. I give in joyfully since you quarrel so charmingly with me, but I will never give up the friendship that I have for you, and you give me so many marks of yours that we shall never have any other quarrel but as to which of us shall love the other most, but in this I will never yield to you. I send you this by the hands of Janton who is the best girl in the world. We talk of you every day and wish a thousand times in the day to be with you. . . . Let me know, I pray, how you pass your time, for if you have been for some time at Chaillot in this inclement weather you will have found it somewhat tedious. In future, I beg of you, do not treat me with so much ceremony in according me so many 'Majesties', for I do not wish there to be anything else between us two but friendship.[13]

On 21 February, under the direction of Monk, the 'secluded members' of the House of Commons took their seats once more with the Rump. They had long ago been expelled by Oliver Cromwell as being antagonistic to his republican form of government. Their return was one more step towards the restoration of the monarchy. They promptly appointed Monk Captain-General of all the forces by sea and land in England, Scotland and Ireland. Next day a resolution was passed for a new parliament to meet on 25 April.

The new trend in England was quickly reflected in the changed attitude of European powers. The States-General of the United Provinces, which had consistently cold-shouldered King Charles for years, now sent commissioners to him at Brussels, assuring him of their regard and expressing the hope that the ancient friendship of England and the Netherlands would be maintained. The Marqués de Caracena, Governor of the Spanish Netherlands, also waited on Charles to assure him of King Philip's good wishes. A day or two later Lord Jermyn arrived with messages of good will from the French court, while in Paris the Prince de Condé called on Henrietta Maria to tell her how ardently he hoped to be of service to her son.

Another glittering proposal came the way of James, conveyed by Caracena; 'an offer was made to the Duke, of commanding in Spain against Portugal, and also to be their High Admiral with the title of Principe de la Mare; which office, the Duke has been told, was never given to any but the King's Sons or near Relations, and whoever enjoys it commands the Galleys as well as Ships, and wherever he lands he commands as Vice Roy of the Country whilst he stays in it; he has also the fifts of all Prises, and a great Salary, besides other considerable perquisits. So that this was not only a very honourable post, but also a very advantageous one even as to profit, which was what the Duke then wanted.'[14] James, with the consent of his brother, accepted with alacrity; but he never took up the post. He 'was preparing to go for Spain in the ensuing spring, when that Voyage was happily prevented by the wonderful Changes, which were almost daily produced in England'.[15]

On 16 March the Long Parliament ended its life of twenty years. In the long-past days of its power before the Great Civil War it had passed a resolution, to which Charles I was compelled to give his sanction, that it could not be dissolved without its own consent. Now, after all its strife and vicissitudes, that consent was given. 'We are now at liberty,' wrote one of the members, Sir Roger Burgoyne, 'though much against some of our wills: after many sad pangs and groanes, at last we did expire, and now are in another world.'[16]

Arrangements for new elections were put in hand immediately, and nobody doubted that, in the prevailing climate, the coming parliament would call for a return of the King. On the day after the dissolution General Monk, in an interview with Charles's envoy, Sir John Grenville, at last declared himself in favour of monarchy. 'I am now not only ready to obey his commands,' he said in a message for the King, 'but to sacrifice my life and fortune in his service.'[17]

Monk advised King Charles to leave the King of Spain's dominions as soon as possible. England was still technically at war with Spain; should the negotiations get under way with the principal figure in Flanders, King Philip might take it into his head to detain him there. A fortnight later, having discovered that a scheme was actually on foot to keep him in Brussels, Charles left secretly in the night and galloped across the border to Breda.

There he was reunited with his sister Mary. There were no recriminations now, and she received him with joy. The Dukes of York and Gloucester were already at Breda, and Mary sent for her ten-year-old son, Prince William III of Orange, to present him to his royal uncle. The burghers of the town wanted to give King Charles a public reception but Mary, with characteristic haughtiness, refused the offer and took the honours on herself. Meanwhile royalist exiles flocked into Breda in such numbers that it was difficult to find food for them.

King Charles now issued the Declaration of Breda, the manifesto of the Restoration. Drawn up by Hyde, it promised a free and general pardon to all who should publicly declare their loyalty, apart from those specifically excepted by Parliament. Liberty for tender consciences in religion was pledged, and the King proclaimed his willingness to assent to such an Act of Parliament as should be passed to that effect. Copies of the Declaration were addressed to the Speakers of both Houses, the Lord Mayor of London, and General Monk; and Grenville was deputed to take them to England.

All was now decided. The new parliament met on 25 April, Grenville presented the King's letters and the Declaration, and on 1 May England declared itself a monarchy once more. Resolutions were passed 'that, according to the ancient and fundamental Law of this Kingdom, the Government is, and ought to be, by King, Lords and Commons'.[18] The Commons voted the King a gift of £50,000, with £10,000 for the Duke of York and £5,000 for the Duke of Gloucester, and orders were issued for arranging the King's return to England as quickly as possible.

A surge of loyalty swept the country, and London was lit from end to end by bonfires. Maypoles, banned by the Puritans as a mark of popery and frivolity, were set up all over the country, and in the ports the sailors celebrated in their own familiar fashion. Samuel Pepys, in the diary which he had started at the beginning of 1660, recorded on 2 May that 'our seamen, as many as have money or credit for drink, did do nothing else this evening'.[19]

King Charles remained calm. In a letter to his youngest sister, dated 29 April from Breda, there is no hint of the stirring news that was now reaching the Continent daily:

> I wrote to you last week and thought to send this letter in Janton's packet, but she had closed hers so that I was obliged to give my letter to Mason. I have yours of the 23rd in which I find so many marks of friendship that I know not how to find words with which to express my joy. In return I assure you that I love you as much as is possible and that neither absence nor any other thing can ever cause me to depart in the slightest manner from that friendship I have promised you;

and have no fear that those about me will have advantage over you, for, believe me, the friendship I have for you cannot be shared. I have sent to Seurseau to make me some clothes for the summer and I have given him orders to bring you some ribbon so that you may choose the trimming and feathers. I thank you for the song you have sent me. I do not know if it is pretty, for Janton does not know it yet. If you knew how often we talk of you and wish you here you would say we are longing to see you, and do me the justice to believe that I am entirely yours.

For my dear dear Sister.[20]

The days when Minette would be King Charles II's closest confidante and collaborator in weighty matters of international affairs were as yet far distant.

All business now, on both sides of the Channel, was subordinated to the overriding priority of arranging for the return of Charles II to his kingdom. Edward Montagu, the royalist admiral who was now in command of the English fleet, was directed to supply naval transport and escort for the King and his train, while a state reception at Dover was planned under Monk.

At Breda likewise arrangements were in hand. All possible speed was being urged from London. Henry Coventry wrote to Ormonde: 'I pray, my Lord, hasten his Majesty over as soon as may be, to prevent the town's running mad; for betwixt joy and expectation the people hardly sleep.'[21]

On 14 May the royal party left Breda. The States-General and the States of Holland, who now could not do enough to show their support for the English monarchy, had sent deputies to wait on the King and beseech him 'that he would grace that province [Holland] with his royal presence at the Hague, where preparations should be made for his reception, in such a manner as would testify the great joy of their hearts for the Divine blessings which Providence was showering upon his head'.[22] Charles, no doubt with his tongue in his cheek, accepted the invitation gracefully. Magnificent coaches were provided for the King, the royal dukes and the Princess Royal, and the route was lined by soldiers.

At Moerdijk they were met by a fleet of yachts, and the party divided. James and Henry went together in one boat. The Princess Dowager, now smiling on all her relations, had sent her own yacht for the King, and in this he and Mary embarked. Unfortunately the sea was rough, and the Princess Royal retired to her cabin, prostrated by sea-sickness, as soon as the craft set sail.

They anchored at Dordrecht, where they were met by Sir John Grenville. He had brought the money voted by Parliament with him in cash, and King Charles, never having seen so large a sum before, excitedly called his sister to come and look at it. Then the voyage continued to Delft, where the royal family again took coach for the final journey to The Hague, where they were splendidly received. The Princess Dowager and the Queen of Bohemia were among those who met them.

The next day, 16 May, the King received a number of delegates from England. They included Lord Fairfax, who asked his pardon for his past offence in bearing arms against his sovereign. Another visitor, even more welcome, was Captain Tattersall, in whose ship Charles had sailed from the Sussex coast to safety in France after his escape from Worcester in 1651.

There were further celebrations in The Hague, culminating in a magnificent banquet given to the royal family by the States of Holland. The walls of the palace named after Prince Maurice were hung with cloth of gold, and courses were served on gold plate which was afterwards presented to the King. Charles sat under a gilded crown, with the Queen of Bohemia on his right and the Princess Royal on his left. The Dukes of York and Gloucester and the little Prince of Orange were with him at the high table.

Montagu had meanwhile arrived with the fleet, which anchored in the harbour of Scheveningen. It was arranged that the King and his brothers should each travel in a different ship—Charles in the *Naseby*, James in the *London* and Henry in the *Swiftsure*. On 23 May, after the States of Holland had paid a farewell complimentary visit, the embarkation took place. Charles went to the Princess Royal's palace for a few minutes' private talk with her. Then he and his brothers, with the Prince of Orange, took horse and set forth for Scheveningen. The Queen of Bohemia, the Princess Royal and the Princess

Dowager of Orange followed in coaches, and the procession was joined by the States of Holland and the foreign ambassadors.

Huge crowds lined the route. At Scheveningen Admiral Montagu paid his respects, and the royal party boarded the *Naseby* for a farewell dinner. Then came the intimate farewells. The King gave his blessing to his nephew and took leave of his aunt, the Winter Queen. But it was all too much for the emotions of the Princess Royal. She had lived for this day; now it had come she clung to her brother in a torrent of tears and could hardly be persuaded to leave him. At last the company parted. The royal ladies and Prince William were rowed to the shore, and the Dukes of York and Gloucester embarked in their respective ships.

Charles was left alone in the *Naseby*. The title of the vessel, taken from the crowning Roundhead victory, was not propitious, and the King then and there renamed her the *Royal Charles*. Two days later, early in the morning, the fleet arrived at Dover. The reception was tremendous. John Dryden, soon to be Poet Laureate, was to write in his paean in honour of the Restoration:

> Methinks I see those Crowds on Dovers Strand
> Who in their hast to welcome you to Land
> Choak'd up the Beach with their still growing store,
> And made a wilder Torrent on the shore.
> While spurr'd with eager thoughts of past delight
> Those who had seen you, court a second sight;
> Preventing still your steps, and making hast
> To meet you often where so e're you past.

At Canterbury King Charles conferred the Garter on Monk and Montagu. And he wrote to Minette:

> Canterbury 26 May.
> I was so plagued with business at the Hague that I could not write to you before my departure. But I left instructions with my sister to send you a little present from me which I hope you will soon receive. I arrived yesterday at Dover where I found Monk with a great number of the nobility who almost overwhelmed me with friendship and joy at my

return. My head is so prodigiously dazed by the acclamation of the people and by quantities of business that I know not whether I am writing sense or no, therefore you will pardon me if I do not tell you any more, only that I am entirely yours.

C.[23]

After a day's rest the journey proceeded, and on 29 May, the King's thirtieth birthday, a glorious summer day, he rode with his brothers to Whitehall Palace, through London streets hung with tapestry and lined with deliriously cheering crowds, while the conduits ran claret.

'I stood in the strand,' wrote John Evelyn in his diary, '& beheld it, & blessed God: And all this without one drop of bloud, & by that very army, which rebell'd against him: but it was the Lords doing, *et mirabile in oculis nostris:* for such a Restauration was never seene in the mention of any history, antient or modern, since the returne of the *Babylonian* Captivity, nor so joyfull a day, & so bright, ever seene in this nation: this hapning when to expect or effect it, was past all humane policy.'[24]

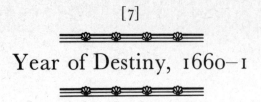

7

Year of Destiny, 1660–1

By the end of 1660 every surviving member of the family of Charles I had put in an appearance in England. They were not all there together, and before the year closed their ranks had been further depleted by death.

It was seven years since Henry Duke of Gloucester, the last to leave the country, had been allowed to make his way to the Continent; and he had then been in durance vile for almost the whole of his young life. The long years of exile had left its mark on all of them.

At the age of thirty King Charles II's character was fully formed. He had been through more varied experiences than come the way of most men, let alone those of royal blood who by the nature of their position tend to live lives cut off from the general run of humankind. Charles had known triumph and disaster, had become acquainted with the most splendid of royal courts and had been a fugitive with a price on his head. He had been brought up in the cultivated and ordered ceremonial of his father's aesthetic regalism, and had been a wanderer short of clothes and compelled almost to beg his bread. He had known all sorts and conditions of men, had been bullied by his elders and cheated by needy courtiers. He had been in battle before he was in his teens, and had known the bitterness of defeat soon after his twenty-first birthday.

No experience had been more enlightening than those weeks of wandering after the loss of the Battle of Worcester. He had then made his way through an England in the hands of his enemies, evading capture by donning disguise, finding shelter wherever he could and hiding in hovels and priest-holes. No English monarch since Alfred the Great had come into such close contact with the humblest of his subjects.

Charles II. Miniature by Samuel Cooper

All this had left him a whimsical, witty, shrewd, humorous man of the world; tolerant, cynical, devoid of illusions. He trusted no man, preferring to rely on his own judgement, which was singularly acute. Women had more influence over him than men. Regarding them in general as intended for one purpose only, he was capable of giving in to their caprices in humiliating fashion when he failed to get his way with them. But this particular unregal trend had not yet been made manifest in any marked degree.

He was highly intelligent; not bookish, for he lacked the application for deep or sustained reading, but capable of quickly mastering the details of any subject that concerned or interested him. While he never tried to cultivate his father's knowledge of art, he had benefited from his early training in that direction. He was a man of taste and discernment, who made his court a pattern of elegance. He encouraged artists both English and foreign; Samuel Cooper the miniaturist, the finest native artist of his time, and the Flemish Peter Lely were among the many who basked in the light of his patronage. His personal tastes, however, were more in the realm of scientific advances, in which he took an informed interest; and his knowledge of nautical matters and of naval architecture was of the highest order. He loved music, brought musicians to England from the Continent, and interested himself in the development of new musical instruments which was one of the features of the time.

In appearance King Charles was a regal figure, tall, slim and dark, with the small moustache that has become so famous. His expression was saturnine, and he was not considered handsome. In his babyhood his mother had complained that he was so ugly that she was ashamed of him. 'Odds fish, I am an ugly fellow!' he said of himself at a later date. But what he lacked in conventional good looks he made up for in grace and dignity; he had the royal gift of putting people at ease with a geniality that was at once free from patronage and redolent of natural authority.

Whether the effect on the character of King Charles of the years of trial had been beneficial or the reverse is a matter of opinion. The next in age, Mary the Princess Royal, had certainly been soured by her experiences. So far as material prosperity went, she had been better off than the rest of the family. But her unpopularity in Holland, the troubles of her widowhood, and the enmity of her mother-in-law, a stronger personality than herself, had brought forth her less noble characteristics. A certain cantankerousness, emphasized perhaps by the ill-health she suffered towards the end of the 1650s, had become more marked with the years. She was touchy and quick to take offence, while her behaviour to the rulers of her husband's country was, to say the least, undiplomatic. It would be a mistake to make too much of what to a modern eye must seem the absurdity of her insistence on trivialities of rank and precedence, for seventeenth-century courts were obsessed with such matters; many princesses of the time went further than she did in this respect. But Mary, in her ostentatious determination to use her title of Princess Royal, thereby displaying her contempt for that of Princess of Orange, went out of her way to antagonize the States-General of the Netherlands. In such conduct she did much to jeopardize the fortunes of her young son, whose interests in the Netherlands were one of her chief concerns. There was a strain of wilful obstinacy, amounting to spite, in the character of Mary of Orange which went far towards obviating her own chances of happiness.

Even her appearance had not improved with the years. In her portraits towards the end of the period in question, showing her long Stuart nose and the contemptuous curl of her lips, there is a hint of sourness and petulance which detracts from the nobility of her features. The fresh openness of the lovely child of the Van Dyck likenesses at the time of her marriage seems to have faded.

Yet at her best she remained the gayest and most vivacious of the family. Hers was an extrovert nature; in her good moods she bubbled over with laughter and good humour, and she was the soul of generosity and of loyalty where her friends and relations were concerned. She had an infinite capacity for affection, and this was lavished in the fullest measure on those of her own family who were the prime objects of her devotion. All the ardour of her nature was expended on the welfare of the Stuart exiles during the dark days of the interregnum.

Mary had few cultural pretensions. Literature hardly existed for her, and her appreciation of art, though not negligible, was superficial. Yet she possessed the indefinable Stuart sense of style, and her court was dignified and elegant. She was not the daughter of Charles I for nothing.

It would be hard to find two brothers more widely different from each other than the King and the Duke of York. In appearance there was a certain resemblance in that both were tall, graceful and well-made. James, however, was better-looking than Charles, fair where the elder brother was dark and with well-formed features. He looked what he was, a soldier and an athlete, physically strong and capable of endurance.

In temperament the contrast was complete. James had none of the quick wit and keen intelligence that were so marked in King Charles. He was slow and obtuse, yet at the same time earnest and conscientious, with an infinite capacity for taking pains. It was this that had made him so valuable a staff officer to Turenne. Charles in his limited military experience had proved himself a spirited and inspiring commander. James's talents were those of a brave and reliable subordinate.

Adversity had increased the natural flexibility of the King's character. The Duke of York was by nature rigid, and his rigidity was accentuated by the hardships he had undergone. All his instincts veered towards the maintenance of authority, and of royal authority in particular. He never formulated the doctrine of divine right as had James I and Charles I, but he believed in it as firmly as did they. Like all his generation of Stuarts he honoured deeply the memory of his martyred father; but the later disasters of the Civil War had convinced him that his father's troubles had stemmed from weakness in dealing with his enemies. Strength and firmness were his ideals, and he never ceased to criticize his elder brother for what he regarded as his lack of vigour when confronted with opposition.

James's slow-wittedness amounted to stupidity, but he had his gifts. His conscientiousness and his capacity for mastering detail made him an admirable administrator, and as such he was greatly valued by King Charles. The elder brother regarded him always with affection, though undoubtedly he was frequently exasperated by his slowness and obstinacy. In the future he was to fight with unwonted tenacity, to the point of putting his own crown at risk, to maintain the rights of his junior; at the same time he doubted, correctly as it turned out, the capacity of James to keep his throne when his own influence was removed.

The main difference between the two brothers was neatly

summed up by the Duke of Buckingham, the brilliant and effervescent crony of King Charles. 'The King' (he said) 'could see things if he would, and the duke would see things if he could.'[1]

The King, at least according to Gilbert Burnet, was less fond of James than he was of the youngest of the three brothers, Henry Duke of Gloucester, whose temper was more akin to his own. Henry, wrote the future Bishop of Salisbury, 'was active, and loved business, was apt to have particular friendships; and had an insinuating temper, which was generally very acceptable'.[2]

Henry of Gloucester was at the time of the Restoration nearly twenty years old. Like his elder brothers he was tall and graceful, and contemporaries bear witness to his charm and vitality. At the age of twelve he had been suddenly transported from close imprisonment to the luxury of a court where he basked in the adulation of two adoring women. It was scarcely to be wondered at that for a time he became insufferable. This was a passing phase; he had since proved himself steadfast in will and of good sense, while when serving in arms in Flanders he had established himself as a brave and capable soldier. He had, in fact, some of the finer qualities of his brother James, with at the same time something of the intelligence and light-heartedness of the eldest of the family, which James so conspicuously lacked. He was eager and ambitious, and amid the bright hopes of the restored monarchy he was regarded as a young man of the highest promise.

Across the water the youngest of the family, Princess Henrietta Anne, Charles II's 'Minette', was the darling of the French court. She was now in her sixteenth year and in the bloom of radiant youth, with a charm and a spontaneous gaiety that won all hearts. The young King Louis XIV was just beginning his dazzling career as *le Roi Soleil*, and in his glittering court there was no brighter ornament than the little princess, English by birth and ancestry but entirely French in upbringing. She was small and frail-looking, and certainly not beautiful; but of the fascination of her personality there is abundant testimony. Men and women alike gave her unstinted praise. 'One loved her,' said one of her admirers, the Abbé de Choisy, 'without thinking that one could do otherwise.'[3]

Minette had all the social graces so prized at the court of the Sun-King; she danced and sang beautifully, and could play the guitar and the harpsichord. But there was more to her than this. She had the gift of unaffected kindness and of both showing happiness and bestowing it on others. Her mental qualities, moreover, were of no mean order. She was not a budding scholar as her sister Elizabeth had been, but her taste in literature, art and music was more in evidence than in any other member of the family. Racine and Molière were to benefit from her patronage in the years to come.

Her constant companion was her mother, who watched over her with a jealous eye. Henrietta Maria was another whose character had not improved with the years. Her wilfulness and her love of interfering in other people's business, always prominent, had increased, while her animation and vitality, which earlier had mitigated those defects, were replaced by petulance and ill-temper. She could never get used to the reality that she, who had exercised so great an influence over her husband Charles I, had none where her son Charles II was concerned.

Her beauty, immortalized by Van Dyck, had likewise faded. Princess Sophia, Elizabeth of Bohemia's youngest daughter, had met her at a considerably earlier time than this and was surprised to find 'a little woman with long lean arms, crooked shoulders, and teeth protruding from her mouth like guns from a fort'.[4] The teeth had probably always protruded, but Van Dyck diplomatically ignored them.

That Queen Henrietta loved her children is not to be doubted; her love was possessive, and she felt that it was not returned in the measure that was its due. But in the view of her youngest daughter she could do no wrong. At the Palais Royal, at Colombes and at Chaillot the two were always to be seen together.

To find employment for his younger brothers was one of Charles II's first tasks. As regards the Duke of York there was no problem. James had been designated as Lord High Admiral by his father in early childhood. Since then the office had been held by the Earl of Northumberland and later by Prince Rupert, but these appointments were at the King's pleasure, and it had always been understood that the post would go to the Duke of York when he was ready to take it up. His martial experiences had so far been wholly on land, but this was not regarded as a handicap. In the seventeenth century there was no hard and fast distinction between naval and military administration and tactics, and senior commanders moved from one service to the other as circumstances dictated. James's army training, and the excellent reputation he had acquired, seemed the best possible qualification for his new duties, and he assumed office with general approval. In fact he was to prove one of the finest of naval administrators; all his conscientiousness and capacity for hard work were put into mastering the details of his new job and he became as knowledgeable in seafaring matters as he already was in the art of war on land. He was also to show himself, when the time came, a more than competent naval commander.

There was, however, no obvious post for the young Duke of Gloucester to take up. He was active and ambitious, and he wanted employment. Not unnaturally, seeing his brother put at the head of the Navy, he thought himself entitled to an equal authority over the Army. This, however, was out of the question. It was not just that he was too young; princes normally took on high responsibility at an early age, and Henry had justified himself in arms in the Low Countries. But the Captain-General of the Army was George Monk, now Duke of Albemarle, the chief architect of the Restoration. Albemarle was far too important and too imposing a personage to be superseded by a youth of nineteen, however close to the throne. So there was no Army command for the Duke of Gloucester.

According to Burnet, Henry next went to Lord Chancellor Hyde with the remarkable proposal that he should be recommended to the King as Lord Treasurer. A less suitable appointment could hardly be imagined. The young man had no training whatever in financial matters, and the Treasurership, in the complicated state of the precarious royal finances, called for expertise of the highest order. Moreover, the post was earmarked for the Earl of Southampton, a statesman of judgement and experience. Hyde solved the question by diplomatically objecting that the position was not sufficiently exalted for a royal prince.

Henry therefore was left without employment, pending the

Henry Duke of Gloucester, after Luttehuys

finding of some position worthy of his birth and talents. In the event the question was destined to be solved in tragic fashion.

The royal ladies were all anxious to see England once more. Mary, who of all the family had been longest away from her native land, began making plans almost as soon as she had seen her brother off from Scheveningen. In addition to her natural desire to return to the country of her birth, she hoped that King Charles would help to promote the right of her young son to succeed to his father's honours. The Restoration had brought a more cordial attitude towards the House of Orange from the Netherlands authorities; but De Witt was still adamant against a renewal of the Stadtholdership, and Mary urged King Charles to use his influence with the Dutch Ambassador in London.

At the same time she went on preparing for her visit to England, and she made it clear that she had no intention of making it a brief one. In a message to the States of Holland and West Friesland she emphasized that, 'as she was thus necessitated to be absent some time from the country, her motherly affection and duty alike bound her specially to commend to them the interests of her son; and, though she had not the least doubt that it would be the intention of the States, when he was come of age, in consideration of the laudable deeds, and great services of his ancestors, to reinstate him in his forefathers' offices, yet would it be very acceptable to her, if they would now give her certain hope and assurance thereof, and take henceforward such care of his education that he might as befitting a son of the State, be brought up for the service of the country, in the true reformed Christian religion, and in the laws and statutes of the land, and thus made capable of such high and honourable offices'.[5]

The States were in no hurry to promise such certain hope and assurance. In the meantime King Charles was as eager for his sister's company as she was for his. He wrote to the States:

It cannot be thought strange that we passionately desire to see here, as soon as possible, our dearest sister, the Princess of Orange, in order that she who could not restrain her compassion towards us in our miseries, may also have her share in the happiness we enjoy in our re-establishment.[6]

He was not, however, the only one of her family who wanted to see her. Queen Henrietta Maria was anxious that her elder daughter should visit her in France before going to England, and Mary in her dilemma wrote, early in August, to Charles in a tone savouring of exasperation:

> I received a letter from the queen this last post, wherein she says by the next she will send for me into France. I have let her know your resolution of sending for me directly into England, therefore, for God's sake, agree between you what I have to do, which I hope you will not consider as an unreasonable desire, since I have made this same to the queen; and pray do not delay it, for I have great impatience to be gone from hence, and yet rather than displease either of you, I would suffer the greatest punishment of this world (that is to live all my life here), for I know what it is to displease both of you; God keep me from it again: I am sure I will have as much care of it as I can.[7]

Henrietta Maria had herself been hoping to visit England. But she had not received a formal invitation and she was apparently not sure of a welcome, owing to the antagonism between herself and Hyde. There was now a further development in the situation, in the shape of the projected betrothal of her younger daughter. The prospective bridegroom was none other than Philip Duke of Anjou, younger brother of Louis XIV.

It would be a splendid match from the worldly point of view, the only drawback being the personality of the Duke, two years younger than King Louis and now twenty years old; he was a mincing transvestite whose only noticeable interests were in clothes and jewels. Such matters, however, hardly entered into consideration where a royal marriage was concerned, and Princess Henrietta herself had no objection to the character of her suitor; the marriage would at least enable her to stay in her beloved France. Philip had fallen in love with her before the Restoration—surprisingly, since he was not usually addicted to passion for the opposite sex. Any suggestion of marriage was opposed by Cardinal Mazarin for the usual reason; the sister of a penniless prince was no fit bride for the brother and heir

presumptive of the greatest monarch in Christendom. Once
King Charles was back in England, however, the position was
changed and all objections were withdrawn. On 14 August
1660, the Queen Mother of France, Anne of Austria, visited
Henrietta Maria to ask formally for the hand of the Princess for
'Monsieur', as the King's brother was known at the French
court.

The Kings of France and England were in accord on the
suitability of the union. Louis at first thought little of Princess
Henrietta, despising her for her thinness and frailty; he 'one day
observed to Monsieur, that he need not be in so great a hurry to
espouse the bones of the Innocents [*les os des Sains Innocens*]'.[8] He
also told Philip that it would be well for him to marry her, since
nobody else wanted her. But this again was before the Restoration. King Louis soon changed his mind, not only on the
desirability of the match but also, perhaps to his own surprise,
on the attractiveness of the proposed bride.

Queen Henrietta was more than ever desirous for her two
daughters to be together at this time, and she wrote to Mary:

> I sent to you last week to be in readiness to start; now I
> earnestly beg and invite you to come as soon as you can; they
> will be very glad here to receive you. As the marriage of your
> sister is in a manner concluded, that is to say, the king your
> brother and I sincerely desire it, and it will accordingly be
> hastened in England,—on this account you could not do
> better than come. I shall perhaps be able to go into England
> myself: if that happens, you will be ready for the journey; if I
> do not go, you can leave from here to join him; and even if he
> wishes, as I have heard, that you should go at once, my
> answer will be resolute, to send him word that you wished to
> see me in passing, and to see your sister.[9]

Mary in growing perplexity forwarded her mother's letter to
Charles, who now decided it was time to put his foot down. He
wanted his sister in England, and he peremptorily ordered her
to ignore Henrietta's wishes and come at once. At the same time
he and James made diplomatic representations to the Netherlands administrators, as a result of which the States of Holland
and West Friesland accepted the charge of the education of

Prince William, settling a substantial income on him and promising to reconsider his exclusion from the offices held by his father.

Queen Henrietta was thus disappointed of her hope of seeing her elder daughter in Paris. But she could still be united with her in England. She had financial as well as sentimental reasons for wanting to visit her son, for in England she could arrange for payment of the jointure she had been promised. To arrive with both her daughters would have facilitated her welcome, but she now at least had an adequate pretext for taking the younger with her. Charles II had given his informal consent to the union of Philip and Henrietta Anne, but to put the marriage contract on an official basis it was desirable that the young princess should approach her brother in person. For his part the King was longing to see his beloved Minette, so the plans were agreeable to all parties with the exception of the lovelorn Duke of Anjou, who was not invited to England and moaned bitterly at the prospect of being parted from his betrothed.

During this time Minette had been corresponding regularly with her eldest brother. The letter he had written at Canterbury reached her at the beginning of June. She was then at Colombes, and she hastened to reply:

> I have received the letter you wrote me by Mr Progers which gave me no little joy, for to know that you were arrived in England and at the same time that you had remembered me gave me the greatest joy imaginable, and in truth I would I were able to express what I think and you would see that it is true that nobody is more your servant than I.[10]

Other letters written this summer which have survived were mostly in recommendation of exiled Cavaliers who wanted favours from the restored king. Both Henrietta's kindness of heart and her influence with her brother were well known, and many suitors went to Colombes to solicit her help. In these letters there is no mention of her proposed marriage. This was a matter the management of which she left to her elders.

Charles certainly answered her, but his replies have not been preserved. There is, however, one particularly affectionate epistle dated August 27, though it is not certain that this was the year:

I should thinke my selfe much to blame if I lett this bearer see you without a letter from me. I know not whether the long time we have been a sunder doth not slacken the kindnesse you had for me, I am sure nether that or any thing else can alter me in the least degree towards you. Deare sister, be kinde to me for assure your selfe there is no person living will strive to deserve it more then him that is and ever will be most truly yours.

C.[11]

King Charles was now ready for the full family reunion. Mary was to come from Holland, and at the beginning of September Edward Montagu, now Earl of Sandwich and Vice-Admiral of England, set off from Deal to conduct her to England. Henrietta Maria was to bring her younger daughter from Paris, though arrangements in her case were not in quite so advanced a state. But before either journey started there occurred two events in England which vitally affected the royal family.

The first, a bombshell of the first order, was known at the time to only a handful of people. On 3 September, at Worcester House in the Strand, the home of the Lord Chancellor, the Duke of York was secretly married to Anne Hyde.

The episode has never been satisfactorily unravelled in all its details. When exactly the love affair between James and the Chancellor's daughter began is not known, but it appears that he formally committed himself to matrimony in November 1659. According to James's biographer, Anne 'shew'd both her witt and her vertue in managing the affaire so dexterously, that the Duke overmaster'd by his passion, at last gave her a promise of marriage some time before the Restoration'.[12] By September 1660 the lady was in an advanced state of pregnancy; this fact seems surprisingly to have escaped general notice, though probably her mother knew. Lady Hyde may indeed have been in the secret all along.

The Worcester House ceremony took place during the night, performed by Dr Joseph Crowther, the Duke of York's chaplain. Anne was given away by Lord Ossory, son and heir of the Marquess of Ormonde, and the only other witness appears to have been her maid, Ellen Stroud. Sir Edward Hyde had no knowledge of what was going on in his own house.

It was unquestionably a misalliance by seventeenth-century standards. Princes were expected to marry princesses, and vice versa; however exalted his position in the state, Hyde, who was not yet even a peer, had neither the right nor the wish to ally himself by marriage with the royal family. He had, moreover, plenty of enemies in high places, pre-eminently Queen Henrietta Maria, who would be only too glad to make capital of any apparent attempt by him to seek honours above his station. He himself was punctilious to excess in such matters. All this helps to account for his hysterical behaviour when he learned what had happened behind his back.

When exactly the storm broke is uncertain. The secret was not kept for long, and it was probably within a week that James, 'with many Tears'[13] according to Clarendon, went to the King, confessed what had happened, and asked for royal permission to acknowledge his wife.

Charles was troubled; less, it would appear, from any disapproval of the marriage than because he was afraid of the effect it would have on Hyde. He decided to call on two old and trusted friends, the Marquess of Ormonde and the Earl of Southampton. He asked them to come to Whitehall Palace and break the news to Sir Edward, with whom they were both on intimate terms; he himself and the Duke of York would not make their appearance until the Chancellor knew the worst.

The interview was more disconcerting than anybody could have expected. Ormonde, warning Hyde that what he had to say might be unwelcome, began by saying that the Duke of York had a great affection for the Chancellor's daughter, who was now with child by him; the King therefore wanted advice on what action to take.

Hyde immediately burst into a torrent of rage. He said that he would go straight home, turn his daughter out of his house as a strumpet, let her shift for herself and never set eyes on her again. Ormonde thereupon told him that James and Anne were believed to be married, and that he must really take a calmer view of the situation.

The mention of marriage only made matters worse. Hyde, whose attitude was hardly that of a loving father, said he would rather Anne was the Duke's whore than his wife, for in that case nobody could blame him for discarding her; he was not obliged to keep a whore for the greatest prince alive. But if she was married he could suggest a solution. Many years later he set down in cold blood, and with not a hint of regret, what he had then proposed: 'that the King should immediately cause the Woman to be sent to the *Tower*, and to be cast into a Dungeon, under so strict a Guard, that no Person living should be permitted to come to her; and then that an Act of Parliament should be immediately passed for the cutting off her Head, to which He would not only give his Consent, but would very willingly be the first Man that should propose it.'[14]

At this point in the proceedings King Charles entered the room and asked how matters stood. Southampton answered that the King had better consult with soberer men, as Hyde was plainly mad. Charles, who alone among those most intimately concerned kept his head and his sense of decency throughout this distressing business, did his best to calm the injured father, telling him that since the thing was done they had all better make the best of it; but his gentleness had little effect on Hyde. When the Duke of York appeared his brother quickly took him away for a private discussion, while Hyde stumped off home to tell his wife that Anne was to be confined to her room, to receive no visits, and not to appear at meals. He did not, however, turn her out of the house; nor was any more heard of her being deprived of her head by Act of Parliament.

In the midst of this furore there occurred the second momentous event in the royal family's fortunes. This was the death of the Duke of Gloucester. He had been taken ill at the beginning of September, and it was soon known that he had smallpox. He rallied, however, and when his brother James set out on 11 September for the coast to meet their sister Mary he was reported to be out of danger. Then came a sudden relapse, and on the evening of the 13th he died—'by the great negligence of the Doctors',[15] according to Pepys.

The death of the promising Henry at the age of twenty, 'in prime of youth, a Prince of extraordinary hopes',[16] plunged the nation into mourning. King Charles, wrote Burnet, 'was never in his whole life so much troubled, as he was on that occasion'.[17] Minette wrote to him after she had heard the news:

Since I last wrote to you so cruel a misfortune has occurred that until this hour I could not make up my mind to speak of it

to you, not finding fit terms in which to do so. The sorrow
which it has caused you is so just that one can but take one's
part in it, and I have the honour to share it equally with you.
Besides I think it is best to be silent, which I shall be when I
have told you that the thing I desire most on earth is to have
the happiness of seeing you, which I hope will be soon; . . .[18]

Mary's voyage had been delayed by stormy weather, and it
was not until 20 September that she was able to embark in
Sandwich's flagship. She had just set foot on board when the
news was brought her of her youngest brother's death. She had
the tenderest memories of Henry when he had stayed with her at
The Hague, and she spent the whole voyage in her cabin,
bathed in tears. The sea off the English coast was rough, and
there was danger of shipwreck; but Mary, absorbed in her grief,
hardly noticed. On 23 September she landed at Margate. James
had returned to London when he heard of his brother's death;
he and Charles now hastened to Margate to meet their sister.

It was an affectionate reunion, and the Princess Royal was
given a triumphal reception into London; she sailed in the
King's barge from Gravesend, and vessels in the river fired
salutes all the way from the Tower to Whitehall Stairs. But it
was not the joyous homecoming to which she had looked
forward. She had been deeply affected by Henry's death, and
now there was this scandal of James's marriage. Whether she
received the news when she landed or later is not known; but
when she did she was furious. Matters of precedence were all in
all to her, and the thought that her former maid of honour
would now rank above her brought out all the worst in her
character. She bitterly upbraided the Duke of York and told the
King that she would never yield precedence to a woman who
had stood as a servant behind her chair.

Henrietta Maria heard about the marriage early in October.
The news affected her, apparently, much more than did that of
the death of her youngest son. Her reaction was similar to
Mary's, and she determined to set off immediately for England
with her daughter in the hope of breaking the marriage. She
wrote to her sister Christine, the Duchess of Savoy:

To crown my misfortunes, the Duke of York has married

without my knowledge, or that of the king, his brother, an English miss who was with child before her marriage. God grant that it may be by him. A girl who will abandon herself to a prince will abandon herself to another. I leave for England to-morrow to try and marry my son the king and unmarry the other. *Le Bon Dieu* does not wish that I shall enjoy complete tranquillity.[19]

The unfortunate King Charles found himself, through no fault of his own, assailed by shrieks of anguish and fury from his friends and relations. And at this point the Duke of York behaved in a manner that reflected as little credit on him as it did on his friends.

Harassed on all sides, he began to have second thoughts and to wonder if he could legally repudiate the marriage. There could be no doubt that the ceremony had taken place, but it might be possible to declare it null and void as having been performed without the King's consent. And it was now that James's friend Sir Charles Berkeley, from what would appear to have been a perverted sense of loyalty, devised a scheme calculated to influence King Charles towards compassing his brother's design to escape from the ties of matrimony. He told the Duke 'that He was bound in Conscience, to preserve him from taking to Wife a Woman so wholly unworthy of him; that He himself had lain with her; and that for his Sake He would be content to marry her, though He knew full well the Familiarity the Duke had with her'.[20]

Berkeley, nothing if not thorough, went further in traducing Anne's reputation. He produced a group of friends who were all prepared to boast of having enjoyed the lady's sexual favours. The author of the Gramont Memoirs asserts that they were the Earl of Arran (a younger son of Lord Ormonde), young Harry Jermyn, Richard Talbot and Henry Killigrew; in a singularly inappropriate phrase the author of the Memoirs describes them as 'all men of honour'.[21] Of these only Killigrew claimed actually to have been to bed with Anne Hyde, but all spoke of 'minor tendernesses, or what are known as the small change of affection'.[22]

Armed with these unsavoury confessions, James approached his brother with a view to the annulment of his marriage. But

Charles would have none of it. He was himself fully convinced of the validity of the Worcester House ceremony, and he believed not a word of the confessions; he bluntly told the Duke of York that 'he must drink as he brewed, and live with her whom he had made his wife',[23] and ordered him to send for Lady Ormonde and other high ladies of the court to witness the birth which was now imminent, as was the custom in the royal family.

James's better feelings were revived by his brother's uncompromising attitude, helped by Berkeley's confession that what he and his friends had said was false. Anne swore before witnesses that her child was the Duke of York's and that she had never been unfaithful. When a son was born in the last week of October, James wrote her a letter of reconciliation and she was publicly acknowledged as the Duchess of York.

Meanwhile the most virulent enemy of the match was approaching England. On 24 October the Duke of York and the Princess Royal set out together for Dover to await the arrival of their mother. They must have been uneasy travelling companions at this time. Mary had been compelled to acquiesce in the King's judgement on the marriage, but she still resented the position of her former maid of honour; and both she and James knew well what their mother's attitude was likely to be.

The two Henriettas arrived with a train of attendants who included two of the Queen's most faithful followers—Henry Jermyn the elder, now Earl of St Albans, and Father Cyprien de Gamache. James, attentive to his mother to the point of obsequiousness, set out with the whole fleet to meet her at sea and to minister to her every wish. Father Cyprien was particularly gratified by the Duke's consideration in arranging for a supply of sturgeon for the Catholic voyagers when he found that it was a day of abstinence.

The Queen was at least in part mollified, and the reunion passed off pleasantly enough. King Charles, who with Prince Rupert had joined Mary, met his mother and sister when they landed on 30 October. He was overjoyed to see his beloved Minette again, and there was a triumphal procession to London, muted only by the mourning for the Duke of Gloucester. On 2 November the royal family reached Whitehall, where apartments had been made ready for everybody. For the first time since the dark days of 1641, all the surviving members of the royal family were under one roof again.

There was general harmony. The family dined together daily at Whitehall, though the Duchess of York remained discreetly in the background. Henrietta Maria received Sir Edward Hyde with marked coldness, but King Charles made a particular point of honouring him. It was at least partially in compensation for the Queen's enmity that at this moment the Chancellor was created Baron Hyde of Hindon.

Queen Henrietta had never been popular in England, and she was no more so now. The English people, however, took her youngest daughter to their hearts. Minette's unaffected charm was irresistible, and soon she had as many admirers in London as she had in Paris. The House of Commons voted her a present of £10,000 (a similar sum had already been granted to Mary), and when a deputation waited on her to tell her what had been resolved she 'with great affection acknowledged the kindness of the House; excusing herself that she could not do it so well in the English tongue, which she desired to supply with an English heart'.[24]

King Charles was enchanted with her company. He could hardly bear to be away from her, and when she went for a brief stay to Tunbridge Wells he passed a note to Hyde at the council table saying he proposed to pay her a visit. When Hyde said he supposed he would go with a light train, the King in high spirits said he intended to take nothing but his night bag. Hyde then protested that he must be attended at least by forty or fifty horse. 'I count that part of my night bag,' replied the happy monarch.[25]

With the rest of the family she was on equally affectionate terms, and it was her influence above all that made their relations with each other now so harmonious. A member of the suite of the French Ambassador, the Comte de Soissons, wrote to Mazarin of a meeting with Queen Henrietta soon after the arrival at Whitehall:

The princess her daughter was so wearied with her voyage, that she kept to her room: however, the queen her mother wished the count to see her, in whatever condition she might be. The King himself led him to her apartments. We found her in a cornette [a mob head-dress], wrapped in an Indian shawl of a thousand colours, playing at ombre with the Duke of York and the Princess of Orange. Monsieur may be told that he never saw her, even in full dress, more beautiful than she was that day.[26]

It seemed to be all sunshine. Henrietta Maria had received satisfactory assurances concerning her jointure, and the King had given his official consent to Minette's union with Philip of Anjou.

In another matter the Queen failed to get her way. As she had hinted in her letter to her sister, she was hoping to arrange a match for her eldest son. The bride proposed was once again Hortense Mancini, niece of Cardinal Mazarin. Henrietta apparently saw no inconsistency in her objection to one of her sons marrying the Chancellor's daughter and her advocacy of a union between his elder and another commoner; but Hortense was a lady of great wealth, and that made all the difference. Charles, however, was in no hurry to marry, and he gently brushed aside his mother's match-making project. But this was a small setback.

The mood of euphoria, however, was too good to last. As so often happened with this family, content was shattered by an unexpected development. Since her arrival in England the Princess Royal had appeared little in public. She took occasional airings on the Thames, in a richly adorned boat given her by King Charles, and she sometimes went out riding. But she was in fact far from well. She had never enjoyed continuous good health, and the air of London disagreed with her. She complained of an oppression in her chest, thought to be caused by the smoke of the city.

Shortly before Christmas her condition worsened, and on 20 December the physicians feared the malady to be once more the dreaded smallpox. She was given a draught of beer, which relieved the irruption in her chest; next day Lord Craven, lifelong admirer of the Queen of Bohemia, wrote to Mary's beloved aunt:

I believe your majesty will hear the hot alarm of the princess royal's being in great danger of death, which, indeed, this morning was sadly apprehended by many; but because your majesty should not be frighted by what news perchance you may hear, I have just now been with her, and, God be praised, she is much better. The doctors do not yet know whether it is the pox or the measles, but I fear it will prove the small-pox.[27]

The improvement was only momentary. Mary's strength ebbed, and there was now no doubt that she had smallpox. Soon her life was despaired of. Henrietta Maria whisked her younger daughter away from Whitehall to St James's, though she vainly sought permission herself to visit Mary. Charles would not let his mother or sister enter the sick-room, but he himself hardly left his sister's side. He had always been devoted to her, and her unfailing help in the days of misfortune had filled him with the deepest gratitude. No fear of infection would keep him from her at the end. Others who stayed with her were her faithful friend the Countess of Chesterfield, the former Lady Stanhope, and the Countess's son the young Earl.

Mary died on Christmas Eve. 'I could not but admire', wrote Lord Chesterfield, 'her unconcernedness, constancy of mind and resolution, which well became the grandchild of Henry the Fourth of France.'[28]

Whether the Princess had been reconciled to the Duchess of York before her final illness is uncertain, but probably she had; Father Cyprien de Gamache records that towards the end she and her sister dined regularly at the same table in Whitehall Palace as the Duke and Duchess. At any rate in her last hours Mary expressed heartfelt contrition for the part she had played in the sufferings endured by Anne Hyde. At the funeral in Westminster Abbey on 29 December the Duke of York was chief mourner for his sister.

So the crowded year of 1660, which had seen the great triumph of the Stuart dynasty, closed in tragedy. The King withdrew himself from all company, and no foreign ambassador was able to approach him to offer condolences. The Duke of York was observed to be plunged in melancholy, and Queen Henrietta, seeing no reason for her presence in England any longer, decided to leave at the beginning of 1661.

Before she went, finding herself in a minority of one, she too made peace with the Duchess of York. The Duke 'presented his

Wife to his Mother, who received her without the least Shew of Regret, or rather with the same Grace as if she had liked it from the Beginning, and made her sit down by her'.[29] When Anne's son, named Charles and created Duke of Cambridge, was christened at Worcester House on New Year's Day, the godfathers were the King and the Duke of Albemarle and the godmothers Queen Henrietta Maria and the Marchioness of Ormonde.

In the following month the Duke of York issued a declaration which he signed before the Privy Council:

I, James, Duke of York, do testify and declare, that after I had for many months solicited Anne my now wife in the way of Marriage, I was contracted to her on the 24th of November, 1659, at Breda in Brabant, and after that time, and many months before I came into England, I lived with her (though with all possible secrecy) as my Wife. And after my coming into this kingdom, and that we might observe all that is enjoyned by the Church of England, I married her on the third of September in the night between eleven and two at Worcester House, my chaplain, Dr Crowther, performing that Office according as is directed by the Book of Common Prayer, the Lord Ossory being then present and giving her in Marriage. Of the truth of all which I do take this my corporal oath this 18th day of February, 1660 [1661].

James.[30]

The sordid episode was thus brought to a happy conclusion, leading the way to an extremely successful marriage. That this was so was due in large degree to the good sense, restraint and dignity shown by Anne Duchess of York. She was a woman of character who in the years to come was to have considerable influence on her husband, an influence that was entirely beneficial.

On 9 January Queen Henrietta Maria and her daughter, having been conducted to Portsmouth by King Charles, embarked in the *London*, a warship commanded by Lord Sandwich. The Queen's usual luck at sea followed her. A violent storm blew up; the vessel ran aground and had to put back into harbour. The Princess then fell ill; smallpox was suspected, and for some days it was feared that she might follow her brother and sister to the grave. She was taken ashore and for a fortnight remained seriously ill at Portsmouth; but it turned out to be measles, and after King Charles had sent his own physician to her she recovered. On 25 January the royal travellers set out once more, to be given a splendid reception at Havres.

At the Palais Royal in Paris on 30 March, 1661, Henrietta Anne Stuart and Philippe de Bourbon were married. Louis XIV's uncle Gaston had recently died, and he had conferred on his brother the dukedom of Orleans, the traditional title of the King's next brother. Henceforth Minette, according to the curious French royal custom, would be known at court simply as Madame, the wife of Monsieur the King's brother.

Three weeks earlier Cardinal Mazarin had died at Vincennes, his death ushering in a new era in the history of France.

8

Eldest and Youngest, 1661–70

The devotion of King Charles II to other members of the royal family was never more clearly shown than at the moments of death. The news of his father's terrible end had shattered him completely. His sister Elizabeth he had hardly known, but the depth of his grief when first Henry and then Mary had died during the months that followed the Restoration was attested by contemporaries.

The loss intensified his love for his one remaining sister. The meetings of Charles with his adored Minette were few and far between, but despite separation their devotion grew with the years, to such a degree that in some quarters it was suspected of being incestuous. Burnet, who wrote with anti-Stuart prejudice, hinted at this when he said that the King 'was so charmed with his sister, that every thing she proposed, and every favour she asked, was granted: it did not pass without the severest censures'.[1] The insinuation was ridiculous, but it was apparently sufficiently prevalent to worry Minette. According to a note against this passage in an early edition of Burnet's *History*, before her death she 'sent for Mr. Ralph Montague, the English ambassador, and discovered to him the object of her interview with her brother, swearing in the most solemn manner, that the suspicion of having entertained too familiar an attachment to any of her own blood was utterly groundless'.[2]

The interest of Charles II's family relationships during the nine years following Mary's death consists almost exclusively in the series of letters that passed between the King and the Duchess of Orleans.

His feelings towards the other survivor among the children of Charles I, his brother James, are more difficult to fathom. The two were close companions, not only on state occasions; and

Coronation of Charles II

undoubtedly they had a strong regard for one another. James was in administrative matters his brother's right-hand man, and Charles respected his efficiency and his thoroughness; but he was often irritated by his slowness, his rigidity, his hectoring and his determination to have a finger in every pie. James for his part despised his elder brother's flexibility; it seemed to him that Charles was always apt to play into the hands of adversaries and was prone to the same mistakes that had characterized their father's rule. Temperamentally the two were poles apart: alike only, it would seem, in their sexual promiscuousness (James had fewer mistresses than Charles, but was never faithful for long to his much loved wife).

The brothers had been brought up together, and latterly were always closely associated. But there was probably less personal fondness between them than there was between any of the others.

There was affection between James and his youngest sister, as was shown on the rare occasions on which they met. But there was nothing like the intimacy that existed between Charles and his Minette. If letters passed between them, they have not survived.

Minette was settling down happily in her new status as 'Madame'. She was always liable to be plagued by unwelcome suitors, and in the early stages of her return to France the Duke of Buckingham made a nuisance of himself. It was a characteristic of the Villiers dukes to fly high in their love aspirations, always with ineptitude. George Villiers the elder had endangered Anglo-French relations by his designs on the virtue of the then Queen of France, Anne of Austria. His son, after the death of William II of Orange, had tried to force his attentions on the widowed Princess Royal, but was quickly choked off. Now he transferred his affection to her younger sister. When Henrietta Anne and her mother left England he wormed his way into their company, and joined the ship in which they were to sail. Then the Princess was taken ill, and Buckingham, in the words of the late C.H. Hartmann, 'had carried on like a maniac in despair, and ever since he had been playing the part of a distracted lover'.[3] Queen Henrietta was furious, and sent the Duke on ahead to Paris; but it was not till representations had been made by the Duke of Orleans to King Charles that he was got rid of and recalled to England.

This, however, was a passing irritation. Minette was now a married princess, the second lady of France, and she soon acquired an admirer of greater lustre than the ducal buffoon, and of even more imposing status than her strutting, effeminate husband.

Louis XIV's young queen, the Spanish Maria Teresa, or Marie-Thérèse as she was now known, was shy and retiring, not to say dull and stupid: not the sort of girl who could grace as first lady the dazzling court that her husband was establishing. Minette, on the contrary, was eminently capable of so doing. She was admired by everybody; she loved gaiety and cere-monial, and without displaying ambition or indulging in intrigue she stepped effortlessly into the position which should have been occupied by the Queen.

In the summer of 1661 the court moved to Fontainebleau for a round of hunting expeditions, banquets, masquerades and moonlit water parties. And it was here that King Louis, the sun about which all the splendour of France revolved, fell under the spell of his sister-in-law. She was no longer 'the bones of the Holy Innocents' but the inseparable companion of the King in all the splendid revelry that filled the summer days and nights.

It is unlikely that she was Louis's mistress. This was one of a number of flirtations in which Minette indulged in the atmo-sphere of gallantry that characterized the French court; but C.H. Hartmann, who made a particular study of her and may be regarded as the best authority on her life, came to the conclusion that her love affairs 'were chiefly of the mind and the imagination'.[4] Her husband's love for her lasted, by his own confession, for about a fortnight after they were married; but there is no reliable evidence that she was ever unfaithful to him.

The intimacy between the King and Madame was, however, sufficient to cause a certain amount of gossip. There was always plenty of that in Paris and Fontainebleau, and nobody worried very much about it; but any suggestion of a liaison between the King and his brother's wife was undesirable. It was decided, therefore, to distract the attention of the scandal-mongers through Louis's making a show of attachment to one of the Duchess's maids of honour, a young country girl named Louise de la Vallière. The result was not quite what Madame had intended. Louis became genuinely attracted to the gentle Louise, who for her part fell deeply in love with him. Before long she was installed as the first *maîtresse en titre* of the reign of Louis XIV.

Minette was not unduly downcast. King Louis remained a faithful friend, and she found consolation in the devotion of another admirer, the Comte de Guiche, son of the respected and influential Marshal de Gramont. This too was to lead to trouble. Not only was Monsieur jealous, in spite of his own neglect of his wife; another who was jealous was the Marquis de Vardes, who himself aspired to Madame's favours. Vardes was an unscrupulous courtier, whose spite led him to go to the Marshal and persuade him that his son was in danger through his indiscretion and would be safer away from Paris. Guiche was therefore exiled by being put in command of the Marshal's troops in Lorraine.

Such was the atmosphere of intrigue in which the youngest of the Stuarts now found herself compelled to move. It did not particularly displease her; she was very much part of the French court scene. But coupled with the enmity of her husband it was all to cause her much heartache in the years to come.

Whatever the feelings of Monsieur towards his wife, there was never a break of any duration in their sexual relations. Madame became pregnant for the first time in the winter of 1661; at the same time the feverish gaiety of her life was too much for her always delicate health. She was taken seriously ill, and there was fear of a miscarriage. In November she was taken in a litter from Fontainebleau to the Tuileries in Paris, where she was tenderly nursed by her mother. Her brother Charles, told about it all by his envoy Lord Crofts, wrote to her on 16 December:

I have been in very much paine for your indisposition, not so much that I thought it dangerous, but for feare that you should miscarry. I hope you are now out of that feare too, and for gods sake, my dearest Sister, have a care of your selfe and beleeve that I am more concerned in your health then I am in my owne, which I hope you do me the iustice to be confident of, since you know how much I love you. Crofts hath given me a full accounte of all you charged him with, with all which I am very well pleased, and in particular with the desire you

have to see me at Dunkerke the next summer, which you may
easily beleeve is a very welcome proposition to me, betweene
this and then we will adiuste that voyage, I am sure I shall be
very impatient till I have the happynesse to see ma chere
minete againe. I am very glad to finde that the K of France
does still continue his confidence and kindnesse to you, which
I am so sensible of, that, if I had no other reason to grounde
my kindnesse to him but that, he may be most assured of my
frindship as long as I live, and pray upon all occasions assure
him of this. I do not write to you in french because my head is
now closed with businesse, and do intend to write you very
often in English that you may not quite forgett it. [5]

After their separation at the beginning of 1661 Charles and
Minette were always hoping to arrange another meeting; and as
time passed political motives were added to personal. But one
obstacle after another intervened, and it was many years before
they could be united again.

Minette made a slow recovery, but in March 1662 she was
well enough to appear in public once more. On the 27th of that
month she gave birth to a daughter, christened Marie-Louise.
This was the first granddaughter of Charles I. Before the
Restoration the only married member of the family was Mary,
and her only child was a boy, born after his father's death.
James's first son, Charles Duke of Cambridge, who made his
appearance so soon after the clandestine wedding of his parents,
had lived only till May 1661.

Two months after the birth of Marie-Louise Charles II was
himself married. His bride was the Portuguese Princess Catherine of Braganza, and the match had been arranged partly
through the instrumentality of Louis XIV, who saw in it a
chance of drawing the King of England into the anti-Spanish
camp. In England a Protestant alliance would have been
preferred, but there was a lack of Protestant brides available,
German princesses being ruled out by Charles; 'Odd's fish, they
are all foggy',[6] he is quoted as saying of them. Catherine was at
least not connected with one of the great Catholic powers,
France or Spain.

The betrothal was announced in the autumn of 1661, and

there was immediate competition for the posts of maid of honour to the new Queen. One of the successful candidates was a young girl of singular beauty named Frances Stuart, who had been brought up in France. She was sent over to England by Minette, who seemed fated to provide potential mistresses for monarchs. On 4 January, 1662, she wrote to Charles, referring once more to the prospect of seeing him:

> I would not miss this opportunity of writing to you by Madame Stuart who is taking her daughter to be one of the maids of the Queen your wife. Had it not been for this purpose I assure you I should have been very sorry to let her go from here, for she is the prettiest girl imaginable and the most fitted to adorn a Court. I received yesterday a letter in reply to that which I sent you by Craf [Crofts] and it would be impossible to be more delighted than I am at the very thought that I may see your Majesty once more. In truth that is the thing I most desire, and that you should believe me your very humble servant.[7]

Catherine reached England in May. Charles met her at Portsmouth, and the wedding took place at once. She was hardly 'dull and foggy', but at fifteen she was shy and gauche, and in the years to come would be unable to compete with the sexual attractions of her many rivals in her husband's affections. On first acquaintance he was pleased with her, and on the day after the wedding he wrote to Hyde, now Earl of Clarendon:

> It was happy for the honour of the nation that I was not put to the consummation of the marriage last night; for I was so sleepy by having slept but two hours in my journey as I was afraid that matters would have gone very sleepily. I can only give you an account of what I have seen a-bed; which, in short, is, her face is not so exact as to be called a beauty, though her eyes are excellent good, and not anything in her face that in the least degree can shock one. On the contrary, she has as much agreeableness in her looks altogether, as ever I saw: and if I have any skill in physiognomy, which I think I have, she must be as good a woman as ever was born. Her conversation, as much as I can perceive, is very good; for she

Catherine of Braganza, by Lely

has wit enough and a most agreeable voice. You would much
wonder to see how well we are acquainted already. In a word,
I think myself very happy; but am confident our two humours
will agree very well together.[8]

On 23 May he wrote more explicitly to Minette on the subject
of the wedding night:

My Ld St Albans will give you so full a description of my wife
as I shall not go about to do it, only I must tell you that I
thinke my selfe very happy, I was married the day before
yesterday but the fortune that followes our famally is fallen
upon me, car Monr Le Cardinal m'a fermé la porte au nez,
and though I am not so furious as Monsieur was, but am
content to lett those passe over before I go to bed to my wife,
yett I hope I shall intertaine her at least better the first night
than he did you. I do intend on Monday next to go towards
hamton court, where I shall stay till the Queene comes. My
dearest sister continue your kindnesse to me and beleeve me
to be intierly Yours.[9]

'The Queene' mentioned in this letter was Henrietta Maria,
who returned at this time. The payment of her jointure was
conditional on her taking up residence in England, and now
that her daughter was married she could at least make an effort
to comply. But she was an ageing and a tired woman now, and
the climate did not agree with her. She made her home at
Denmark House and was treated with affection and respect by
her sons. She was, moreover, delighted with her unsophisticated
daughter-in-law, whose ardour for the Catholic faith was equal
to her own. At their first meeting she begged Catherine 'to lay
aside all compliments and ceremony, for she would never have
returned to England but for the pleasure of seeing her son's wife,
loving her as a daughter and honouring her as a queen'.[10] A new
gentleness was noticeable in her manner. Her love of intrigue
and of interfering in other people's business had faded; she lived
unobtrusively and made few public appearances.

It was not long before King Charles's marriage ran into
difficulties. The trouble was caused by his principal mistress,
Barbara Countess of Castlemaine. Barbara was a dominating

character, a termagant of the first order. What she wanted she insisted on getting, and the King was as wax in her hands. What she wanted now was an official position as lady of the bedchamber to the new Queen. Charles promised that she should have it; but Catherine, little as she knew of England, had been told all about Lady Castlemaine, and when the list of proposed attendants was submitted to her she struck Barbara's name out with her own hand. The result was a furious row between husband and wife, in which Catherine was eventually worsted. Bullied by his mistress, Charles insisted on the appointment, and Catherine, too naïve and innocent to deal with such matters diplomatically, had to give way.

The rift took time to heal; but heal it did. Catherine in due course learned to be philosophical about such royal foibles as marital infidelity, and the relationship between King and Queen developed into an affectionate regard more satisfying than sexual passion. Lady Castlemaine for her part, though she remained a formidable figure, lost some of her influence as Charles began to interest himself in Frances Stuart.

For the moment, however, King Charles's behaviour to his wife was insulting and indefensible. Even Minette seems to have been of this opinion. Charles tried to justify his conduct by blaming others for interference, and apparently suggested this in a letter to his sister which has disappeared. With gentle raillery she replied:

Paris 22 July.
The courier I sent you returned two days ago and brought me the worst news I could ever receive after the hopes I had had of seeing you by informing me of the contrary. Everyone here was not of the same opinion, and those in the highest quarters were as pleased as I was miserable, and I was only consoled by the hopes you gave me that it is but a postponement. I have so much faith in your word that I would not doubt it after what you have told me, and also because of my hope that you have a little affection for your poor Minette, who assuredly has more for you than she can say. You tell me that someone has spoken maliciously about a person near to the Queen your wife. Alas! How can one possibly say such things? I who know your innocence marvel

at it. But jesting apart I pray you tell me how the Queen takes this. It is said here that she is grieved beyond measure, and to speak frankly I think it is with reason.[11]

As time went by the idea took root in King Charles's mind that his sister would be an ideal unofficial intermediary between himself and Louis XIV. During the years of exile he had been much impressed with French culture and civilization, and the notion of a close alliance between England and France was dear to his heart. His aspirations were not shared by his subjects, who distrusted France as a country of popery and absolutism. Hatred of the French was in fact endemic in the English people, and it behoved Charles to move warily so far as open diplomacy went. Contact through Minette was the solution. Not only was she discreet and intelligent; she was highly thought of by both monarchs and in their confidence.

A new note in the correspondence made its appearance before the end of 1662. In October King Charles sent young Ralph Montagu, a son of the Earl of Manchester, over to Paris as a special envoy, and sent by him a letter to Minette which with its formal tone, so different from his usual style, was plainly meant to be shown to Louis. 'I have charged this bearer,' he wrote, 'to acquaint you and the King my brother with the present state of my affairs and with the procedure which I propose to adopt. He will assure you of all the respect that I have for your person and of the desire I have that you should be the witness and pledge of the friendship between the King my brother and myself, and for this I refer you more particularly to the bearer.'[12]

Montagu returned to London in February 1663, bringing glowing accounts of the splendid gaiety of the French court and of the charm of Minette. Charles wrote a cheerful letter to his sister:

Mr Montagu is arrived heere, and I wonder Monsieur would lett him stay with you so long, for he is undoubtedly in love with you, but I aught not to complaine, haveing given me a very fine sword and belt which I do not beleeve was out of pure liberality but because I am your brother. He tells me that you passe your time very well there. We had a designe to have a masquerade heere, and had made no ill designe in the generall for it, but we were not able to goe through with it, not haveing one man heere that could make a tolerable entry. I have been persuading the queene to follow Q mother of frances example and goe in masquerade before the carnavall be done. I beleeve it were worth seeing my Ld St Albans in such an occasion. My wife hath given a good introduction to such a businesse, for the other day she made my Ld Aubigny and two other of her chaplins dance country dances in her bedchamber. I am just now called for to goe to the Play so as I can say no more at present but that I am intierly

Yours.[13]

One of the reasons why Montagu had been sent to France was that an exchange of new ambassadors had recently been made, and neither was a good choice for Charles's purposes. The French Ambassador was Gaston Comte de Cominges, a blunt, irascible man; his English counterpart was Lord Holles, who long ago had been one of the 'Five Members' whom Charles I had wanted to arrest in the House of Commons. He had made his peace with Charles II, but his aggressive temper had not changed with the years. Neither envoy was blessed with tact; both were obsessed with those matters of etiquette and precedence that so bedevilled international diplomacy in the seventeenth century, and each had a profound dislike and distrust of the country to which he was accredited.

In the circumstances unofficial contact was desirable if Charles was going to achieve his aim of an alliance with Louis. Ralph Montagu and the Duchess of Orleans would be more useful than Cominges and Holles.

For the next two years the possibility of an alliance with France was complicated by the boiling up of hostilities between England and the Netherlands. The causes of the Second Dutch War were commercial and maritime; there was constant friction over herring fisheries and the wool trade, while English claims to sovereignty at sea were resented by the Dutch with their growing naval power. King Charles was not anxious for war, but his subjects were; the Duke of York was especially belligerent. It soon became clear that hostilities sooner or later were inevitable. And by a treaty of 1662 France had bound herself to come to the aid of the Netherlands.

Meanwhile Minette had a further mishap. She was pregnant again, and caught her foot in some ribbon while taking part in a masque at the Louvre. She fell and twisted an ankle and was badly shaken, but this time she made a good recovery. Charles wrote on 29 February 1664:

I was in great paine to heare of the fall you had least it might have done you preiudice in the condition you are in, but I was as glad to finde by your letter that it had done you no harme. We have the same disease of sermons that you complaine of there, but I hope you have the same convenience that the rest of the family has, of sleeping out most of the time, which is a great ease to those who are bounde to heare them. I have little to trouble you with this post only to tell you that I am now very busy every day in prepareing businesse for the Parliament that meetes a fortenight hence. Mr Mountegu has had the seatique but is now pritty well. I thanke you for the care you have taken of the snufe, at the same time pray send me some wax to seale letters that has gold in it, the same you seald your letters with before you were in mourning, for there is none to be gott in this towne.[14]

All went well with the pregnancy, and on 16 July Madame gave birth to a son. He was christened Philippe-Charles and created Duc de Valois, but was not destined to grow up.

From this time onward King Charles's letters to his sister took on an increasingly serious turn, being more occupied with the coming war with the Dutch and with hopes that friendship with France would not be interrupted. On 2 June he wrote:

. . . Sr George Downing [English Ambassador at The Hague] is come out of holland, and I shall now be very busy upon that matter. The States keepe a great braging and noise, but I belieeve when it comes to it they will looke twice before they leape. I never saw so greate an appetite to a warre as is in both this towne and country, espetially in the parlament men, who I am confident would pawne there estates to mainetaine a warre, but all this shall not governe me, for I will looke meerely what is iuste and best for the honour and good of England, and will be very steady in what I resolve, and if I be forced to a warre, I shall be ready with as good ships and men as ever was seene, and leave the successe to God. I am iust now going to dine at Somerset house with the Queene [Henrietta Maria], and tis twelve a clocke, so I can say no more but that I am

Yours[15]

On 23 August, in an exceptionally long letter, King Charles entered on the question of a treaty with Louis. The matter had already been broached, but had been retarded by irritating questions of etiquette, difficulties having been raised by Lord Holles on his precedence as Ambassador over the French Princes of the Blood. Charles lamented this nuisance to his sister, and continued:

> . . . But now that I am upon this matter I must deale freely with you, and tell you that nothing can hinder this good aliance and frindship which I speake of, but the king my brother's giving the Hollanders some countenance in the dispute there is betweene us, for I assure you they brag very much already of his frindship and it may be they would not be so insolent as they are, if they had not some such hopes. . . . I am very glad that the king my brother is so kind to you; there can be no body so fitt to make a good correspondence and frindship betweene us as your selfe. I take the occasion of this safe messenger to tell you this, because I would not have this businesse passe through other hands then yours, and I would be very willing to have your opinion and councell, how I shall proceede in this matter. I do not doute but that you will have that care of me, that I ought to expect from your kindnesse, and as you are an Exeter woman; and if you are not fully informed of all things as you complayne of in your letters, it is your own faute, for I have been a very exact correspondent, and have constantly answered all your letters, and I have directed my Ld Hollis to give a full account of our dispute with holland if you will have the patience to heare it.[16]

Madame thus became established as the personal intermediary between Charles II and Louis XIV. She was completely in the confidence of both monarchs, and was hencefor-

Henrietta, Duchess of Orleans. Miniature by Samuel Cooper

ward entrusted by them with secrets kept from their respective ambassadors.

Louis was as anxious for a treaty as Charles. But there remained the difficulty of the Franco-Dutch pact. War was rapidly approaching, and though there was as yet nothing more than armed neutrality in Europe the English and Dutch were already embarking on hostilities in their colonial territories overseas. On 24 October 1664, Charles mentioned, in a letter to his sister about more important matters, a skirmish on the other side of the Atlantic:

> . . . You will have heard of our takeing of New Amsterdam which lies iust by New England. Tis a place of great importance to trade, and a very good towne. It did belong to England heretofore but the Duch by degrees drove our people out of it, and built a very good towne, but we have gott the better of it, and tis now called New Yorke. He that tooke it and is now there, is Nicols my brothers servant who you know very well.[17]

A town which has since achieved considerable international fame was thus restored to English rule and was renamed after the King's brother, James Duke of York.

Once again special envoys were exchanged between England and France. Charles's choice was Viscount Fitzhardinge; this was the title now borne by Charles Berkeley who had played so disreputable a part in the affair of the Duke of York and Anne Hyde. In spite of that scandal he was still much in the confidence of both the Stuart brothers. Louis's envoy was Henri de Massué, Marquis de Ruvigny, who knew England well. The pretext for his mission was to discuss a French marriage alliance with Portugal. When he left France in November 1664 Minette sent by him a short letter in which for the first time the possibility was mooted of a secret pact between the two kings. In Hartmann's view it was 'entirely her own idea; there is no reason to suppose that she had Louis' authority to make the suggestion'.[18] She wrote:

> I could not let Ruvigni leave without giving him this letter to show you that you will see by what he tells you how much

your friendship is desired and even necessary here. In God's name take advantage of this and do not lose any time in obtaining the King's secret promise that he will not help the Dutch; for you understand that he cannot promise you this openly because of his engagements with them, though it is notorious that they are only worth what one makes them worth as the saying is. But as in this world appearances must be kept up and this affair requires them, you ought, as I have already said, to content yourself with a secret agreement which in this way will be much more solid. I promise you to see to it that it is done in good faith, for I so much fear the contrary in anything with which I concern myself that I would have nothing to do with it were it not so.[19]

Those engaged in international diplomacy have never been remarkable for a rigid adherence to principles of personal honour. It is clear that Madame had as elastic a view of the sanctity of treaties as had her brother and brother-in-law.

This was underlined in another letter a week later, in which Minette emphasized to Charles that a secret agreement would be the best means of reaching a true understanding with Louis. 'You see how long great treaties are kept,' she added, 'but this one ought to be inviolable being concluded between two friends.'[20]

Madame was at this time involved in the court intrigues that were always apt to plague her. Her admirer the Comte de Guiche was back in Paris, still hoping to throw himself at her feet; but the man who was causing trouble was once more the Marquis de Vardes. He was still jealous of de Guiche and still resentful towards Madame over the earlier episode, and he went out of his way to insult her. The Chevalier de Lorraine, one of Monsieur's favourites, was believed to be in love with one of Minette's maids of honour, Mademoiselle de Fiennes; and one day in the Queen's apartments Vardes said loudly to the Chevalier: 'I do not understand why you bother about the maid when you could easily have the mistress.'[21]

This was the sort of insolence that could not be overlooked, and Minette took it very seriously indeed. She complained to King Louis, and at the same time asked King Charles to intervene. He did so through Fitzhardinge, and eventually Vardes found himself in prison.

Some of the correspondence between brother and sister was of a lighter and pleasanter nature. A comet had made its appearance. 'By the letters from paris,' wrote Charles on 15 December, 'I perceave that the blasing starr hath been seen there likewise. I hope it will have the same effect heere as that in Germany had, and then we shall beate our neighbour turkes as well as they beate thers.'[22] On Christmas Eve a comet was seen again, and there was argument on whether it was the same or another one. Charles, always interested in such matters, asked his sister to consult the pundits in Paris.

Minette had little faith in astronomers. On 12 January 1665, she replied to her brother:

> . . . The last time I wrote to you I asked what they thought of the Comet in England, and two hours later I received the letter in which you ask me the same thing. I will tell you then that there have been meetings at the Jesuits' observatory which were attended by all the learned persons and also by those who are not. The former disputed according to their beliefs which were nearly all at variance, some say it is the same comet returned and others that it is a new one. And as one would have to get there to discover the truth I suppose it will remain undecided as well as the substance of which it is composed which was also discussed. This is all that my ignorance permits me to tell you, and I think it is enough to satisfy your curiosity, since these learned gentlemen are beyond question all mad or very nearly so.[23]

Two months later the expected war broke out. Louis did all he could to prevent it. He wanted the English alliance, but doubted if he could get out of his obligations to the Dutch; and war would force his hand. Charles tried to defer hostilities, but the pressure of parliament and people was too much for him. On 4 March, 1665, he declared war on the United Provinces; it was bound to be a purely naval conflict, and on 23 March the Duke of York as Lord High Admiral hoisted his flag in the *Royal Charles* at the Gunfleet.

The Second Dutch War dragged on for two years. There were a number of naval battles, some of them on a considerable scale, but in the end the issue was indecisive. The first great engagement, the Battle of Lowestoft in June 1665, was a splendid victory for the Duke of York. Through no fault of his it was not exploited; if it had been the war might have ended there and then. As it was, Lowestoft marked the cessation, for the time being, of James's fighting career at sea. He had been so much in the thick of the action that two of his comrades—one of them was his old friend Charles Berkeley, now Earl of Falmouth—were killed at his side; James was bespattered with their blood. This, it was decided, could not go on. Catherine of Braganza had consistently failed to provide the King with a family, and James was still the heir to the throne. Lord Clarendon, his father-in-law, represented that he must not be allowed to continue to risk his life in battle, and Queen Henrietta Maria added her plea on behalf of her younger son. Charles agreed, and the supreme naval command was entrusted jointly to Prince Rupert and the Duke of Albemarle.

James therefore returned to the Admiralty and from this time devoted himself, with the expert assistance of Samuel Pepys among others, to the building up and administration of the Royal Navy which was perhaps his greatest service to his country.

King Louis during the early hostilities managed to keep out of the struggle, and indeed expressed almost undiplomatic delight at the result of the Battle of Lowestoft. His brother and sister-in-law made no secret of their joy; Minette, pregnant again and nearing her time, had been racked with anxiety. 'I doe protest,' wrote Holles, 'I thinck Madame would have dyed if things had gone ill, I speake it seriously. Monsieur is the most joyed man that ever I saw, but the Bourgeois is generally no frend to us, their having so much dealing with the Hollander doth wholy backbyas them that way, and much the interruption of their trade by our Men of Warr.'[24]

Louis could not maintain his neutrality indefinitely. He tried hard to make peace, communicating with Charles II through Madame. But he was being pressed to fulfil his treaty obligations, and when his overtures came to nothing he declared war on England in January 1666. The part his navy took in the fighting, however, was half-hearted. When what became known as the Four Days Battle took place just a year after Lowestoft the French fleet failed to arrive in time. King Louis later admitted that the dilatoriness was deliberate.

The European scene was now being altered by the departure of some of the older figures who had played prominent parts in their time. Mazarin was already dead; so was Elizabeth of Bohemia. In September 1665 the Spanish King Philip IV died after reigning for forty-four years, leaving his throne to a small child, delicate and mentally retarded, whose death was expected at any minute. In the event the young Charles II of Spain lived for thirty-five years, but throughout his precarious life there were manoeuvrings for the succession.

Four months later, in January 1666, Philip's sister Anne of Austria, the widow of Louis XIII who had played so large a part in the affairs of France, followed him to the grave.

Henrietta Maria had still a few years to live, but she was feeling her age and the severe winter of 1664–5 taxed her strength. She announced that she must spend the next New Year in France. When the Great Plague broke out in London in the summer of 1665, she decided that she could stand it no longer. On 29 June Pepys reported 'the Queene-mother setting out for France this day to drink Bourbon waters this year, she being in a consumption—and entends not to come till winter come twelvemonths.'[25] She was destined not to see England again.

The climax of the war came with the Medway calamity. London had suffered two great misfortunes—the Plague and the Great Fire of September 1666 which virtually destroyed the City. These disasters, coupled with the expenses of war, had crippled the country's finances. King Charles was at odds with his Parliament, which was unwilling to grant him money except in return for concessions to its views, which were principally involved with religion. The upshot of it all was the decision to lay up the fleet in the summer of 1667; the Dutch were also war-weary, and it was hoped there would be a lull in hostilities.

It was a fatal decision. The great Dutch Admiral de Ruyter saw his chance, and in May his fleet sailed unopposed up the Medway, attacked Sheerness and Chatham, and burned some sixteen ships of the line, towing the *Royal Charles*, the pride of the Navy, away as a prize.

It was the greatest humiliation ever inflicted on the Royal Navy; yet in spite of the loss in naval shipping its results were moral rather than strategic. Negotiations for peace were already in hand, and the outcome was hardly affected by the Medway episode. The Peace of Breda which followed recognized capture of territory on both sides; England retained New York and the Netherlands Surinam. The treaty settled nothing except the certainty of another war. England was burning for revenge, and the Netherlands were as great a menace to her supremacy at sea as ever.

One result in England was the fall of the Earl of Clarendon, yet another of the older generation to disappear from the European scene. Clarendon was no war leader, and he knew little of naval affairs. Younger aspirants to power were howling for his blood, and all the misfortunes of the war were laid, not altogether unjustly, at his door. Charles gave in to popular clamour, as he so often did. Clarendon was driven from office, in spite of vigorous efforts by his son-in-law the Duke of York to save him; and the King connived at his fleeing the country to escape impeachment.

During the Second Dutch War correspondence between King Charles and his sister had languished, though it had never altogether ceased. Now it was resumed on a new note. The question of an agreement, secret or otherwise, between the Kings of England and France took on fresh urgency, and for the first time religion entered the discussion.

Both Charles and James Stuart had been veering for some time towards the Church of Rome. If we are to believe Burnet, James even before the Restoration had come to the conclusion that truth in religion was to be found there. All his instincts tended in that direction, and as the 1660s wore on the conviction spread throughout England that he was a crypto-Catholic. It was this, coupled with the impression he gave of being inclined towards an authoritarian method of government, that brought about the rapid decline in his popularity. In spite of the services he had rendered at sea and at the Admiralty, he was increasingly distrusted in the country, and this distrust developed as time went on into hatred, at least among certain influential circles in political society. The suspicions were unquestionably true. James's was an uncomplicated nature, and having convinced himself that the Catholic Church was the true church he moved steadily and steadfastly towards his goal, though he did not take the final step till almost the end of the decade. He was aided by his wife, who with a keener intellect and at least as forthright a nature was moving in the same direction. Detailed evidence is lacking, but it seems probable that she was received into the Catholic Church at an earlier date than her husband.

Charles's motives were more complex. He was not, like his brother, a fundamentally religious man. By nature he was a sceptic, distrustful of all rigid beliefs; and he wanted no creed that interfered with his private life. He could not, he said, think that God would damn a man for taking a little irregular pleasure by the way.[26] One thing, however, in which he did believe was religious toleration. He had fought for it since the Restoration, and he was constantly trying to curb the persecuting ardour of his subjects. This alone was sufficient to create in him sympathy towards the Catholics, the harmless victims of persecution. And he always had in mind the splendid loyalty he had experienced from these same Catholics in his hunted days after Worcester in 1651. All this inclined him towards the feeling, without any deep doctrinal conviction, that Catholicism was the only reasonable faith for a civilized man.

The hope that her brothers might be reconciled to Holy Church was very dear to Minette, herself a fervent Catholic from her earliest years. And she was whole-heartedly supported by King Louis. It is not to be supposed that Louis was much concerned with the welfare of his brother monarch's immortal soul. Good Catholic though he himself was, his motives were above all political. A Catholic monarchy would help to bind England to the French interest; and he was keener than ever on an English alliance. Now that Philip IV was dead, and the Spanish monarchy weakened, his chief interest lay in gaining possession of the Spanish Netherlands; he had already invaded the territory. Here his chief enemy was the Dutch Republic: English support was of the highest importance.

The religious issue was not raised immediately. When the correspondence between Charles and Minette resumed its full flow, it was at first concerned with lighter matters. King Charles sent his much loved illegitimate son by Lucy Walter, James Duke of Monmouth, over to Paris and was most grateful to his sister for taking him under her wing. Then there was some talk about the King's old love Frances Stuart, who had been recommended to him by Minette. She had angered him by eloping with, and marrying, the Duke of Richmond, and

Charles, who was sincerely devoted to her, found it hard to forgive her. But when she developed smallpox, and it was feared that her beauty would be marred, his chivalrous instincts were aroused. In the event the disease had little effect on her.

Then there was the matter of the Triple Alliance. Pursuing the principle of the balance of power, Charles countered Louis's campaign in Spanish Flanders by entering into an alliance with the Dutch, which was later joined by Sweden. Louis was not unnaturally indignant at this breach of the tacit understanding between him and Charles, and Minette was much exercised to keep the peace between them.

Madame herself was by no means happy at this time. The chief trouble was her husband's infatuation with the Chevalier de Lorraine. Philip's homosexual tendencies had increased with the years, and he now cared for nothing and nobody but the Chevalier. His wife he treated with cruelty and contempt, while at the same time watching her with an obsession of jealousy. Lorraine on the other hand was bisexual, and was still in love with Mademoiselle de Fiennes. When, in the summer of 1668, Monsieur discovered some letters between them containing insulting references both to him and to his wife, he dismissed the maid of honour from Madame's service without consulting her. This led to further estrangement, accentuated by Monsieur's conduct in holding the Chevalier in no way to blame. It was all very difficult for Minette.

It was the Duke of York who took the initiative in bringing the religious issue into the discussions with the King of France. James was received into the Church of Rome some time in 1669, but he was of course already a convinced Catholic and it was only for political reasons that he delayed taking the final step. Towards the end of 1668 he approached his brother and asked him if he would himself be willing to be reconciled to the faith. He found the King, according to his biographer, 'resolv'd as to his being a Catholick, and very sensible of the uneasiness it was to him to live in so much danger and constraint'.[27] A meeting was therefore arranged with three trusted friends—Lord Arlington, Lord Arundell of Wardour and Sir Thomas Clifford. At this time Charles's principal political councillors were the five known from the initial letters of their names as the 'Cabal'— Clifford, Arlington, Buckingham, Ashley and Lauderdale. Of those admitted to the secret of the King's religious intentions, therefore, two were members of the ruling clique. Neither was at this time a publicly declared Catholic: of the five in the secret, only Lord Arundell, who had nothing to do with the government, was this.

The meeting duly took place in the Duke of York's quarters at Whitehall on 25 January, 1669. The King professed his eagerness to declare himself a Catholic, and it was decided 'that there was no better way for doing this great work, then to do it in conjunction with France and with the assistance of his Most Christian Majesty, The House of Austria not being in a condition to help in it; and, in pursuance of this Resolution, Monsr. de Croissy Colbert, the French Embassador, was to be trusted with the secret in order to inform his Master of it, that he might receive a power to treat about it with our King.'[28]

Whether or not King Charles ever intended to make a public declaration of Catholicism has been a matter of controversy since that day. He was nobody's fool, and he cannot have been under any illusion about the reception of such a declaration by the country at large; the opposition aroused would certainly endanger his throne, whatever support he received from abroad. On the other hand it is not easy to see why he should make so much of the design if he had no intention of carrying it out. Louis was certainly keen to bring England into the orbit of Catholic Europe, but this was not a *sine qua non*; agreement between the two monarchs could have been reached without any mention of religion. Money was undoubtedly a consideration, but again Charles could probably have arranged for a cash contribution from Louis in some simpler way. Minette was overjoyed at the new development. In her case at least religious considerations were paramount. The thought that she might help to bring about the conversion of her beloved brother, and thus save his soul, was heaven to her. Charles sent Lord Arundell, head of an old English Catholic family, as his envoy, to Paris, and by him Louis was told of his brother monarch's intentions.

Minette was wholly in the secret from first to last, and her correspondence with her brother was from now on as much diplomatic as personal. In dealing with such matters brother and sister now disguised the names of the persons most involved in a cipher devised by Charles.

Details of the proposed alliance were worked out. The

principal object was a joint war against the Dutch, with the French attacking on land and the English by sea. At the same time Charles undertook to make his declaration of Catholicism, and asked Louis to aid him with troops and money in the event of insurrection among his subjects. An important point in the negotiations was the English sovereign's insistence on the naval supremacy of his kingdom; Charles asked that Louis should curtail his own programme of fleet expansion, which was causing some alarm in England. Discussions on this aspect of the alliance were spun out for many months, but eventually Louis was brought to agreement.

During the remainder of the year 1669 the negotiations, nearly all conducted through Minette, were intensified. At the same time lighter topics as usual cropped up in the correspondence. One of Louis's envoys was the Abbé Pregnani, an Italian monk who had won fame at the French court with his gift for astrology and telling fortunes. Charles invited him to join him at Newmarket, but the Abbé's skill deserted him when he was required to act as a racing tipster. Charles wrote to his sister on 22 March:

> I came from Newmarkett the day before yesterday where we had as fine wether as we could wish, which added much both to the horse matches as well as to hunting. L'abbé pregnani was there most of the time and I beleeve will give you some account of it, but not that he lost his mony upon confidence that the Starrs could tell which horse would winn, for he had the ill luck to foretell three times wrong together, and James [Monmouth] beleeved him so much as he lost his mony upon the same score.[29]

There had been a further change of ambassadors. Louis's representative in London was now Charles, Marquis de Croissy; he was the brother of the French King's chief minister, Jean Baptiste Colbert, Marquis de Seignelay, and was usually known as Colbert de Croissy. The tiresome Lord Holles had retired from Paris, and was succeeded by Ralph Montagu; but Montagu was not in the great secret of the proposed treaty.

The hope of her brother's conversion was the one ray of light in Madame's rather dismal existence. Monsieur was treating her more callously than ever. He was besotted with Lorraine, and it was the Chevalier who ruled the Orléans household, behaving to its nominal mistress with contemptuous insolence. Henrietta Maria visited her when she could, but her health was failing and she was unable to be with her daughter when Minette gave birth to a baby girl on 17 August—the second of her children to survive.

She had hardly recovered from the effects of the birth when she heard of her mother's death. Queen Henrietta died at Colombes in the early hours of 1 September 1669. She was not quite sixty, but she seemed older. She had grown apart from her two sons, though never estranged; but her death added to the grief of her remaining daughter.

That daughter's married life became increasingly miserable. Even the departure of the Chevalier de Lorraine made the situation worse rather than better. The Chevalier's intrigues and insolence multiplied to the point where he overreached himself. Baulked of the revenues of some church lands which Monsieur had promised him, he made disparaging remarks about the King—a fatal thing to do where Louis XIV was concerned. He was arrested at the end of January 1670, and sent first to Pierre Encise, near Lyons, and then to the bleak Château d'If, on an island off Marseilles.

Philip of Orleans, predictably, had hysterics. He fainted when he heard the news; then threw himself at his brother's feet in tears and implored him to release his favourite. Louis was inexorable, and the Chevalier remained in distant and close custody. Monsieur attributed the whole affair to his wife, who was totally innocent. He carried her off in high dudgeon to his country estate of Villers-Cotterets, where he treated her more brutally than ever.

Her one consolation lay in the negotiations for the Anglo-French alliance, and her exile from Saint-Germain (where the court was in residence) was particularly awkward as proposals were revived at this time for her to visit England. Charles wanted her to come for personal reasons, but Louis had also decided that details of the terms in the proposed treaty could be worked out only by direct contact; nobody but his sister-in-law had the qualities necessary for this. First, however, she must return to the royal circle.

Diplomacy was brought into play. King Charles and the Duke of York both wrote to Monsieur at Villers-Cotterets asking him to allow his wife to pay a social visit to her brothers. King Louis, so high-handed to others, was always indulgent to the whims of his contemptible young brother; instead of peremptorily commanding him to bring his wife back to court, he made the concession of allowing the Chevalier de Lorraine to live in Marseilles as a prisoner on parole. Further than that he would not go, but Philip was mollified. Towards the end of February the Duke and Duchess of Orleans returned to Saint-Germain.

The business of the treaty could now go ahead. The chief difficulty lay in preventing Monsieur from knowing what was going on. There were in fact two treaties in view—the secret pact and one for public consumption. Indulgent as Louis was towards his brother, he had no illusions concerning his discretion or his political judgement. To admit him into the secret was out of the question, though he knew about the plan for the other treaty. It was essential, however, for constant discussions to take place, and the King now took a firm attitude. Philip was put in his place as regards his authority over his wife, and a room was placed at Madame's disposal near the King's own apartments in the Palace of Saint-Germain; here Louis and Minette held their private meetings.

Territories in Flanders had been ceded to the King of France in the Treaty of Aix-la-Chapelle concluded with Spain in April 1668. It was proposed that in the spring of 1670 the French court should pay a ceremonial visit of inspection to these territories, and from there it would be convenient for Madame to sail over to Dover to meet her brothers. But there were yet more complications. Monsieur at first flatly refused to allow his wife to go, and once again his brother was reluctant to coerce him. Then, cajoled into consent, he insisted that he must go too. A treaty was to be negotiated, and he considered that he, not his wife, was the proper person to play the leading part. He further insisted that neither he nor Madame should go further into England than Dover.

It was a delicate situation. The presence of the Duke of Orleans would ruin the project of a secret treaty. King Charles solved the problem. It would not be etiquette, he maintained, for the brother of the King of France to visit him unless at the same time his own brother paid a similar courtesy to King Louis; and unfortunately the Duke of York's commitments at home made it impossible for him to go to France at this time. This did the trick. Questions of ceremonial procedure were paramount with Monsieur. With an ill grace he gave his consent to the trip; but he reiterated that the Duchess should not go beyond Dover, and that she should not stay more than three days.

The court with all its trappings set out for Flanders on 18 April. It was a journey of the greatest discomfort; the weather was appalling, and the roads as bad as could be. The carriages of the nobility were constantly getting stuck in the mud.

Minette's health was wretched, and by the time Flanders was reached she was so exhausted that she could hardly stand. Her husband, moreover, behaved as callously as even he had ever done. One of her closest friends at this time was Anne-Marie de Montpensier. La Grande Mademoiselle had been jealous of Madame's predominance at court in earlier days; but with all her eccentricities she had a kind and an impulsive nature, and the misfortunes of her rival touched her heart. In her memoirs she bore witness to the sufferings Minette endured on the progress to Flanders:

> Madame appeared extremely low-spirited during the whole of the journey, and was ordered a milk diet. The moment she alighted from the coach she retired to her own room, and for the most part, to bed. The King went often to see her, and on every occasion showed a great regard for her. It was not so with Monsieur; when in the coach he would say very disagreeable things even to her face, and, among others, when we happened to speak of astrology, he observed, smiling, that it had been predicted that he should have several wives, and from the state Madame was in he had now reason to put some faith in it. All this appeared to me as silly as it was hard-hearted, and our silence showed what we thought of him—remonstrance would only have recoiled upon poor Madame.[30]

She rallied on arrival at Courtray, with the prospect of soon seeing her brothers. English envoys met her with the news that King Charles was already at Dover and that the English fleet under Lord Sandwich was waiting for her at Dunkirk. The French royal family accompanied her as far as Lille, and from there she went on with her train to the port. On the evening of 14 May she embarked at Dunkirk.

On the 16th, close to Dover, the English royal barge appeared, carrying the King, the Duke of York and Prince Rupert; after nine years the surviving members of the family were together again.

It was a brief enough reunion. Louis managed to persuade his brother to agree to an extension of the visit for a further ten or twelve days, and they all made the most of their time. Queen Catherine and James's wife came to Dover to meet their sister-in-law. Minette later told Mademoiselle that 'the Queen had appeared to her a worthy woman; not handsome, but so affable and full of piety, that she gained the friendship of all. The Duchess of York had a vast deal of wit and sense, with which she was herself perfectly satisfied.'[31] There were banquets and entertainments, and one day Charles took his sister to Canterbury to see a ballet and a comedy. 'Many of our expeditions are on the sea,' wrote one of Minette's attendants, 'where Madame is as bold as she is on land, and walks as fearlessly along the edge of the ships, as she does on shore.'[32]

But time was short, and inevitably much of it had to be spent on arranging the final details of the Secret Treaty of Dover. On 22 May it was signed by Lord Arlington, Lord Arundell of Wardour, Sir Thomas Clifford and Sir Richard Bellings for England, and by Colbert de Croissy for France.

The main article of the treaty provided that war should be declared on the United Provinces by both monarchs, the timing of the declaration being left to King Louis. The French king was to conduct the war on land, the English by sea. The vital article on religion said that the King of England, being convinced of the truth of Catholic doctrine, would make a public declaration of Catholicism as soon as possible. To enable him to do so he was to receive the sum of two million *livres tournois* from the King of France, who also agreed to provide him with a military force of six thousand men if this should prove necessary. The date of the declaration, however, was left entirely to King Charles's discretion.[33]

The official object of her voyage accomplished, Minette had no excuse for staying longer, but she managed to spin out the visit till the beginning of June. Charles gave her presents of jewellery and money, including two thousand gold crowns to build a chapel at Chaillot in memory of their mother. Madame wanted to give him something in return, and called to one of her maids of honour, a pretty Breton girl named Louise de Kéroualle, to bring her jewel-case so that her brother could choose a present. Charles's reply was that Louise herself was the only jewel he coveted, and he asked his sister to leave her in England. Minette refused; she was responsible to the girl's parents, she said, and she must return her to them. But King Charles did not forget, and once again Minette had unwittingly played the rôle of Cupid.

The final scene took place on 2 June. The King and the Duke of York went on board with their sister, and sailed with her for some distance. Minette wept bitterly, and Charles said good-bye to her three times before he could bear to let her go. Colbert de Croissy wrote that 'he had never witnessed so sorrowful a leave-taking, or known before how much royal personages could love one another'.[34]

Three weeks later Minette was dead.

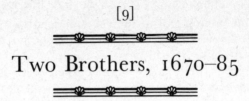

[9]

Two Brothers, 1670–85

At first it seemed that the trip had done Minette good. Buoyed up with the joy of having seen her brothers once more, she arrived in France looking radiant. 'Madame now returned from England', wrote Mademoiselle de Montpensier, 'where it seemed she had at least found health, for she was looking very pretty and happy. Monsieur actually declined to go to meet her, and requested the King also to waive it. But if the King failed in this civility, he received her with the greatest marks of esteem. Not so with Monsieur.'[1]

Fêted by the King and Queen, and cosseted by Mademoiselle, Minette arrived in Paris on 10 June. From there next day she wrote to Sir Thomas Clifford, who had played a leading part in the Dover negotiations, one of her most delightful letters, referring to her brother's promises of advancement for Clifford and Arlington:

> When i have write to the King from Calais i praid him to tel milord Arlington an you what he had promised mi for bothe. his ansers was that hi gave mi againe his word, that hee would performe the thing, but that hi did not thing it fit to exequte it now.
>
> I tel you this sooner than to Milord Arlington because I know you ar not so hard to satisfie as hee. I should be so my self, if I was not sure that the King would not promis mee a thing to faille in the performance of it.
>
> this is the ferste letter I have ever write in inglis. you will eselay see it bi the stile and ortograf. prai see in the same time that i expose mi self to be thought a foulle in looking to make you know how much I am your frind.
>
> for Sr Thomas Clifort[2]

Three days later the Duke and Duchess of Orleans left for their house at Saint-Cloud, and there, facing once again her husband's unkindness, Minette immediately began to feel ill again. On Thursday, 16 June, King Louis ordered his brother to bring his wife to Versailles for the day; Monsieur obeyed with his usual bad grace, and sulked when the King insisted on a private conversation with Madame to discuss the Dover mission. Minette looked terribly ill and was seen to be in tears when she left for Saint-Cloud.

The following day was a very hot one, and Madame disregarded her doctor's orders to the extent of bathing in the Seine. On the Saturday she indulged in more activity, but her health was bad and on Sunday afternoon she was taken suddenly and painfully ill. She asked for a glass of iced chicory water, which was always kept for her, but when she drank it she was seized with most violent pain and cried out that she had been poisoned.

Minette's last hours have often been described in detail.[3] The news that she was dying soon spread, and the King and Queen and Mademoiselle hurried to Saint-Cloud. When Louis embraced his sister-in-law with tears, she said: 'Ah, do not weep, sire, or you will make me weep too. You are losing a very good servant, who has always feared to lose your good graces more than she has feared death itself.'[4] To Monsieur she said: 'Alas! Monsieur, it is long since you have ceased to love me. That was unjust of you; I have never failed you.'[5] When King Louis ordered his brother to send for a priest, Monsieur asked the characteristic question: 'Whom can we send for whose name will look well in the Gazette?'[6] In the event Madame's very good friend the eminent Bishop Bossuet was held to satisfy the condition, and it was he who consoled her dying hours.

One of her last visitors was the English Ambassador, Ralph Montagu. 'You see the sad condition I am in,' she said to him. 'I am going to die. How I pity the King my brother. For I am sure he is losing the person in the world that loves him best.'[7]

Minette died in great agony in the early hours of Monday, 19 June 1670. There were immediate outcries, based largely on her own words, that she had been poisoned. Monsieur's attitude, though hardly that of a heartbroken husband, had not suggested guilt; but it was widely believed that agents of the

Chevalier de Lorraine had put poison in her chicory water.

Charles II, in the first paroxysm of grief that followed the receipt of the news from France of his sister's death, immediately believed the worst. In a torrent of tears he denounced his brother-in-law as a villain guilty of the murder of his wife. But time brought calmer thoughts, and he realized that there was no evidence at all against Philip. Louis XIV did everything that could be asked of him. On the day after Madame's death he wrote to his cousin of England:

> My Brother,——The tender love I had for my sister was well known to you, and you will understand the grief into which her death has plunged me. In this heavy affliction, I can only say that the part which I take in your own sorrow, for the loss of one who was so dear to both of us, increases the burden of my regret. My only comfort is the confidence I cherish that this fatal accident will make no change in our friendship, and that you will continue to let me enjoy yours as fully as I give you mine.[8]

Louis immediately ordered a thorough and open inquiry into the circumstances of Madame's last hours, assuring King Charles that, 'if there were the least imagination that her death had been caused by poison, no severity should be wanting either towards the discovering or the punishing of so horrid and infamous a fact.'[9] A post-mortem examination was held, and the most eminent doctors in France declared that death was due to natural causes.

Their verdict has been endorsed by modern medical historians. It is generally accepted that Henrietta Duchess of Orleans died from acute peritonitis caused by the perforation of a duodenal ulcer.

And now, out of the nine children born to King Charles I and Queen Henrietta Maria, only two remained—the two eldest sons if we except the first-born of all, the infant who had died on the day of his birth in 1629. The remainder of the reign of Charles II was a time of many anxieties. The bright dawn of the Restoration had faded, and for many years the King found himself involved in a battle of wits against constantly mounting opposition, from which he was eventually to emerge victorious. And one of the main elements of the battle was his unwavering fight to overcome the unpopularity of his brother and to ensure that that brother was not deprived of his right of succession.

The unpopularity of James Duke of York was due, almost entirely, to the fact that he was now widely known to be a Catholic, although as yet there had been no official pronouncement on the subject. Since the reign of Mary Tudor the fear of popery in England had reached paranoiac proportions, and the dread of a papist on the throne amounted almost to hysteria. In James's case, however, there was also the feeling that his was a fierce and dictatorial nature, that his goal was absolute monarchy, and that he already had too much power over his brother. Among his admirable qualities tact and diplomacy had no place, and he did little to quieten the fears of the future displayed by his many influential opponents.

He was still the heir to the throne. Queen Catherine had consistently failed to provide her husband with offspring, and there was now virtually no hope that she would ever do so. James himself and his wife, the former Anne Hyde, had had a number of children, but only two daughters survived: Mary, born in 1662, and Anne, three years younger. Anne was short-sighted and not in the best of health.

There was therefore nothing certain about the succession. It was always possible that Catherine might die, and Charles find a more fertile bride; it was obvious that the lack of royal issue was not his fault, since the number of his illegitimate children increased annually. And as time went on suggestions began to be heard in high places that he might find some pretext for putting away his barren wife and making a more suitable marriage— anything, in the view of some members of the political opposition, rather than the succession of James. Any mention of an annulment, however, was firmly and flatly rejected by King Charles. He might be unfaithful to his queen, but was never disloyal.

In these circumstances no objection was raised to the Duke of York's resuming his active naval career. Henrietta Maria was dead, and Clarendon in exile; there was nobody else to fear for James's life. His death in command of the English fleet would be a matter of rejoicing to those who dreaded his succession to the throne. And while King Charles certainly wished for no such thing there can be no doubt that the removal of his brother would make his political task easier.

The Third Dutch War was the direct result of the Secret Treaty of Dover, and also of the open or 'simulated' treaty, which was not signed until the beginning of 1672 and which provided for an Anglo-French alliance but omitted the more contentious clauses.

Early in this year King Charles set about implementing the terms of the Secret Treaty. On 15 March, as a preliminary to his acknowledgement of Catholicism, he issued his Declaration of Indulgence which suspended the penal laws against Catholics and nonconformists. Its terms were mild enough, but sufficient to raise a hornets' nest about his ears.

Two days later he declared war, in conjunction with Louis XIV, against the United Provinces. The pretext for hostilities was flagrantly devoid of moral scruple. Sir Robert Holmes was instructed to get himself embroiled with a Dutch naval escort to a merchant convoy, and though the English were palpably the aggressors a *casus belli* was provided. The Lord High Admiral was promptly chosen to command the fleet, which included a French contingent. On land his two illustrious former comrades in arms, the Prince de Condé and the Vicomte de Turenne, led the French army across the Rhine.

At the same time the King rewarded the members of the Cabal. As Minette had mentioned in her 'English' letter to Clifford, promises had been made to him and Arlington at the time of Dover. Arlington, at this time a baron, was now given an earldom, while Sir Thomas Clifford became Lord Clifford of Chudleigh. Lord Ashley was made Earl of Shaftesbury, and John Maitland Earl of Lauderdale, the Scottish member of the Cabal, received a dukedom. There was nothing for Buckingham; he already enjoyed the highest rank in the peerage.

The Cabal were far from being a cabinet in the modern sense. They were simply a collection of advisers to the King, frequently at loggerheads with each other. Charles consulted now one, now another, as circumstances made convenient. He was himself the framer of policy, and he kept his own secrets.

In April James hoisted his flag in the *Prince* at the Buoy of the Nore, and led his fleet forth to meet the Dutch, whose fleet was commanded by the formidable de Ruyter.

He fought only one action. Early in the morning of 28 May he was attacked by de Ruyter at Southwold Bay, close to the scene of his Lowestoft victory of seven years before. The Battle of Sole Bay, as it was generally called, was a furious struggle in which both fleets engaged with determination throughout the day; but the result, as so often in these encounters, was indecisive. There was nothing remarkable about James's tactics, but he himself fought with the greatest gallantry, as he had done in the previous war; he shifted his flag twice as his flagships were disabled.

There were no more major engagements in 1672, and in the following year the Duke of York was no longer in command. This time his departure from the scene of action had nothing to do with the question of his risking his life at sea.

King Charles was desperately in need of money to carry on the war, and for this he perforce had recourse to Parliament. The House of Commons was ready to oblige, but only at a price. The House was now overwhelmingly antagonistic to the heir to the throne and his religion. Anne Duchess of York had died in 1671, and at her death it became known that she had been a Catholic for some years; Burnet wrote that 'the change of her religion made her friends reckon her death rather a blessing than a loss at that time to them all'.[10] There was no longer any doubt in any quarter that her husband had followed her into the Church of Rome.

The price that the Commons demanded for their financial support was the withdrawal of the hated Declaration of Indulgence. To these devout Christians it was plain that to allow papists to worship God as they chose in the privacy of their own homes was to strike at the roots of the Church of England, of the English Constitution, of civilization itself. That Protestant nonconformists were allowed the greater privilege of holding public worship in approved places was a further provocation, if a lesser one. Sir John Reresby, a firm supporter of the Stuarts, described the Declaration as 'the greatest blow that ever was given, since the King's restoration, to the Church of England'.[11]

Charles, as was his custom, bowed to the storm; the Declaration of Indulgence was withdrawn on 8 March 1673. But the Commons were not yet satisfied. They voted the necessary money, but followed up their advantage by allying the financial concession to a bill to introduce tests of religious orthodoxy which would oust Catholics from the King's counsels and force the Duke of York from office.

The Test Act, 'for preventing changes which may happen from popish recusants and quieting the minds of His Majesty's good subjects',[12] was passed on 29 March. Under its provisions any person holding public office in the Government or in the armed services was required to take the oaths of supremacy and allegiance, to receive the sacrament according to the Church of England in public on or before 1 August following, and to abjure the doctrine of transubstantiation. Failure to comply made the offender ineligible.

James refused to take the sacrament in the Anglican rite, and on 19 June laid down all his official appointments, including that of Lord High Admiral. He was not the only eminent victim of the Test Act. Lord Clifford, who had become a Catholic at some recent but unknown date, resigned his office of Lord Treasurer and retired to his Devon estates, where he died a few months later.

Prince Rupert succeeded the Duke of York in the command of the fleet, though without the title of Lord High Admiral. The war dragged on for another year, the most notable event being the rise to power in the Netherlands of the young Prince William, son of William II and Mary of Orange, now in his early twenties. Attacked by sea and on land, the United Provinces in their extremity turned once more to the House of Orange which had served them so well in the past. William was made Captain-General in command of the national defences; he was not, however, as yet restored to his father's office of Stadtholder.

His leadership was effective, and the Dutch held off the Anglo-French assault. The result was once again stalemate, and in February 1674 the war was ended by the Treaty of Westminster.

In England the policy initiated by the Secret Treaty of Dover was in ruins. And so was the rule, such as it was, of the Cabal. Without his ally Clifford, Arlington lost influence; he was unpopular in Parliament and in the country. Buckingham drifted from group to group, mercurial and ineffective as ever. Shaftesbury, who had been for a brief period Lord Chancellor, went into opposition. Lauderdale retained his grip on Scottish affairs, but with little power in London. The new chief minister was Sir Thomas Osborne, who took Clifford's place as Lord Treasurer.

The Duke of York now held no official position in the state. The fact remained that he was a royal prince and heir presumptive to the throne, and his most implacable enemies could not prevent him from giving advice to his brother or that brother from taking it. Charles and James were as close in counsel as ever.

The most important event in James's life in the early 1670s was his second marriage. His union with Anne Hyde had been a love match, and a consistently happy one; but he was both amorous and uxorious, and he wanted a replacement. Moreover a marriage was dynastically desirable. There was no male heir to the throne beyond himself. William of Orange, Charles I's only grandson, was junior in the line of succession to James's own daughters; in addition he was a foreign prince whose accession, if it ever came about, might cause international complications.

More than one candidate was considered for the bridal bed. James himself fell in love with a young widow, Susan Lady Belasyse; but he had impulsively married a commoner before, and his brother was not going to allow another misalliance. 'The king sent for the duke, and told him, it was too much that he had played the fool once: that was not to be done a second time, and at such an age'.[13] So the Earl of Peterborough was sent off to the Continent to find a more suitable bride. Ultimately the choice fell on Mary the young daughter of the Duke of Modena. She was tall, dark and lovely, but could hardly seem the ideal partner for a roué of forty. As James's own biographer recorded,

. . . It was with no litle difficulty that the young Princess consented to it, she being then but fifteen years old, and so innocently bred, that till then she had never heard of such a place as England, nor of such a person as the Duke of York. Besides she at that time had a great inclination to be a Nun, in so much that the Dutchess her Mother was obliged to get the Pope to write to her, and perswade her to comply with her Mother's desires, as most conducing to the Service of God and the publick good.[14]

Mary of Modena, by Wissing

The young Princess arrived in England on 21 November 1673. James met her at Dover, and 'they were married and bedded the same night'.[15]

James was fortunate in his matrimonial alliances. In the first days of marriage Mary was reported to have cried every time she saw her husband; but in the years that followed she became as devoted and as loyal to him as Anne had been. In the tribulations of his later life she was his unfailing supporter and his constant comfort.

This marriage to a papist princess of course doubled the fury of the anti-York brigade. It was now that Lord Shaftesbury emerged as the leader of the opposition to the Stuarts and their court. Anthony Ashley Cooper, Earl of Shaftesbury, was one of the ablest politicians, and at the same time most slippery, who existed in that or any other age. He had a genius for intrigue and for manipulating men, and he was totally without scruple. He had served Charles I, Oliver Cromwell, and Charles II, and he was always ready to change sides when it suited him. The Poet Laureate John Dryden, in his devastating satire *Absalom and Achitophel*, summed him up in the character of Achitophel:

> For close Designs and crooked Counsels fit,
> Sagacious, Bold, and Turbulent of wit,
> Restless, unfixt in Principles and Place,
> In Pow'r unpleased, impatient of Disgrace; . . .
> In Friendship false, implacable in Hate,
> Resolv'd to Ruine or to Rule the State.

Whether or not Shaftesbury was resolved to ruin the state, he was certainly determined to ruin the Duke of York. And if he hated the Duke and all he stood for, he certainly disliked the Duke's brother. For the next eight years the internal politics of the reign of Charles II took on the character of a prolonged duel of wits between the King and his former Lord Chancellor.

Diplomatically and politically, the period following the Third Dutch War was distinguished by intrigue and manoeuvre rather than any decisive action. King Charles still hoped for a close association with Louis XIV, but his chief adviser Sir Thomas Osborne, soon created Earl of Danby, was anti-French, and there was Shaftesbury, with strong Parliamentary support, in the background. Future trends were not easy to discern.

The King, however, continued to enjoy himself. He was a man who found it easy to put aside public cares, and his private life was not much altered. He played tennis regularly, and went racing at Newmarket. He frequented the theatre, and he ate and drank heartily though with discrimination. And his indulgence in his favourite occupation increased rather than diminished.

Charles had always had a good supply of mistresses, but in the 1670s his love affairs came more into the public eye. Lady Castlemaine, who had so dominated the scene in the early days of the Restoration, was no longer a power to be reckoned with, though that forceful lady never quite faded out of sight. But three principal successors to her position, all colourful in their different ways, now competed for places in the royal bed.

The first of the three was the one who has most caught the imagination of posterity. It was King Charles's fondness for the theatre that brought him into contact with Nell Gwyn, already well known for her talent as a comic actress, for wit and good nature in private life, and for looseness of morals. By the end of the 1670s she was well established as a royal mistress, and she never lost her hold on her lover's heart. Nell was an illiterate, cheerful, irrepressible cockney who made the King and most other people laugh with her happy and usually bawdy humour; and she was exceptional in that she never sought honours, or influence in high quarters and in affairs of state, though she was not averse from gifts of hard cash.

A different type was Louise de Kéroualle, the Breton girl whom Minette had brought to England as a maid of honour in 1670 but had refused to leave behind with her brother. Minette's death left Louise without employment, and Louis XIV, knowing that his brother of England had been attracted to her, thought what an excellent agent she might be for the French interest in England. So he arranged for her to be given a place among Queen Catherine's attendants, and that patient lady, who had long ceased to worry about rivals in her husband's affections, raised no objection. From there the next step was easy. By 1671 she was installed in Whitehall as *maîtresse en titre*, and soon afterwards was created Duchess of Portsmouth.

Louise was baby-faced and doll-like (Charles called her

'Fubs'), but she had a shrewd brain. She was hated in England as 'the French whore', and Nell Gwyn, while neither jealous nor malicious, heaped good-humoured ridicule on her; but she maintained her position to the end and had more influence over the King than any of his other mistresses. Charles was genuinely devoted to her.

In 1675, however, Louise had a violent shock to her ambitions. A worthy rival suddenly swept into England.

This was none other than that Hortense Mancini, Cardinal Mazarin's niece, who had been proposed as a bride for the King in days both before and after the Restoration. Since then she had had a bizarre and spectacular career. Married to the eccentric Charles de la Porte de la Meilleraye, created Duc Mazarin (without the usual 'de') in honour of his wife's uncle, she left him when he developed religious mania. Thereafter she flitted about Europe picking up and discarding lovers of both sexes and various classes of society; they included the Duke of Savoy and a page named Couberville, by whom she had a child. She was related to the new Duchess of York, and ostensibly to visit her she appeared in London (in man's clothes) in January 1675.

The black-haired Hortense was one of the loveliest women of her time, and her dashing personality and complete contempt for convention of any sort brought the English courtiers, with King Charles at their head, to her feet. She was soon reckoned among the royal mistresses, and Nell Gwyn went into mourning for her rival Louise's prospects. But though the affair went on for some years it did not prove the threat to the Duchess of Portsmouth's supremacy that was envisaged. The Duchesse Mazarin was too volatile and too indifferent to her own interests to aspire to feminine dominion. The more dedicated Louise soon found that she had no need to worry.

In 1677 the court scene was enlivened by a royal marriage. The Duke of York's daughters, Mary and Anne, had been brought up as Protestants, and largely under the influence of Danby a betrothal was negotiated between Mary, now fifteen, and her cousin William III of Orange. James would have preferred a Catholic alliance, and at first demurred to the proposal. But the King was adamant. 'God's fish,' he said, 'he must consent.'[16] And eventually James did.

William came over to England, and the wedding took place in Whitehall, where Mary's aunt and namesake had married the other William thirty-five years before. The Princess was a reluctant bride, and the King was not much taken with his solemn, earnest nephew. But he did his best to infuse some jollity into the proceedings. He urged on the young man to drink, and putting the bridal pair to bed, a ceremony he always enjoyed, he drew the curtains with the words: 'Now, nephew, to your work; hey! St George for England!'[17]

But such high jinks as these, shining through the uneasy gloom of the mid-1670s, were thrown into eclipse in the following year. In the summer of 1678 the bombshell fell; and it was a bombshell of the first magnitude.

Walking in St James's Park on 13 August, the very approachable King Charles was approached by a nondescript individual, Christopher Kirkby, who warned him of a plot against his life. He shrugged the suggestion aside, but in the ensuing weeks the story spread until it engulfed the country. Its principal authors were a crackbrained clergyman named Israel Tonge and a more sinister figure, Titus Oates, an unprepossessing mountebank with a huge face and a braying voice, who had once been a Jesuit novice but had been dismissed for homosexuality. He would seem in the light of history to have been a man by whom no sane person could have been expected to be taken in; but he plainly had a mesmeric gift for impressing the impressionable.

Tonge and Oates proclaimed their sensational information to the Privy Council. Its essence has been summarized by Sir Arthur Bryant:

. . . Gradually the wondrous tale unfolded: the Pope, the French King, the General of the Jesuits, the Provincials in England, Spain and Ireland, the Archbishops of Dublin and Tuam, and the Rectors of the Jesuit Colleges, linked together in a mighty plot to kill the King, set up the Duke of York, plunge Ireland in blood, impose Catholicism by the sword, and destroy English commerce; the four Irish ruffians who were to do the bloody work at Windsor, the Lancashire incendiaries to fire London, and the three thousand cutthroats to massacre the sleeping citizens; the poisoners in attendance, who included Wakeman, the Queen's physician, and Coleman, the Duchess of York's secretary.[18]

The ramifications of the 'Popish Plot' are beyond the scope of the present narrative. The whole extraordinary episode has been the subject of major works and is recounted at length in every book dealing with the reign of Charles II. Little need be said beyond the unquestionable facts that it represented a conspiracy to deprive the Duke of York of his right to the succession (and of his life if possible); that it was extended to embrace a personal attack on the Queen; and that it led to an outbreak of mass hysteria that has seldom been equalled, bringing in its wake an orgy of murder, false witness, and the shedding of innocent blood.

No historian now believes in the reality of any such plot, and Titus Oates has been described as virtually the only character in English history whom nobody has tried to whitewash. Whether the story originated in the fertile brain of Shaftesbury cannot be determined; but certainly he exploited the situation to the full, making all the capital possible out of the wave of unreasoning anti-Catholic fury that for a time made England a madhouse.

One person who was not deluded was King Charles, who never for a moment believed in the fantastic 'revelations' of Tonge and Oates. Nevertheless his conduct was not to his credit. Unable to control events, he followed his custom of giving them their head and allowing them to burn themselves out. It was perhaps the only policy which he could follow to preserve his throne, but it led him into providing Oates with a pension and lodging him in Whitehall, and into signing the death warrants of men—Jesuit priests and others—whom he knew to be innocent.

The terror lasted for a full two years, continuing to draw victims to the scaffold. And its repercussions affected the history of England for a decade at least; it could be argued that the whole story of the end of the Stuart dynasty might have been vastly different but for the events of 1678.

Further plots followed. There was the Meal Tub Plot of 1679 (incriminating papers were said to be hidden in a meal tub) and the Rye House Plot of 1683 to assassinate the King and the Duke of York. The latter at least had far more reality than the 'Popish Plot'. But the immediate and most important development was the drawn-out episode known as the Exclusion Crisis.

The monarchy, shaken as it was by the extraordinary events of 1678, had not been outwardly affected. King Charles had been firm in his support of his wife and his brother. But the Popish Plot had provided a formidable foundation on which Shaftesbury could work in his overmastering design, that of preventing the Duke of York's succeeding to the throne of England. He was in a powerful position. Besides his own standing in the House of Lords he had a large following in the Commons, where the fear of popery threw the members into the hands of the Protestant champion. He also held wide authority in the City of London, the centre of the nation's wealth; there he presided over the Green Ribbon Club, headquarters of the opposition party, now becoming known as the Whig Party. It was actually in the City that Shaftesbury could depend on his most powerful support.

On one point he and his minions were not united. If James could be excluded from the succession, who would take his place? The next heir was Princess Mary, his elder daughter; and some of the party were in favour of her and her husband. But there was no unanimity on the advisability of giving power to a Dutch ruler who might be as dictatorial a ruler as the Stuart heir was expected to be.

There was, however, another candidate, King Charles's eldest illegitimate son. James Duke of Monmouth was a lightweight who had grown too big for his boots. He was now a man of thirty, foolish and ambitious, devoid of political capacity but with a superficial talent for intrigue. He was handsome and he had proved himself a good soldier, and he was greatly loved by his indulgent father.

Monmouth was Shaftesbury's favourite for the succession, for obvious reasons. William of Orange was intelligent and strong-willed, and once on the throne would follow his own course. The stupid, vainglorious Monmouth, on the other hand, would be easy for an adroit politician to control. Shaftesbury could look forward to at least a period of supreme power during which he could shape his country's destiny.

His first move was to set up the young man as the legitimate heir to the monarchy. Reports were circulated that the King had been legally married to Monmouth's mother, Lucy Walter, and rumours were sedulously fostered of the existence of a mysterious 'black box' which would be found to contain the marriage certificate.

Shaftesbury next turned his attention to getting rid of the King's chief minister. Danby was a staunch Protestant and conspicuously anti-French, and thus far was in accord with Shaftesbury's line of thought; but he was also a loyal supporter of the King and the court, and so by implication of the Duke of York. The arch-intriguer wanted him out of the way.

Chance played into his hands. Ralph Montagu had lost his post of Ambassador in Paris through Danby's agency, and in revenge he threatened to reveal the contents of some secret letters in which reference was made to French subsidies to the English government, a legacy of the Treaty of Dover. The affair was blown up, and Shaftesbury arranged for impeachment proceedings to be started against Danby.

To meet the threatening situation the King took two important decisions. The first was to dissolve Parliament. The Cavalier Parliament had sat since 1661; its eighteen years of life were exceeded only by the 'Long Parliament', which in its twenty suffered so many changes and vicissitudes that in 1660 it was hardly recognizable as the body which had met in the crisis of 1640. The existence of Charles II's great parliament was continuous, but by the beginning of 1679 it was certainly not 'Cavalier'. Opposition to the court had been building up for years, and now was intense.

Its successor met in January. Shaftesbury had had no difficulty in manipulating the elections, and the new body was predictably as Whiggish and anti-court as its predecessor. Charles now took his second step. This amounted to no less than sending his unpopular brother into exile, with orders to stay abroad until the position was clarified. On 28 February 1679, the King wrote to James:

> My dear Brother. I have already fully told you the reasons which oblige me to send you from me for some time beyond the sea.
>
> As I am truly sorry for the cause of our separation, you may

also assure yourself that I shall never wish your absence to continue longer than is absolutely necessary for your good and my service. I find it, however, proper to let you know under my hand that I expect you will satisfy me in this; and that I wish it may be as soon as your conveniency will permit. You may easily believe that it is not without a great deal of pain I write you this, being more touched with the constant friendship you have had for me than with anything else in the world; and I also hope that you will do me the justice to believe for certain that neither absence, nor anything will hinder me from being truly and with affection yours.[19]

At the same time King Charles issued a declaration denying that he had ever been married to the Duke of Monmouth's mother or to any woman other than Queen Catherine.

On 3 March, therefore, James with his wife Mary reluctantly departed for the Continent. The official purpose of his journey was to visit his elder daughter and her husband, and so he first went to The Hague. But after a brief stay there he moved to Brussels, where he settled down to await events.

The new Parliament carried on where the old one had been interrupted. The impeachment of Danby proceeded, and though Charles tried to save him the minister, fearful that resistance would imperil his life, preferred to resign. Lords and Commons differed on what should be done with him, and finally he was committed to the Tower.

The King now had no chief minister. Bowing in his fashion to opposition, he made Shaftesbury Lord President of the Council, and brought into the administration a group of comparatively inexperienced and comparatively uncommitted politicians of whom the most competent was George Savile, Earl of Halifax. Lord Halifax was one of the most brilliant men of the age, with a wit and a brain which rivalled those of his sovereign. The trouble with him in politics was that nobody ever quite knew where he stood. His principal associates were Arthur Capel, Earl of Essex, and Robert Spencer, Earl of Sunderland; these three became known as the Triumvirate.

Charles saw to it, however, that neither Shaftesbury nor Halifax nor anybody else had any real authority. The monarchy was now in danger, and he knew it; he met the menace by keeping power in his own hands, playing off his ministers and his opponents against each other in the old familiar way.

The Commons proceeded on their self-appointed task. In April a bill was introduced for disabling the Duke of York as a papist from succeeding to the throne, and this first exclusion bill was given its second reading on 21 May. Charles made his position clear. He told the House that he was ready to accept any law that might safeguard the Protestant religion, provided there was no interference with 'the Descent of the Crown in the right line';[20] with this he would have no tampering. Here he was adamant, and this remained his attitude to the end.

The Commons were unimpressed by the King's unequivocal statement of policy, and made it clear that they intended to prevent his brother from coming to the throne. Thereupon he prorogued, and on 10 July dissolved, his short-lived Parliament. The bill had failed to reach the House of Lords.

The King's health was not what it had been, though he continued to be an active man. In August, after a hard game of tennis, he caught a severe chill, and for a time his life was in danger. The Duke of York was hurriedly sent for, but Charles recovered and James went back to Brussels. Not for long, however; with Shaftesbury and Monmouth sedulously pushing the young duke's claim to the throne, Charles felt that his brother must be closer at hand if the worst should befall. James was brought home and sent to take charge of the administration in Scotland.

Monmouth was also exiled. When he went too far in his efforts to stir up the London mobs in demonstrations against his uncle, he was told to leave London. He went off to The Hague, there to seek the support of the Prince of Orange. William and the young James were rivals in the matter of the succession, but they were at one in their design to have the Duke of York excluded. The wily William, ostensibly on the friendliest of terms with his father-in-law, was happy to make use of the younger and stupider claimant for the moment. He himself could afford to bide his time.

So the plotting continued. Charles for his part, hard up as he was for money to carry on the government, explored the prospects of renewed aid from France. But Louis XIV, seeing how precarious was the position of the British monarchy, was not now prepared to help unless the King promised to rule without Parliament. Charles might have been well advised to agree, but he felt that he could not cut himself off from all possibility of further supplies of cash.

Yet another parliament was therefore elected, designed to meet in November. It proved to be of the same complexion as its predecessors, and in October King Charles made it known that he intended to prorogue it at least till January 1680. Shaftesbury reacted with fury. He asserted the legitimacy of the Duke of Monmouth, and threatened not only to force the issue of exclusion of the Duke of York but to prosecute the Queen and the Duchess of Portsmouth. The only connection between these three was the fact that they were all Catholics.

Shaftesbury had in his turn gone too far, and was dismissed from the Presidency of the Council. His reply was to stage a massive demonstration in the City of London against popery. It was organized by the Green Ribbon Club, and took place on 17 November, the anniversary of the accession of Queen Elizabeth I.

Throughout 1680 the crisis continued to move towards its climax. Monmouth returned without permission; his father was furious, but he was always indulgent to his wayward son. The young man was ordered away from Whitehall, but was left at liberty and continued his nefarious activities. Shaftesbury went on working for exclusion, and he and his minions agitated incessantly for a meeting of Parliament. King Charles, however, managed to keep going on his revenues and by a series of prorogations prevented that body from meeting until almost the end of the year.

He maintained his wonted calm throughout these dangerous months when his crown was in the balance. It seems likely that he, if hardly anybody else, discerned the beginnings of a change in feeling in the nation at large which in fact marked the turn of the tide. The hysterical fury of the Popish Plot was burning itself out, and the relentless anti-monarchism of the Shaftesbury party was defeating its own object. Time might yet be on the King's side.

He reshuffled his ministry, bringing in his 'second triumvirate' of Sunderland, Sidney Godolphin and Clarendon's younger son Laurence Hyde. He brought his brother back from

Scotland, a move which aroused little opposition. And he himself spent most of the summer at Windsor and Newmarket, giving faction its head in London. 'Give them but rope enough,' he said of the exclusionists, 'and they will hang themselves.'[21]

In May, at Windsor Castle, he was again taken ill, suffering from ague and fits. Lord Bruce, son of the Earl of Ailesbury, a new and devoted attendant, described the malady as apoplexy. The King soon recovered, but it was now realized that sudden death was an ever-present possibility. The exclusionists had no time to lose.

The Whigs were themselves divided. Many followed Shaftesbury in demanding total exclusion of the Duke of York from the succession; but others maintained that it would be enough, in the event of his inheriting the throne, to place limitations on his power and thus safeguard the Protestant supremacy. This line of thought, which had already been implicitly sanctioned by the King, was now extending its influence.

The exclusionists, however, were in the majority, and when Parliament at last met, at the end of October 1680, the second exclusion bill was quickly passed, few members daring to oppose it. Shaftesbury laid his plans for a public demonstration as soon as it should become law, with a mob marching on Whitehall in whipped-up frenzy. King Charles could not face the risk of revolution should he dissolve Parliament again, and the bill was taken to the Lords. The atmosphere was electric.

It was cooled in an unexpected manner. Shaftesbury spoke in the Lords for exclusion, never doubting that he would win the day. But he was opposed by the peers' most eloquent speaker, the Earl of Halifax, hitherto regarded as a supporter of exclusion. Halifax, 'the Trimmer', now threw all his powers of debate into the scale in support of the law and constitution of England and in defence of the rights of the heir to the throne. He was in favour of the limitation of powers if a Catholic should become king, and even advocated the banishment of James from the kingdom during the lifetime of his brother; but the correct hereditary succession must, in his view, be maintained. He spoke sixteen times in the long and furious debate, maintaining reason and moderation in the face of the frenzy of the exclusionists, and when at last the House rose, shortly before midnight, the bill was thrown out by thirty-three votes.

Revolution had been averted. Shaftesbury tried to keep up

the pressure, now advocating the annulment of the King's marriage and his alliance with a bride who might give him a Protestant heir apparent. But the heat had gone out of the opposition. Charles now felt strong enough to dispense with his unruly advisers. On 10 January 1681, he prorogued Parliament, and a week later announced its dissolution.

He had not yet despaired of finding a House of Commons that would see reason. Immediately on dissolution he issued a proclamation for a new Parliament. But he would not allow it to meet at Westminster, where Shaftesbury could inflame the mob and rely on his support in the City of London. The new body was appointed to meet at Oxford on 21 March.

What followed was one of the most dramatic episodes of the reign. The battle was not yet won by either side, and the threat of a civil war was a real one. There was furious electioneering, but inevitably the new parliament was as exclusionist as its predecessors. In the words of Lord Bruce, who was himself M.P. for Marlborough, it 'was filled with more fiery members and their adherents than were in that dissolved'.[22] Shaftesbury and his followers were convinced that the King would now be compelled to submit to their demands; but they were ready for all eventualities. Those who could took armed retainers to Oxford, and Bruce, riding out of the town, 'on the bridge met the Duke of Monmouth, with thousands after him, on horseback and on foot'.[23] The King himself lined the road from Windsor to Oxford with soldiers, while troops were quartered in the villages.

Charles maintained his customary calm. He set out from Windsor on 12 March, and on arrival in Oxford took up residence at Christ Church. James was back in Scotland, but with the King were the Queen, Nell Gwyn and the Duchess of Portsmouth. Pending the opening of Parliament the court amused itself with dances and plays.

The session began as arranged on 21 March. Charles opened it with a conciliatory speech, alluding directly to the subject in everybody's mind. 'To remove all reasonable fears', he said, 'that may arise from the possibility of a Popish successor's coming to the Crown; if means can be found that in such a case the administration of the government may remain in Protestant hands, I shall be ready to hearken to any such expedient, by which the religion might be preserved, and the monarchy not destroyed.'[24] In the next few days he elaborated on his concession, even to the extent of proposing a regency under Mary and William of Orange.

The Commons would have none of it. Exclusion was the objective, and nothing less would do. On Saturday, 26 March, the third exclusion bill was given its first reading.

There can be little doubt that Charles knew this would happen. He had laid his plans, and was following his own precept of giving his opponents rope with which to hang themselves. What the Whigs did not know was that he had concluded a new secret agreement with the King of France. Louis was now satisfied that Charles was in control of the situation, and agreed to pay him a subsidy which would enable him to dispense with Parliament for the next three years.

He accepted the introduction of the exclusion bill with serenity, suggesting amiably that as the Commons' quarters in Convocation House were not too comfortable they might meet on Monday in the Sheldonian Theatre. The next day, Sunday, he assembled the Privy Council at Merton College and told them his plans. He then quietly sent the royal coaches out of Oxford on to the road to Windsor.

The Lords were meeting in Christ Church Hall, and on Monday, 28 March, King Charles walked over from his quarters. He was wearing his ordinary clothes, and the Whigs were in no doubt that he had come to declare his capitulation. He had, however, given orders for his crown and royal robes to be sent over, hidden in a sedan chair. Arrived at the chamber, he sent to the Sheldonian for the Commons, and when they arrived they found their sovereign arrayed in all his regalia, as the constitution demanded for a dissolution.

He made the briefest possible announcement:

My Lords and Gentlemen: That all the world may see to what a point we are come, that we are not like to have a good end, when the divisions at the beginning are such: therefore, my Lord Chancellor, do as I have commanded you.[25]

Lord Bruce was present among his fellow members. Later, when he was Earl of Ailesbury, he described the scene:

> The King ordered my Lord Chancellor Finch to do his duty; on which he declared, in the usual manner, it was the King's pleasure that this Parliament should be dissolved. I was witness of the dreadful faces of the members, and the loud sighs. I went up the House to attend the King at the putting off his robes, and with a most pleasing and cheerful countenance he touched me on the shoulder with this expression, 'I am now a better man than you were a quarter of an hour since; you had better have one king than five hundred;' and bid us all go to our own houses and there stay until further orders.[26]

Shaftesbury and his friends were caught hopelessly on the wrong foot. Before they could lay new plans or organize any sort of demonstration the King was on his way to Windsor.

He had judged the moment to perfection. The nation was tired of Shaftesbury and his plots, and there was a tremendous reaction in favour of the monarchy.

> This unexpected vigor in the King struck them like thunder with confusion and amazement, and gain'd his Majesty exceeding great reputation, his friends now began to take courage again, and those turbulent and fiery men were left in the last degree of rage and despair, not only vext at their disappointment, but asham'd after so much undutifull behaveour to be thus exposed and baffled; for they saw there was no more hopes of a Parliament in hast, without which, all their well laid projects were like to vanish into smoke.[27]

The King's first act on reaching Windsor was to send an express to Scotland to tell his brother the good news. Nothing further was heard of exclusion, and though King Charles decided that for the moment it would be better for James to stay in Scotland he returned to Whitehall in March 1682.

Mopping-up operations proceeded apace. Shaftesbury soon found himself in the Tower, charged with high treason. He was acquitted by a London jury, but after a final attempt to stir up the mob, an attempt which failed hopelessly, he fled the country, like Clarendon before him, and like Clarendon died in exile.

Monmouth made abject submission to his father, and was even graciously received by the Duke of York; but he continued to make trouble, and in the aftermath of the Rye House Plot, in which he was clearly implicated, he was finally banished to the Continent.

King Charles was at last able to relax and to indulge himself to his heart's content. He spent much of his time at Newmarket, and both there and at Westminster he was able to enjoy his sport and his pleasures; his principal mistresses were faithful to him. He was a tired man, and he probably knew that his time was short. James was constantly at his side, and it seemed to many that it was he who was now the real ruler of the country.

At the same time the King had no illusions about his brother's intractable character or about what was likely to happen after his own death. William of Orange paid another visit to England in the summer of 1681, and according to Burnet his uncle confided his fears to him.

. . . The king assured him, that he would keep things quiet, and not give way to the duke's eagerness, as long as he lived: and added, he was confident, whenever the duke should come to reign, he would be so restless and violent, that he could not hold it four years to an end.[28]

To Sir Richard Bulstrode, English Resident in Brussels, he said much the same, and in even more explicit terms. According to Sir Richard,

. . . he said, that during his exile abroad he had seen many countries, of which none pleased him so much as that of the Flemings, which were the most honest and true-hearted race of people that he had met with, and then added, *But I am weary of travelling, I am resolved to go abroad no more: but when I am dead and gone, I know not what my brother will do. I am much afraid, that when he comes to the crown, he will be obliged to travel again. And yet I will take care to leave my kingdoms to him in peace, wishing he may long keep them so. But this hath all of my fears, little of my hopes, and less of*

my reason; and I am much afraid, that when my brother comes to the
crown, he will be obliged again to leave his native soil.[29]

The winter of 1683-4 was particularly severe, and the King's
health was further weakened. But he continued to enjoy himself.
As late as 1 February 1685, the austere John Evelyn was present
at Whitehall and observed with pious horror 'the unexpressable
luxury, & prophanesse, gaming, & all dissolution, and as it were
total forgettfullnesse of God (it being Sunday evening) . . .; the
King, sitting & toying with his Concubines Portsmouth,
Cleveland, & Mazarine, etc.: A french boy singing love songs, in
that glorious Gallery'.[30]

Louise, Barbara and Hortense all together in Whitehall,
listening to French love songs—it is a delightful picture, even if
Evelyn did not think so. Doubtless Queen Catherine, quite
reconciled now to the constant presence of her rivals, was not far
away. Only Nell Gwyn seems to have been absent. But Nelly
was never really at home in the Whitehall circle.

This, however, was the end. That very night the King suffered
another apoplectic fit, and before the next day was out it was
clear that he was dying.

The death-bed of Charles II was wholly in character. He was
in great pain for the four days that followed his seizure, but his
good humour never left him. He apologized for taking so long to
die; his speech was badly affected, but when he could speak he
was gracious to the courtiers who thronged the bedchamber and
affectionate to his intimates. To Bruce, who was in constant
attendance, he said: 'I see you love me dying as well as living.'[31]
The Queen, unable after a time to bear the sight of his suffering,
sent a message asking his pardon if she had ever offended him.
When he received it his reply was: 'Alas! poor woman! she beg
my pardon! I beg hers with all my heart.'[32]

The Duke of York was with him to the end. At the first onset of
illness Bruce ran to fetch him, and the Duke came so hurriedly
that he arrived wearing one shoe and one slipper. He was deeply
affected by the scene, of which he now took charge. There was
one urgent duty to be done.

Charles had never fulfilled the clause in the Secret Treaty of
Dover which bound him to make a public declaration of his
Catholicism. There was no question of his doing so now, but he

could still make a private submission to the Church of Rome. His brother knelt down by his bed and asked him in a whisper if he would like him to send for a priest—'to which the King immediately replyd, For God's sake Brother doe, and pleas to loos no time; but then reflecting on the consequence, added, But will you not expose yourself too much by doing it?'[33]

James brushed aside the question of the danger to himself, and a priest who by good fortune was in the palace was brought secretly to the sick-room. The Duke of York cleared the chamber and admitted him to the bedside.

By a remarkable chance the priest was none other than Father John Huddleston, of the Order of St Benedict, who more than thirty years before had befriended Charles when he was on the run after the Worcester defeat. The King had since given him his protection, and now when he saw him he said: 'You that saved my body is now come to save my soul.'[34] Huddleston received his sovereign into the Catholic Church and gave him the Last Sacraments. He was then smuggled out again, and the court was readmitted.

There remained only the King's final farewell to his brother and successor.

He gathered all his strength to speak his last words to the duke, to which every one hearkened with great attention. He expressed his kindness to him, and that he now delivered all over to him with great joy. He recommended lady Portsmouth over and over again to him. He said, he had always loved her, and he loved her now to the last; and besought the duke, in as melting words as he could fetch out, to be very kind to her and to her son. He recommended his other children to him, and concluded, Let not poor Nelly starve; that was Mrs Gwyn.[35]

On Friday, 6 February 1685, in the words of the faithful Bruce, 'my good and gracious king and master, and the best that ever reigned over us, died in peace and glory, and the Lord God have mercy on his soul.'[36]

The last survivor of Charles I's nine children was now King James II.

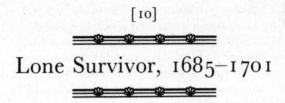

Lone Survivor, 1685–1701

With the death of Charles II the story of the relationship of the Stuart brothers and sisters towards each other comes to an end. The disastrous reign of the last of the family, and its melancholy aftermath, are beyond the limits of this study. A brief summary and a few comments will not be out of place.

King James II began well. He had recovered his popularity; he was a dignified figure, he had a record of efficiency and of gallantry on sea and land, and the seriousness of his disposition appealed to the more solemn elements of the nation after the levity and dissipations of his brother, which, greatly as he was loved, had caused grave shakings of heads in some influential quarters. In the matter in which the deepest misgivings were felt, moreover, James promised well. He lost no time in assuring his subjects that he intended to maintain and defend the Church of England as by law established.

When in the summer of 1685 the Duke of Monmouth invaded England to wrest the throne from his uncle, he got little support. James's army had no difficulty in defeating him, and the victory was generally approved though James lost some of his popularity through the severity which followed suppression of the rebellion. It was all right to cut off the futile young duke's head, but too many of his misguided followers were sent to follow him into the next world.

Thereafter King James committed blunder after blunder. He was totally without political subtlety, and compromise was foreign to his nature. He had one overriding aim—the attainment of religious toleration. And the impetuousness with which he pursued his goal, charging blindly against obstacles instead of trying to circumvent them, brought about his downfall.

The Test Act was still in force, making it illegal for anybody

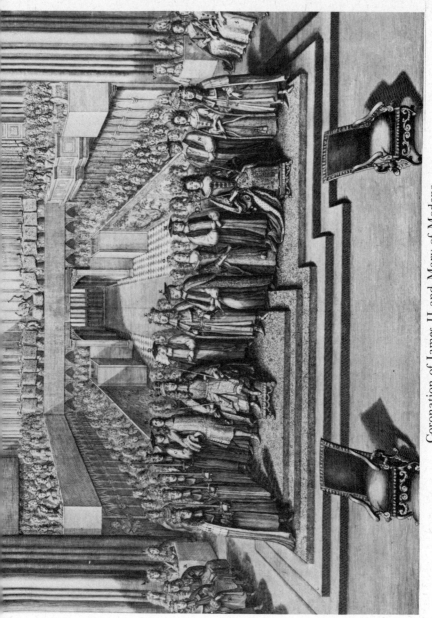

Coronation of James II and Mary of Modena

other than a practising Anglican to hold public office; and no parliament was likely to be persuaded to repeal it. James's way of circumventing it was to dispense individuals from its provisions. The royal right of dispensation had been a bone of contention in the preceding reign, and King Charles's opponents had had the better of the argument. James now multiplied individual dispensations to an extent that alarmed the opposition, who now saw non-Anglicans—mostly the King's co-religionists—appointed to high positions in defiance of the law of the land.

King Charles had issued Declarations of Indulgence. They were mild enough, simply allowing dissenters from the national creed a discreet privilege of private worship; but they were enough to produce furious and successful opposition. James now went much further. In his Declaration of Indulgence of 1687 he proclaimed the right of all his subjects to worship God after their own way and manner, in public or in private, only on the condition 'that they take special care that nothing be preached or taught amongst them which may any ways tend to alienate the hearts of our people from us or our government; and that their meetings and assemblies be peaceably, openly and publicly held, and all persons freely admitted to them; and that they do signify and make known to some one or more of the next justices of the peace what place or places they set apart for those uses'.[1]

To modern ideas such a decree would seem unexceptionable. To the seventeenth-century mind it was revolutionary and subversive to the ultimate degree. The Anglican establishment saw itself threatened to the core of its being, and the Whig lords began to turn their eyes towards The Hague in the hope of salvation.

There was further provocation in the following year. James re-issued the Declaration of Indulgence and ordered it to be read in churches. The famous 'Seven Bishops', led by Archbishop William Sancroft of Canterbury, refused to comply, and King James had the bad judgement to send them to the Tower. Martyrs had been created.

Then, on 10 June 1688, the Queen gave birth to a son. Other children had been born to James and Mary of Modena, but all had died in infancy; the Protestant Mary of Orange had remained the heir to the throne. Now there loomed the prospect of a papist dynasty.

It was the last straw. The leading Whigs sent an invitation to William of Orange, who had been in readiness for some months. In November there was another invasion of England, and this time the King's supporters deserted him in droves.

In this supreme crisis of his life King James lost his head. First, before invasion was an accomplished fact but too late to achieve any useful result, he tried to appease his enemies; reversing his policies, dismissing Catholic officials, and offering to call a new parliament. Then, when William of Orange had landed at Torbay, he showed himself unable to make up his mind how to confront him. He delayed his advance towards the west country, made a half-hearted move to Salisbury, and then turned back. In the meantime his most trusted military adviser, Lord Churchill, the future Duke of Marlborough, defected to William. The cruellest blow of all came when his younger daughter Anne, now married to Prince George of Denmark but at this time in England, left him to join her brother-in-law.

Broken by these desertions, James sank into desperation. He tried to flee the country in disguise, having sent his wife and baby son ahead of him; but he was recognized and sent back to London in circumstances of the deepest humiliation. He fled again and this time reached France, sailing with the connivance of his nephew who was only too glad to see the last of him. In the new year William and Mary were declared joint sovereigns of the British dominions.

There followed King James's futile attempt to recover his throne through a campaign in Ireland. In subsequent years there were other bids for restoration, but none came to anything. James lived for most of the rest of his life in the palace of Saint-Germain, which Louis XIV generously put at his disposal.

His latter days were warmed by the loving care of his wife and the affection of his children. James Prince of Wales, whose birth had precipitated the usurpation of William III, grew up to be a dutiful son; but the King's chief joy in his old age lay in the company of his youngest child, Louise, born in France, whom he named his *Consolatrix*, the consolation of his exile.

He grew more deeply religious as the years went by; prayer and pious exercises occupied the greater part of his time. But his faith never led him to that calm and peace of mind that religion can bring. He became more and more gloomy, obsessed with the sense of failure, tortured by the contemplation of his sins which he was convinced had brought about his misfortunes.

That King James was the victim of religious intolerance there can be no reasonable doubt. It is equally certain that the disaster that overtook him was primarily caused by his own stupidity and incompetence. Had he possessed a tithe of the finesse habitually shown by his elder brother he could have kept his throne, and the subsequent history of his country would have been different.

But a mystery remains about James II. How did he come to fail so ignominiously when the débâcle came? He had always seemed to be the firmest and strongest in character of his family. He had proved his worth in administration, his gallantry in action. Throughout his life he had been constant and consistent, facing opposition with unwavering courage. Yet when the crash came all his decisiveness left him. Disconcerted by the desertion of his friends, and deeply distressed by the treachery of both his daughters, he wavered and dithered, and even his physical bravery was suspect. All the fine qualities that had distinguished him seemed suddenly reversed.

Some historians have attributed his failure to ill-health. At the moment when he was opposing Prince William in arms he was overcome by violent nose-bleeding. The complaint sounds trivial, but in his case it appears to have amounted to a haemorrhage. He was incapacitated for hours at a time.

Yet this is hardly a sufficient explanation. The trouble was temporary, and James remained in general a strong and healthy man. Some other cause must be sought.

No suggestion can be more than conjecture. But it may be that not enough consideration has been given to family circumstances. James may or may not have been the strongest of the Stuarts, but he was certainly the least intelligent. And it may be that, like his father, he was unable to stand without leaning on some personality more powerful than his own. The flexible Charles II, often bowing to the storm, had seemed the weaker character of the two; but what seemed weakness could equally be construed as shrewdness. James may have depended more than he knew on the worldly wisdom of his brother. Without it he lost his head and could not make up his own mind.

His kindest epitaph was written by Thomas Bruce, Earl of Ailesbury, who served him as loyally as he had served his predecessor:

> . . . I do affirm he was the most honest and sincere man I ever knew, a great and good Englishman, and a high protector of trade, and had nothing so much at heart as the strength and glory of the Fleet and Navy; and it was never in so high a pitcch, nor in so great lustre, as during the time of his administration, not only when Duke of York, but the same after his coming to the Crown, until he was obliged to retire out of the nation.
>
> In fine, he wanted for nothing but the talent of his Royal Brother, who certainly was a great master of that art called king craft, and no one knew men better, and this good king less. In former days he had been very amorous, and more out of a natural temper than for the genteel part of making love, which he was much a stranger to. He was at last truly sensible of that error, and became a hearty penitent, which certainly was most agreeable to God.[2]

James II died on 5 September 1701. He was a month short of his sixty-eighth birthday.

The period from the birth of King Charles I to the death of the last of his children covered, almost exactly, the entire course of the seventeenth century.

References

1 The Father

1 *Memoirs of Robert Carey*, p. 68.
2 Ibid., p. 69.
3 *Vide* Ellis Waterhouse, *Painting in Britain, 1530–1790*, pp. 33–8.
4 *Vide* David Mathew, *James I*, pp. 230–4, and Ethel Carleton Williams, *Anne of Denmark*, pp. 124–32.
5 Waterhouse, op. cit., p. 35.
6 Mathew, op. cit., p. 292.
7 Apparently an allusion to a fancied resemblance to a picture of St Stephen. *Vide* J.P. Kenyon, *The Stuarts*, p. 50, and John Bowle, *Charles I*, p. 53.
8 Gilbert Burnet, *History of his Own Time*, vol. I, p. 34.
9 Edward Earl of Clarendon, *History of the Great Rebellion*, vol. I, p. 28.

2 Raising a Family

1 Thomas Birch, *Court and Times of Charles I*, vol. I, p. 30.
2 Ibid., p. 31.
3 Ibid.
4 Ibid., p. 32.
5 Ibid.
6 Ibid., vol. II, p. 294.
7 Sir Charles Petrie, *Letters of King Charles I*, p. 40.
8 Ibid., pp. 40–1.
9 Ibid., p. 45.
10 Birch, op. cit., vol. I, p. 120. *Vide* also Carola Oman, *Henrietta Maria*, pp. 45–9.
11 *Vide: Memoirs of Madame de Motteville*, vol. I, pp. 34–5.
12 Birch, op. cit., vol. I, p. 355.

13 Ibid., pp. 355–6. The letter is dated 'May 20, 1628', but this is obviously a mistake. There is no question but that the birth took place on 13 May 1629. *Vide: Calendar of State Papers Domestic, 1628–1629*, p. 548.

14 John Rushworth, *Historical Collections*, vol. II, p. 50.

15 John Dryden, *Astraea Redux*.

16 Oman, op. cit., p. 67.

17 Mary Anne Everett Green, *Lives of the Princesses of England*, vol. VI, p. 103.

18 C.V. Wedgwood, *The King's Peace*, p. 65.

19 *Vide* Wedgwood, op. cit., p. 67, and Bowle, op. cit., p. 123.

20 J.H. Plumb, *Royal Heritage*, p. 114.

21 Ellis Waterhouse, *Painting in Britain, 1530 to 1790*, p. 53.

22 Plumb, op. cit., p. 113.

23 Henry Ellis, *Original Letters*, ser. I, vol. III, p. 286.

24 Ibid., p. 287.

25 Antonia Fraser, *King Charles II*, p. 14.

26 Vatican Transcripts, quoted by Everett Green, op. cit., p. 103.

27 Thomas Fuller, *Worthies of England*, vol. II, p. 108.

28 Aldous Huxley, *Grey Eminence*, p. 97.

29 Everett Green, op. cit., p. 105.

30 Ibid., p. 337.

31 Wedgwood, op. cit., p. 280.

32 Fuller, op. cit., p. 108.

33 Edward Earl of Clarendon, *History of the Rebellion*, vol. I, p. 337.

34 Wedgwood, op. cit., p. 426.

35 Wedgwood, *Thomas Wentworth, First Earl of Strafford*, p. 375.

36 Ibid., p. 377.

37 Petrie, op. cit., p. 116.

38 *Vide* Everett Green, op. cit., pp. 109–10.

39 Ibid., p. 111.

40 Ibid., p. 115.

41 Ibid., pp. 117–18.

42 *Vide* Elizabeth Hamilton, *Henrietta Maria*, p. 173.

3   Separated by War

1 *Calendar of State Papers Domestic*, 1641–1643, p. 302.

2 Ibid., p. 294.

3 Mary Anne Everett Green, *Lives of the Princesses*, vol. VI, p. 129.

4 Carola Oman, *Henrietta Maria*, p. 135.

5 *Life of James the Second*, ed. J.S. Clarke, vol. I, p. 2.

6 Ibid.
7 Ibid.
8 Ibid., pp. 4–5.
9 Oman, op. cit., p. 136.
10 *Vide* John Aubrey, *Brief Lives*, vol. I, p. 297.
11 *Life of James II*, p. 15.
12 Peter Young, *Edgehill 1642*, p. 301.
13 S.R. Gardiner, *History of the Great Civil War*, vol. I, p. 94.
14 Susan Cole, *A Flower of Purpose*, p. 3.
15 Everett Green, op. cit., p. 341.
16 Cole, op. cit., p. 3.
17 Dict. of Nat. Biography, vol. XXXV, p. 391.
18 Cole, op. cit., p. 5. *Vide* also Everett Green, op. cit., p. 346.
19 Cole, op. cit., p. 6.
20 Everett Green, op. cit., p. 349.
21 Henry Ellis, *Original Letters*, ser. 2, vol. III, p. 316.
22 For the Queen's flight from England, *vide* Oman, *Henrietta Maria*, pp. 159–61, and Elizabeth Hamilton, *Henrietta Maria*, pp. 209–10.
23 Antonia Fraser, *King Charles II*, p. 37.
24 Clarendon, *History of the Rebellion*, vol. IV, p. 78.
25 *Eikon Basilike*, p. 130.
26 Julia Cartwright, *Madame*, p. 8.
27 Ibid., pp. 10–11.
28 Ibid., p. 12.
29 Everett Green, op. cit., pp. 408–9.
30 Thomas Birch, *Court and Times of Charles I*, vol. II, p. 410.
31 Clarke (ed.), *Life of James II*, vol. I, p. 28.
32 Ibid., p. 29.
33 Ibid., p. 30.

4 *In the Depths*

1 *Memoirs of Mademoiselle de Montpensier*, vol. I, p. 23.
2 Ibid., p. 97.
3 Susan Cole, *A Flower of Purpose*, p. 7.
4 Mary Anne Everett Green, *Lives of the Princesses of England*, vol. VI, pp. 145–6.
5 Sir Charles Petrie, *The Letters of King Charles I*, p. 231.
6 Everett Green, op. cit., p. 355.
7 Cole, op. cit., p. 9.
8 Clarendon, *History of the Rebellion*, vol. IV, pp. 250–1.
9 Everett Green, op. cit., pp. 358–9.
10 Ibid., p. 359.

11 *Vide* Everett Green, op. cit., p. 360.
12 Clarendon, *History of the Rebellion*, vol. IV, p. 251.
13 Everett Green, op. cit., p. 362.
14 *Letters of King Charles I*, p. 232.
15 Clarendon, op. cit., pp. 262–3.
16 *Life of James II*, ed. J.S. Clark, vol. I, p. 33.
17 Ibid., p. 36.
18 Ibid., pp. 36–7.
19 Everett Green, op. cit., p. 148.
20 Clarendon, op. cit., p. 338.
21 Ibid., p. 339.
22 Brian Masters, *The Mistresses of Charles II*, p. 14.
23 Carola Oman, *Henrietta Maria*, p. 190.
24 *Letters of King Charles I*, pp. 239–41.
25 *Letters of King Charles II*, pp. 6–7.
26 *Vide* C.V. Wedgwood, *The Trial of Charles I*, p. 170.
27 *Letters of King Charles I*, pp. 272–3.
28 Thomas Herbert, *Memoirs of the Two Last Years of the Reign of King Charles I*, pp. 178–80.
29 Everett Green, op. cit., p. 369.
30 Cole, op. cit., p. 16.
31 For the arrival of the news at The Hague, *vide* Everett Green, op. cit., pp. 151–2; Hester W. Chapman, *The Tragedy of Charles II*, p. 119, and Antonia Fraser, *King Charles II*, p. 78.
32 Thomas Birch, *Court & Times of Charles I*, vol. II, p. 382.
33 *Life of James II*, vol. I, p. 40.
34 Everett Green, op. cit., p. 372.
35 Thomas Birch, op. cit., vol. II, p. 398.

5   Haven in Holland

1 *Life of James II*, ed. J.S. Clarke, vol. I, p. 50.
2 *Five Stuart Princesses*, ed. R.S. Rait, pp. 204–5.
3 James Geddes, *Administration of Johan de Witt*, p. 178.
4 Ibid., p. 173.
5 *Life of James II*, vol. I, p. 51.
6 *Bishop Burnet's History of his Own Time*, vol. I, pp. 304–5.
7 *Life of James II*, vol. I, p. 52.
8 *Memoirs of James II*, p. 80.
9 Clement Walker, *The History of Independency*, Pt. IV, p. 99. (Part IV is not by Walker but is an addition by 'T.M. Esquire', probably Thomas Manley.)
10 *Vide* Eva Scott, *The Travels of the King*, pp. 24–5.

11 Ibid., p. 26.
12 *Thurloe State Papers*, vol. I, p. 397.
13 Scott, op. cit., p. 27.
14 *The Letters of King Charles II*, ed. Arthur Bryant, pp. 29–30.
15 Antonia Fraser, *King Charles II*, p. 138.
16 *Letters of Charles II*, p. 30.
17 Everett Green, op. cit., pp. 217–18.
18 Scott, op. cit., p. 30.
19 *Letters of Charles II*, p. 31.
20 Ibid., p. 32.
21 Ibid., p. 33.
22 Everett Green, op. cit., p. 223.
23 Ibid., pp. 223–4.
24 Hester Chapman, *The Tragedy of Charles II*, p. 280.
25 Scott, op. cit., p. 46.
26 Ibid., p. 49.
27 Everett Green, op. cit., p. 226.
28 Ibid.
29 Ibid., p. 227.
30 Scott, op. cit., pp. 107–8.
31 *Thurloe S.P.*, vol. IV, p. 89.
32 Everett Green, op. cit., p. 233.
33 Ibid., p. 235.
34 Carola Oman, *Henrietta Maria*, p. 250.
35 Ibid., p. 252.
36 *Memoirs of James II*, p. 218.
37 Ibid., p. 223.
38 Ibid., p. 242.
39 Everett Green, op. cit., p. 262.
40 Scott, op. cit., p. 343.
41 *Memoirs of James II*, pp. 266–7.

6 *Turn of the Tide*

1 *Vide* Antonia Fraser, *King Charles II*, pp. 155–6.
2 *Memoirs of James II*, p. 280.
3 Eva Scott, *The Travels of the King*, p. 374.
4 *The Diary of John Evelyn*, ed. E.S. de Beer, vol. III, p. 224.
5 Ibid., p. 228.
6 *Memoirs of James II*, pp. 287–8. The English text of this passage and others is lifted from the *Life*, as being identical in wording with the French manuscript.

7 *The Letters of Charles II*, ed. Arthur Bryant, pp. 76–7.
8 Hester Chapman, *The Tragedy of Charles II*, p. 350.
9 Cyril Hughes Hartmann, *Charles II and Madame*, p. 3.
10 Julia Cartwright, *Madame*, pp. 49–50.
11 Ibid., p. 51.
12 *Vide* Patrick Morrah, *1660: The Year of Restoration*, pp. 35–153. For the period immediately before the Restoration I have repeated some passages from my earlier book, supplemented by other material.
13 Hartmann, op. cit., pp. 10–11.
14 *Memoirs of James II*, p. 291.
15 Ibid.
16 Morrah, op. cit., p. 91.
17 Ibid., p. 94.
18 Ibid., p. 119.
19 *The Diary of Samuel Pepys*, ed. Robert Latham and William Matthews, vol. I, pp. 122–3.
20 Hartmann, op. cit., pp. 12–13.
21 Morrah, op. cit., p. 130.
22 M.A. Everett Green, *Lives of the Princesses*, vol. II, p. 288.
23 Hartmann, op. cit., pp. 14–15.
24 *Diary of John Evelyn*, vol. III, p. 246.

7 *Year of Destiny*

1 Bishop Burnet's *History of his Own Time*, vol. I, p. 304.
2 Ibid., p. 308.
3 Cyril Hughes Hartmann, *The King my Brother*, p. 22.
4 *Memoirs of Sophia, Electress of Hanover*, p. 13.
5 Mary Anne Everett Green, *Lives of the Princesses of England*, vol. VI, p. 307.
6 Ibid., p. 309.
7 Ibid., p. 310.
8 *Memoirs of Mademoiselle de Montpensier*, vol. II, p. 226.
9 Everett Green, op. cit., p. 311.
10 Hartmann, *Charles II and Madame*, p. 15.
11 Ibid., p. 18.
12 *Life of James the Second*, ed. J.S. Clarke, vol. I, p. 387.
13 Edward Earl of Clarendon, *Continuation of Life*, vol. II, p. 53.
14 Ibid., p. 54.
15 *Diary of Samuel Pepys*, ed. Robert Latham & William Matthews, vol. I, p. 244.

16 Evelyn's *Diary*, vol. III, p. 257.
17 Burnet's *History*, vol. I, p. 308.
18 Hartmann, *Charles II and Madame*, p. 21.
19 Carola Oman, *Henrietta Maria*, p. 279.
20 Clarendon, op. cit., p. 61.
21 Anthony Hamilton, *Count Gramont at the Court of Charles II*, p. 59.
22 Ibid., p. 60.
23 Burnet's *History*, p. 303.
24 Hartmann, *The King my Brother*, p. 21.
25 *Letters of Charles II*, ed. Arthur Bryant, p. 104.
26 Everett Green, op. cit., pp. 435–6.
27 Ibid., pp. 324–5.
28 *Five Stuart Princesses*, ed. R.S. Rait, p. 221.
29 Clarendon, op. cit., p. 74.
30 C.H. Hartmann, *The King's Friend*, pp. 55–6.

8 *Eldest and Youngest*

1 Bishop Burnet's *History of his Own Time*, vol. I, p. 550.
2 Ibid.
3 C.H. Hartmann, *The King my Brother*, pp. 25–6.
4 Ibid., p. 30.
5 C.H. Hartmann, *Charles II and Madame*, p. 35. Much of this chapter is based on Hartmann's researches. When quoting the letters I have used *Charles II and Madame*, where they are all transcribed with the original spelling. For the general narrative of the relations between brother and sister I have made more use of Hartmann's later work, *The King my Brother*. I have accepted his translations of Minette's letters, which were all written in French.
6 Arthur Bryant, *King Charles II*, p. 105.
7 Hartmann, *Charles II and Madame*, p. 42.
8 *Letters of King Charles II*, ed. Arthur Bryant, pp. 126–7.
9 Hartmann, *Charles II and Madame*, p. 43.
10 Carola Oman, *Henrietta Maria*, p. 313.
11 Hartmann, *Charles II and Madame*, pp. 50–1.
12 Ibid., pp. 57–8.
13 Ibid., p. 68.
14 Ibid., p. 95.
15 Ibid., p. 102.
16 Ibid., pp. 111–12.
17 Ibid., pp. 121–2.
18 Hartmann, *The King my Brother*, p. 123.

19 Hartmann, *Charles II and Madame*, pp. 127–8.
20 Ibid., p. 129.
21 Bryan Bevan, *Charles II's Minette*, p. 97.
22 Hartmann, *Charles II and Madame*, p. 135.
23 Ibid., pp. 140–1.
24 Ibid., p. 161.
25 *Diary of Samuel Pepys*, ed. Robert Latham and William Matthews, vol. VI, p. 142.
26 *Vide* Bryant, *King Charles II*, p. 287.
27 *Life of James II*, ed. J.S. Clarke, vol. I, p. 441.
28 Ibid., p. 442.
29 Hartmann, *Charles II and Madame*, p. 241.
30 *Memoirs of Mademoiselle de Montpensier*, vol. III, p. 54.
31 Ibid., p. 61.
32 Julia Cartwright, *Madame*, p. 334.
33 *Vide: English Historical Documents, 1660–1714*, ed. Andrew Browning, p. 864, and C.H. Hartmann, *The King my Brother*, p. 314.
34 Cartwright, op. cit., p. 335.

9   *Two Brothers*

1 *Memoirs of Mademoiselle de Montpensier*, vol. III, p. 61.
2 C.H. Hartmann, *Charles II and Madame*, p. 318.
3 *Vide* Julia Cartwright, *Madame*, pp. 344–55; C.H. Hartmann, *The King my Brother*, pp. 326–30, and Bryan Bevan, *Charles II's Minette*, pp. 178–82.
4 Hartmann, *The King my Brother*, p. 328.
5 Ibid., p. 326.
6 Ibid., p. 328.
7 Ibid., p. 329.
8 Cartwright, *Madame*, p. 357.
9 Hartmann, *The King my Brother*, p. 332.
10 Bishop Burnet's *History of his Own Time*, vol. I, p. 568.
11 *Memoirs of Sir John Reresby*, p. 86.
12 *English Historical Documents, 1660–1714*, ed. Andrew Browning, p. 389.
13 Burnet's *History*, vol. II, p. 16.
14 *Life of James II*, ed. J.S. Clarke, vol. I, p. 485.
15 Maurice Ashley, *James II*, pp. 98–9.
16 Burnet's *History*, vol. II, p. 120.
17 Arthur Bryant, *King Charles II*, p. 206.
18 Ibid., pp. 216–17.

19 *Letters of King Charles II*, ed. Arthur Bryant, pp. 304–5.
20 Antonia Fraser, *King Charles II*, p. 367.
21 *Memoirs of Thomas Earl of Ailesbury*, vol. I, p. 40.
22 Ibid., p. 53.
23 Ibid., p. 55.
24 *Letters of King Charles II*, p. 318.
25 Ibid., p. 319.
26 *Ailesbury Memoirs*, vol. I, p. 57.
27 *Life of James II*, vol. I, p. 673.
28 Burnet's *History*, vol. II, p. 415.
29 Ibid.
30 *Diary of John Evelyn*, ed. E.S. de Beer, vol. IV, p. 413.
31 *Ailesbury Memoirs*, vol. I, p. 89.
32 Burnet's *History*, vol. II, p. 468.
33 *Life of James II*, vol. I, p. 747.
34 *Ailesbury Memoirs*, vol. I, p. 90.
35 Burnet's *History*, vol. II, pp. 472–3.
36 *Ailesbury Memoirs*, vol. I, p. 97.

10 *Lone Survivor*

1 *English Historical Documents, 1660–1714*, ed. Andrew Browning, p. 396.
2 *Memoirs of Thomas, Earl of Ailesbury*, vol. I, pp. 131–2.

Bibliography

AILESBURY, THOMAS EARL OF, *Memoirs*, Roxburgh Club, 1890.

AKRIGG, G.P.V., *Jacobean Pageant*, Hamish Hamilton, 1962.

ASHLEY, MAURICE, *Charles II: the Man and the Statesman*, Weidenfeld & Nicolson, 1971.

— *James II*, Dent, 1977.

AUBREY, JOHN, *Brief Lives*, ed. Andrew Clark, Clarendon Press, 1898.

BEVAN, BRYAN, *Charles II's Minette*, Ascent Books, 1979.

BIRCH, THOMAS, (ed.), *The Court and Times of Charles I*, Colburn, 1849.

BOWLE, JOHN, *Charles I*, Weidenfeld & Nicolson, 1975.

BROWNING, ANDREW, (ed.), *English Historical Documents, 1660–1714*, Eyre & Spottiswoode, 1953.

BRYANT, ARTHUR, *King Charles II*, revised edn, Collins, 1955.

BURNET, GILBERT, *History of His Own Time*, O.U.P., 1833.

CAMMELL, CHARLES RICHARD, *The Great Duke of Buckingham*, Collins, 1939.

CAREY, ROBERT, *Memoirs*, ed. F.H. Mares, Clarendon Press, 1972.

CARTWRIGHT, JULIA, *Madame: a Life of Henrietta, Duchess of Orleans*, Seeley, 1894.

CHAPMAN, HESTER W., *The Tragedy of Charles II*, Cape, 1964.

CHARLES I, KING, *Eikon Basilike*, ed. Edward Almack, De La More Press, 1903.

— *Letters*, ed. Sir Charles Petrie, Cassell, 1935.

CHARLES II, KING, *Letters*, ed. Arthur Bryant, Cassell, 1935.

CHARLTON, JOHN, *The Banqueting House, Whitehall*, H.M.S.O., 1964.

CLARENDON, EDWARD EARL OF, *History of the Rebellion and Civil Wars*, ed. W. Duncan Macrae, Clarendon Press, 1888.

— *Continuation of Life*, Clarendon Press, 1759.

CLARKE, REV J.S., (ed.), *Life of James the Second*, Longman, Hurst, Rees, Orme & Brown, 1816.

COLE, SUSAN, *A Flower of Purpose: a Memoir of Princess Elizabeth Stuart*, Royal Stuart Soc., 1975.

EARLE, PETER, *Life and Times of James II*, Book Club Associates, 1972.

ELLIS, HENRY, (ed.), *Original Letters, Illustrative of English History*, Harding, Triphook & Lepard, 1827–46.

EVELYN, JOHN, *Diary*, ed. E.S. de Beer, Clarendon Press, 1955.

FALKUS, CHRISTOPHER, *Life and Times of Charles II*, Book Club Associates, 1972.

FANSHAWE, ANNE LADY, *Memoirs*, ed. Beatrice Marshall, Bodley Head, 1905.

FRASER, ANTONIA, *King James VI of Scotland, I of England*, Weidenfeld & Nicolson, 1974.

— *King Charles II*, Weidenfeld & Nicolson, 1979.

FULLER, THOMAS, *History of the Worthies of England*, Tegg, 1840.

GARDINER, S.R., *History of the Great Civil War*, Longmans 1886–91.

GAUNT, WILLIAM, *Court Painting in England*, Constable, 1980.

GEDDES, JAMES, *History of the Administration of Johan Witt*, Kegan Paul, 1879.

GREEN, MARY ANNE EVERETT, *Lives of the Princesses of England*, Colburn, 1855.

HALKETT, ANNE LADY, *Autobiography*, ed. John Gough Nicols, Camden Soc., 1875.

HAMILTON, ANTHONY, *Count Gramont at the Court of Charles II*, ed. & tr. Nicholas Deakin, Barrie & Rockliff, 1965.

HAMILTON, ELIZABETH, *Henrietta Maria*, Hamish Hamilton, 1976.

HARTMANN, CYRIL HUGHES, *Charles II and Madame*, Heinemann, 1934.

— *The King's Friend*, Heinemann, 1951.

— *The King my Brother*, Heinemann, 1954.

HASKELL, FRANCIS, *Patrons and Painters*, Harper & Row, 1971.

HERBERT, SIR THOMAS, *Memoirs of the Two Last Years of the Reign of Charles I*, Shakespeare Press, 1839.

HUXLEY, ALDOUS, *Grey Eminence*, Chatto and Windus, 1941.

JAMES II, KING, *Memoirs: Campaigns as Duke of York, 1652–60*, tr. A. Lytton Sills, Chatto & Windus, 1962.

JOHN, EVAN, *King Charles I*, Barker, 1933.

KENYON, J.P., *The Stuarts*, Batsford, 1958.

— *The Stuart Constitution, 1603–1688*, C.U.P., 1966.

LEVY, MICHAEL, *Painting at Court*, Weidenfeld & Nicolson, 1971.

McELWEE, WILLIAM, *The Wisest Fool in Christendom*, Faber & Faber, 1958.

MARPLES, MORRIS, *Princes in the Making*, Faber, 1965.

MASTERS, BRIAN, *The Mistresses of Charles II*, Blond & Briggs, 1979.

MATHEW, DAVID, *James I*, Eyre & Spottiswoode, 1967.

MILLAR, OLIVER, *Sir Peter Lely, 1618–80: exhibition in London*, Nat. Portrait Gallery, 1978.

MONTPENSIER, ANNE DUCHESSE DE, *Memoirs*, ed. from the French, Colburn, 1848.

MORRAH, PATRICK, *1660: the Year of Restoration*, Chatto & Windus, 1960.
— *Prince Rupert of the Rhine*, Constable, 1976.
— *Restoration England*, Constable, 1979.
MOTTEVILLE, MADAME DE, *Memoirs*, tr. Katherine Prescott Wormeley, Heinemann, 1902.
OLLARD, RICHARD, *The Image of the King: Charles I and Charles II*, Hodder & Stoughton, 1979.
OMAN, CAROLA, *Henrietta Maria*, Hodder & Stoughton, 1951.
PEPYS, SAMUEL, *Diary*, ed. Robert Latham & William Matthews, Bell, 1970–76.
PLUMB, J.H., *Royal Heritage*, BBC, 1977.
RAIT, ROBERT, (ed.), *Five Stuart Princesses*, Archibald Constable, 1902.
RERESBY, SIR JOHN, *Memoirs*, ed. James J. Cartwright, Longmans, 1875.
RUSHWORTH, JOHN, *Historical Collections*, vol. II, London, 1680.
SCOTT, EVA, *The Travels of the King*, Constable, 1907.
SMEETON, GEORGE, (ed.), *Historical & Biographical Tracts*, Smeeton, 1820.
SOPHIA, ELECTRESS OF HANOVER, *Memoirs*, tr. H. Forester, Bentley, 1888.
THURLOE, JOHN, *Collection of State Papers*, Gyles, Woodward & Davies, 1742.
WARWICK, SIR PHILIP, *Memoirs of the Reign of King Charles I, with Continuation*, Chiswell, 1701.
WATERHOUSE, ELLIS, *Painting in Britain, 1530 to 1790*, Penguin Books, 1953.
WALKER, CLEMENT, *The History of Independency*, Part IV, by T.M. Blome, 1660.
WATSON, D.R., *Life and Times of Charles I*, Book Club Associates, 1972.
WEDGWOOD, C.V., *The King's Peace*, Collins, 1955.
— *The King's War*, Collins, 1959.
— *Thomas Wentworth, First Earl of Strafford*, Cape, 1961.
— *The Trial of Charles I*, Collins, 1964.
WILLIAMS, ETHEL CARLETON, *Anne of Denmark*, Longmans, 1970.
YOUNG, BRIG. PETER, *Edgehill 1642, Campaign and Battle*, Roundwood Press, 1967.
YOUNG, BRIG. PETER, and HOLMES, RICHARD, *The English Civil War*, Eyre Methuen, 1974.

Index

Aix-la-Chapelle (Aachen): Charles II's
    and Mary's visit to, 140, 149; Treaty
    of (1668), 230
Albemarle, Duke of *see* Monk, General
Alfred the Great, 2
Amelia von Soms, Princess Dowager of
    Orange, 161, 177; her bad relations
    with Princess Mary, 64, 75, 122, 135,
    162; and partial reconciliation, 137;
    Charles II's courtship of Henrietta
    Catherine and, 161–2
Andrea del Sarto, 44
Anjou, Duke of *see* Orléans, Duke of
Anne, Princess (Charles I's daughter):
    birth (1637), 41, 46; and childhood,
    44–5, 46; death, 51–2
Anne Hyde, Duchess of York, 150, 199,
    237, 241; first meeting with James in
    Paris, 151; and secret marriage (1660),
    193–5, 196–8; Queen Henrietta makes
    peace with, 201–2; birth of son
    Charles, 202; and daughters (Mary
    and Anne), 237; death (1671), 239
Anne of Austria, Queen, 29, 31, 79, 109,
    146, 152, 191, 206, 223
Anne of Denmark (wife of James I), 5,
    20, 35; children, 5–6; and relations
    with son Charles, 8, 11, 16–17;
    Catholicism, 9, 11, 47; relations with
    James I, 11; her liking for jewellery,
    12; and passion for architecture, 12,
    14; and court masques, 12–13; death
    (1619), 16
Anne of Denmark, Princess (daughter of
    James II), 237, 245, 263
d'Aranjou, Monsieur, tutor, 37
architecture, 12, 13–14
Arlington, Lord, 226, 232, 234, 238, 240
Armorer, Sir Nicholas, 104
Arran, Earl of, 197
art and artists, 40–41, 44; Charles I as
    patron of, 11, 14, 40–42, 44; royal
    encouragement of foreign paintings,
    12, 41, 44; Earl of Arundel's
    collection, 14; Buckingham's

collection, 15, 44; Philip IV's
    collection, 22; Van Dyck appointed
    court painter by Charles I, 41;
    miniaturists, 41, 44, 182; Charles II as
    patron of, 182
Arundel, Thomas Howard, Earl of, 14,
    15, 40, 57
Arundell of Wardour, Lord, 226, 227,
    232
Ashley, Lord *see* Shaftesbury, Earl of
Ashley, Dr Maurice, 4
Aubrey, John, 68
Austria, 17, 19

Balcarres, Lord and Lady, 156
Baltasar Carlos, Infante, 54–5
Bamfield, Colonel Joseph, 107; helps
    Duke of York to escape, 102, 103–5;
    and suspect behaviour of, 105–6
Bassompière, Marshal the Duc de,
    French Ambassador to London, 30
Batten, Captain Sir William, 71;
    knighted and promoted to Rear-
    Admiral, 107
Battles of the Dunes (1658), 157–8
Battle of the White Mountain (1620), 19
Beacon Hill, Battle of (1644), 79
Belasyse, Susan, Lady, 241
Bellings, Sir Richard, 232
Berkeley, Charles *see* Falmouth, Earl of
Berkeley, Sir John, 86, 96, 101, 106, 154;
    Exeter surrendered to Fairfax by, 87
Berwick, pacification of, 50
Bishops' War(s): First (1639), 50; Second
    (1640), 51
Blijenberch, Abraham van, 12
Bohemia: Protestants' uprising against
    Emperor Ferdinand, 17–18; and
    Thirty Years War, 18–19
Booth, Sir George, defeat of Cheshire
    rising led by, 165, 167
'Boscobel oak', Charles II hides in, 129
Bossuet, Bishop, 235
Breda (Brabant), Princess Mary's palace
    at, 125, 134, 150, 156, 157, 158, 174,

176, 202; feast in honour of Charles II, 118; Charles II's Declaration of (1660), 175

Brederode, Count, 56, 57

Brégis, Mme de, 170

Bristol: Prince Rupert's headquarters at, 81; and Prince Charles goes to, 81; surrended to Sir Thomas Fairfax (1645), 82–3

Bristol, Earl of *see* Digby, George, Lord

Bruce, Lord (later Earl of Ailesbury), 253, 254, 256, 258, 259, 265

Bruges, Flanders, Charles II's headquarters in, 152–4, 156, 157, 158, 163

Bryant, Sir Arthur, 4, 246–7

Buckingham, George Villiers, first Duke of ('Steenie'), 20, 26, 36; as favourite of James I, 15–16; art collection, 15, 40, 44; Charles's friendship with, 16, 31–2; Bohemian Protestants supported by, 18; accompanies Charles to Madrid, 20–23; Charles's letters about 'monsieurs' to, 28–30; scandal over attentions paid to Anne of Austria by, 31, 206; rivalry between Henrietta Maria and, 31–2; failure of French campaign, 32; murder of (1628), 32, 34

Buckingham, George Villiers, second Duke of, 52, 185, 226, 238, 240; in Paris with Prince Charles, 94, 135; forces his attentions on Henrietta Anne, 206–7

Bulstrode, Sir Richard, 257

Burgoyne, Sir Roger, 174

Burnet, Bishop Gilbert, 21, 127–8, 185, 187, 195, 204, 224, 239, 257

Cabal: political influence of, 226–7, 240; Charles II rewards members of, 238

Calvinism, 9

Canterbury, William Sancroft, Archbishop of, 262

Capuchins, French, 35

Caracena, Marqués de, 154, 156, 158, 173

Caravaggio, 44

Carey, Lady Elizabeth, 8

Carey, Sir Robert (Lord Rochford), 6–7, 151; Prince Charles entrusted to care of, 7–8

Carings (Keirincx), Alexander, 41

Carisbrooke Castle, Isle of Wight: Charles I imprisoned in, 101, 109, 111, 118–19; Elizabeth and Henry imprisoned in, 120, 136

Castle Dore, Battle of (1644), 79

Castlemaine, Barbara, Countess of (Charles II's mistress), 212–3, 244, 258

Catherine of Braganza, Queen of England, 222, 232, 237, 244, 254, 258; Charles II's marriage to (1662), 209–10, 212; Henrietta Maria's friendship with, 212; and relations with her husband, 212–13; Popish Plot and, 247

Catholicism, Catholics, 21, 26, 47, 143; Anne of Denmark and, 9, 11, 47; Bohemian Protestants' uprising against, 17–18; Henrietta Maria's, 27–8, 47–8, 127, 141; and Princess Henrietta Anne, 127, 225; James II's conversion to, 127–8, 143, 224–5, 237–8; Queen Henrietta fails to convert Prince Henry to, 141–6; Charles II's sympathetic attitude to, 143, 224, 225; and his intention to become Catholic, 226–7, 228, 232, 238, 258; Charles II's Declaration of Indulgence (1672), 238; and withdrawal of Declaration (1673), 239; and Test Act, 239–40, 260, 262; Popish Plot (1678), 246–7; and Exclusion Crisis, 248–57; Charles II's deathbed conversion to, 258–9; James II's Declaration of Indulgence (1687), 262

Cavaliers *see* Royalists

Caversham House, 97, 98

Charles I, King of England, 127, 184, 186; birth at Dunfermline Castle (1600), 5–6; and sickly childhood, 6, 7–8; James I's relations with, 7, 11, 17; entrusted to care of Sir Robert and Lady Carey, 7–8; his relations with mother Anne, 8, 11, 16–17; and with brother Henry, 8; devotion to the Church of England, 8–9, 20, 47–8; marriage of sister Elizabeth, 9, 10; death of brother Henry, 9; his responsibilities as heir to throne, 9–10; created Prince of Wales, 10; his dislike of English court life, 10, 21–2; and filial respect, 10–11; as patron of the arts, and his art collection, 11, 14, 22, 40–42, 44; *Eikon Basilike* by, 13, 118–19; friendship with 'Steenie' Buckingham, 16, 31–2; death of mother, 16; candidates for marriage to, 17, 19–20, 21–3; cause of Bohemian Protestants championed by, 18; Spanish visit to see Infanta, 20–23; and his liking for Spanish Court life, 21–2; Philip IV presents him with *The Venus of Pardo*, 22; death of father, and succeeds to throne, 23–4; and marriage to Henrietta Maria, 4, 24–6; relations between Henrietta and, 26–32, 34, 36, 76; Coronation of

(1626), 28; sends 'monsieurs' packing, 28–30; and bad relations between Queen and Buckingham, 31–2; and murder of Buckingham, 32; premature birth and death of first child, 34–5; birth of son Charles (1630), 35–6; domestic bliss, 36–7; and other children, 37–9, 44–7; cultural atmosphere and court ceremonial, 39–40, 44; appoints Van Dyck court painter, 41; and appoints Laud as Archbishop of Canterbury, 47; methods of raising revenue, 49; imposes new English prayer book on Scotland, 50; and First Bishops' War (1639), 50; and pacification of Berwick, 50; and Puritan opposition in England, 50; sends for Thomas Wentworth, 50–51; Second Bishops' War, 51; trial and execution of Strafford, 52–4; daughter Mary's marriage to William of Orange, 55–8; abortive attempt to arrest five members of Commons, 58–9; and flight with family to Hampton Court and Windsor, 59; Queen Henrietta and Princess Mary leave for Holland, 59–60; goes to York with Prince Charles, 64; and sends three younger children to St James's 64; refused entry into Hull by Hotham, 65–6; Civil War begins, 67; Battle of Edgehill, 68–70; and retires to Oxford, 70; Henrietta Maria rejoins him, 70–71, 76; First Battle of Newbury, 76; Queen leaves Oxford, 77–8; and birth of daughter Henrietta Anne, 78, 79, 80; Battle of Cropredy Bridge, 78, 79; Queen's flight to France, 78–9; successful Cornish campaign of, 79; Battle of Marston Moor, 79–80; Second Battle of Newbury, 80; appoints son Charles Generalissimo of all his forces, 81; Battle of Naseby, 82; and surrenders Bristol to Roundheads, 82–3; letter to son advising him to leave for France, 84; leaves Oxford and surrenders to Scots, 85, 95; handed over by Scots to English Parliament, 91; prisoner in Holmby House, 93, 96; moved by Army to Caversham, 97; and meetings with his children, 97–101; moved to Hampton Court, 99; and flight from Hampton Court, 101; and imprisoned in Carisbrooke Castle, 101–2, 109; Second Civil War (1648), 105, 109; letter to son Charles, 109–11; stands trial and sentenced to death (1649), 111–13; farewell meeting with

Elizabeth and Henry, 113–15; execution of, 115–18

Charles II, King (formerly Prince of Wales), 4, 53, 54, 57, 186; birth (1630), 35–6; childhood, 38–9, 44–6; Van Dyck's portrait of, 41; illness, 45; Anglican religious education, 47–8; at trial of Strafford, 52; education, 52; wedding of sister Mary to William of Orange, 57; and his letter to Mary, 62–3; goes to York with father, 64; Civil War, 67; and Battle of Edgehill, 68–9; in Oxford, 70, 71; Battle of Cropredy Bridge, 78; Second Battle of Newbury, 80; appointed Generalissimo, 81; leaves Oxford for Bristol, 81; and affair with Mrs Wyndham, 81–2; father's letter orders him to leave for France, 84; seeks refuge in Scilly Isles, 85; and Jersey, 85–6; and escapes to Paris, 86; courtship of Princess Anne-Marie, 93–4; and his life in Paris, 94–5; takes over as Admiral of revolted fleet in Holland, 105–8; settles in the Hague, 108; catches smallpox, 108; birth of bastard son, Duke of Monmouth, 108; father's letters from Newport to, 109–11; his frantic efforts to save his father, 111–13; and grief at news of father's death, 117; returns to Paris, 118; lands in Scotland (1650), 126, 127; instructs brother James to return to Paris, 126–7; leads his army into England (1651), 128–9; and defeated at battle of Worcester, 129; escapes back to France, 129–30; seeks terms from Duke of Lorraine, 133–4; temporary rift between Mary of Orange and, 134–5; arrival in the Hague of Prince Henry, 137; and orders Henry to go to Paris, 137–8; illness, 139; leaves France and settles in Germany, 139–41; religious toleration, 143, 225; and opposed to Prince Henry becoming Catholic, 143–5; and sends for Prince Henry in Cologne, 146; letter to Mary asking for money, 147–8; pays secret visit to Middleberg in Zeeland, 148; treaty with Philip IV of Spain, 152; moves his HQ to Bruges, and Flanders campaign, 152–4, 156; quarrel with Mary, 156–7; Battle of the Dunes, 157–8; death of Cromwell and, 159, 160; courtship of Princess Henrietta Catherine, 161–2; and estrangement of Mary, James and Henry from, 162–3; plans for new royalist risings, 165–8; and Turenne's offer of support,

166–7, 168; his visit to Spain, 168–9;
visits his mother at Colombes, 169;
close relation and correspondence with
Minette, 169–71, 172–3, 175–6, 178–9,
192–3, 195–6, 199, 204, 206, 208–9,
213–15, 216–20, 224, 225; General
Monk declares himself in favour of,
174; Declaration of Breda, 175;
returns to England as King (1660),
176–9; character and appearance at
age of thirty, 180, 182; and contrast
between James and, 184–5; appoints
James Lord High Admiral, 186–7; but
finds no suitable position for Henry,
187, 189; Mary's visit to England,
189–90, 191, 196; betrothal of
Henrietta Anne to Duke of Anjou
agreed by, 191, 192, 200; Duke of
York's secret marriage to Anne Hyde,
194–5, 196–7; and death of Prince
Edward, 195–6; Queen Henrietta's
and Minette's visit to England
198–200; death of sister Mary, 201;
relations with James, 204, 206, 257;
marriage to Catherine of Braganza,
209–10, 212; and quarrel over Lady
Castlemaine, 212–13; and relations
with Catherine, 213–14; seeks close
alliance with France, and uses Minette
as intermediary, 214–15, 217, 219–20,
222, 224, 227–8, 229–33; Second
Dutch War and, 215, 216–17, 219,
221–4; and France declares war on
England (1666), 222; fall of Clarendon
and, 224; religious issues and, 224,
225, 226, 239–40; political influence of
Cabal, 226–7, 240; his intention to
become a Catholic, 226–7, 228, 232,
238, 258–9; meets Minette in England,
232–3; and Secret Treaty of Dover,
232; death of Minette, 235, 236;
James's unpopularity and problem of
succession, 237–8; Declaration of
Indulgence by, 238, 239; and Third
Dutch War, 238–9; House of
Commons votes money for war, 239;
and Test Act, 239–40; Treaty of
Westminster, 240; Shaftesbury's
opposition to, 243; private
amusements, 244, 257, 258; and
mistresses, 244–5, 257, 258; arranges
marriage between William III and
Mary, 245–6; Popish Plot, 246–7; and
Rye House Plot, 247–8; and Exclusion
Crisis, 248–57; dissolves Cavalier
Parliament, 249; sends James into
temporary exile, 249–50; appoints
Shaftesbury Lord President of
Council, and the Triumvirate, 250;
illness, 251, 253, 258; his 'second

Triumvirate' of ministers, 252;
concludes new secret agreement with
Louis XIV, 255; and dissolves Oxford
Parliament, 255–6; his fears about
James's future, 257–8; death of (1685),
258–9; and received into Catholic
Church on deathbed, 259
Charles II, King of Spain, 223
Charles, Duke of Cambridge (son of
James II), 202, 209
Charles, Duke of Cornwall, premature
birth and death of (1629), 34–5, 52
Charles Louis, Elector Palatine of the
Rhine, 65
Chateauneuf, Marquis de, 37
Chesterfield, Countess of *see* Stanhope,
Lady
Chesterfield, Lord, 201
Chevreuse, Duchesse de, 31, 48
Choisy, Abbé de, 185
Christina, Princess (sister of Louis XIII),
17, 19, 24, 37, 196–7
Christina, Queen of Sweden, 149, 152
Church of England: Charles I's devotion
to, 8–9, 20, 143; Presbyterians'
antagonism to, 49–50; and new
English prayer book, 50; Prince
Henry's faith in, 143; Test Act,
239–40; James II and, 260, 262;
'Seven Bishops' sent to Tower by
James II
City of London: Shaftesbury's authority
in, 248; demonstration against popery
in, 252
Civil War, Great (1642–46), 67–91:
Charles I raises Royal Banner at
Nottingham, 67; Battle of Edgehill,
68–70; Henrietta Maria rejoins
Charles in Oxford, 70–71, 76; Battle of
Roundway Down, 76; First Battle of
Newbury, 76; Battle of Cropredy
Bridge, 78, 79; Charles I's successful
Cornish campaign, 79; Battle of
Marston Moor, 79–80; Second Battle
of Newbury, 80; Battle of Naseby, 82;
Bristol surrendered to Fairfax by
Prince Rupert, 82–3; Charles I
surrenders to Scots, 85; Exeter
surrendered to Fairfax, 87; and
Oxford surrendered to Fairfax, 90;
Charles I handed over by Scots to
English Parliament, 91
Civil War, Second (1648), 105, 108, 109
Clarendon, Edward Hyde, Earl of, 81,
84, 85, 105–6, 107, 134, 138, 140, 168,
172, 194; antagonism between Queen
Henrietta and, 76, 86, 127, 150, 169,
190, 194, 199; as Lord Chancellor,
145, 187; Declaration of Breda drawn
up by, 175; his reaction to daughter

Anne's marriage to James, Duke of York, 193–5; created Baron Hyde of Hindon, 199; Charles II's letter about his new Queen to, 210, 212; fall of, 224

Clifford, Sir Thomas (Lord Clifford of Chudleigh), 226, 232, 234, 238, 240

Colbert, Jean-Baptiste, 228

Cologne, Charles II's stay in, 140–41, 143, 146, 148, 149, 150

Colombes, Queen Henrietta's home at, 186, 192; Charles II's visit to, 169–71

Cominges, Gaston, Comte de, 215

Commonwealth of England, 92, 108, 118, 125; Dutch States Generals receive ambassadors from, 125, 126; war between United Provinces and (1652–4), 135–6; Cromwell becomes Lord Protector, 136; Battle of the Dunes, 157–8; death of Cromwell, 159, 160, 163–4; rivalries and struggle for power between leaders, 164–5, 171; General Monk marches into England and takes control (1660), 171–2; *see also* Roundheads

Condé, Prince de, 154, 158, 173, 238

Conn, Monsignor George, 46, 47

Cook, Captain Thomas, 166

Cooper, Samuel, 44, 182

Correggio, 44

Covenanters, 50, 125, 126

Coventry, Henry, 176

Craven, Lord, 97, 200

Croafts, Lord, 208, 210

Croissy, Charles, Marquis de (Colbert de Croissy), French Ambassador in London, 227, 228, 232, 233

Cromwell, Oliver, 96; at Battle of Marston Moor, 80; New Model Army and, 81; Battle of Naseby, 82; present at King's meeting with children, 99; dictatorship of, 111; Ireland subdued by, 125; victorious campaign in Scotland, 128–9; and Battle of Worcester, 129; becomes Lord Protector, 135–6; Mazarin seeks agreement with, 139, 153; death of, 159, 160, 163–4

Cromwell, Richard, 160, 164

Cropredy Bridge, Battle of (1644), 78, 79

Crowther, Dr Joseph, 193, 202

Dalkeith, Countess of (later Countess of Morton), Princess Henrietta Anne left in care of, 78, 79, 80, 86–7, 118; and accompanies Princess to Oatlands, 87–8; and escapes to France with Princess, 88–90

Danby, Earl of *see* Osborne, Sir Thomas

Darnley, Lord, 7

Declaration of Breda (1660), 175

Declaration(s) of Indulgence: Charles II's (1672), 238, 262; and withdrawal of (1673), 239; James II's (1687), 262

Denmark House, Queen Henrietta's residence at, 212

Desborough, General John, 164

De Witt, Johan, prime minister of Holland, 123, 189

Dicconson, William, *The Life of James the Second*, 133

Digby, George, Lord (later Earl of Bristol), 77, 154, 168

Dobson, William, 41

Don Juan, Governor of Flanders, 154, 156

Dorislaus (Roundhead agent), murder of, 118

Dorset, Mary Sackville, Countess of, 38, 71, 74

Downing, Sir George, 216

Dryden, John, Poet Laureate, 36, 178; *Absolom and Achitophel*, 243

Dunfermline Castle, 5

Dunkirk, 154, 209, 232; surrendered to French (1658), 157–8

Dunottar Castle, abortive expedition to rescue Scottish regalia from (1652), 134

Duppa, Dr Brian (later Bishop of Salisbury), 38, 84

Dürer, Albrecht, 44

Dyves, Sir Lewis, 65, 66

Edgehill, Battle of (1642), 68–70

Edward VIII, King (Duke of Windsor), 4

Elizabeth, Princess (daughter of Charles I), 48, 55, 56, 57, 87; birth (1635), 37; childhood, 37–8, 39, 44–5, 46; Van Dyck's portrait of, 41; left behind at St James's Palace by father, 64, 65; in custody of Parliament during Civil War, 67–8, 71–5; and her letter to House of Lords, 72–3; intellectual studies, 73–4; removed to Whitehall, 74; placed in care of Earl and Countess of Northumberland, 74–5, 90; letter to Mary in Holland, 75; encourages James to escape, 95, 102–3; moved to Hampton Court, 95; meetings with her father, 97–101; at Syon House, 99, 105, 113, 115, 119; farewell meeting with father, 113–15; illness, 119; moved to Carisbrooke Castle, 120; death of (1650), 120, 126, 136

Elizabeth I, Queen, 2, 6

Elizabeth, Queen of Bohemia ('Winter Queen'), 5, 11, 60, 64, 65, 70, 118, 123, 136, 137, 147, 177, 178, 200–201;

marriage to Frederick V, Elector Palatine, 9, 17; and Bohemian disaster, 18–19; and exile, 19; meets Queen Henrietta and Princess Mary in Holland, 61–2

Essex, Earl of (Roundhead commander), 76, 77, 78, 79, 80; Battle of Edgehill, 68, 69; First Battle of Newbury, 76; Charles I's Cornish campaign against, 79

Essex, Arthur Capel, Earl of, 250

Evelyn, John, *Diary*, 163–4, 179, 258

Exclusion Crisis, 4, 248–57

Exeter, 80, 84; birth of Henrietta Anne, 77–8, 79; siege of, 86; and surrendered to Fairfax, 87

Fairfax, Lord, 80, 81, 171–2, 177

Fairfax, Sir Thomas, 87, 96; at Battle of Marston Moor, 80; appointed supreme commander of New Model Army, 81; Prince Rupert surrenders Bristol to, 82–3; Battle of Naseby, 82; siege and surrender of Exeter to, 86, 87; and of Oxford, 90; arranges for King to meet his children, 97–8; Prince Charles's letter to, 112

Falkland, Lord, 77

Falmouth, Charles Berkeley, Earl of, 154, 197, 219, 221, 222

Felton, John, 32

Ferdinand II, Emperor, 18–19

Ferdinand III, Emperor, 94

Fiennes, Mlle de, 221, 226

Fire of London (1666), 223

Fleetwood, General Charles, 164

Fontainebleau, Louis XIV's court at, 207–8

Four Days Battle (1666), 222

Fox, Sir Stephen, 159

France, 92; England's war with (1627), 32; and Charles I makes peace, 36; Thirty Years War, 75, 92, 132; Queen Henrietta Maria escapes to, 78–9; and Prince Charles joins mother in, 86; the Fronde (civil war), 108–9, 117, 130, 132–4; Charles seeks help for campaign from, 127; and Charles returns to, 129–30; difficult times for royal exiles in, 130, 132; Prince Henry moves to Paris, 138–9; Charles II leaves, in return for pension, 139–40; Princess Mary's visit to Paris, 150–52; Louis XIV's court, 39, 40, 152, 185; Battle of the Dunes, 157–8; and Dunkirk surrendered to, 158; peace treaty with Spain, 169; and betrothal of Louis XIV to Maria Teresa, 169; Charles II seeks closer relations with, 214–15, 217, 219–20, 224, 227–8, 243;

treaty with Netherlands (1662), 215, 219, 222; war declared on England (1666), 222; Louis XIV's campaign in Spanish Netherlands, 226, 227; Treaty of Aix-la-Chapelle (1668), 230; and royal visit to Flanders, 230–31; Secret Treaty of Dover (1670), 232; and open or 'simulated' treaty (1672), 238; and Third Dutch War (1672), 238–40; Treaty of Westminster (1674), 240; Charles II's new secret treaty with, 255; James II's exile in, 263–4

Francis I, King of France, 11

Franco-Dutch Pact (1662), 215, 219, 221, 222

Frankfort, 149, 158

Fraser, Lady Antonia, 4

Frederick II, King of Denmark and Norway, 5

Frederick IV, Elector Palatine, 18

Frederick V, Elector Palatine: Princess Elizabeth's marriage to, 9, 17; elected to throne of Bohemia, 18; and defeated by Emperor Frederick, and exile, 18–19

Frederick Henry, Prince of Orange, 55, 61, 70, 93; helps Queen Henrietta to raise money and arms, 63–4, 67; serious illness, 75; estrangement of William and Mary from, 75–6; death, 95

Fronde (civil war in France), 108–9, 117, 130, 132–4, 151

Fuenterrabia, Franco-Spanish peace treaty signed at (1659), 169

Fuller, Dr Thomas, 52; *The Worthies of England*, 46–7, 80; appointed chaplain to Princess Henrietta Anne, 80

Fyvie, Lord and Lady, 7

Gamache, Father Cyprien de, 27, 35, 89–90, 117, 118, 120, 127, 198, 201

General Assembly of the Kirk, 50

Gentileschi, Orazio, 41

George of Denmark, Prince, 263

Germany: Charles II's stay in, 139–41, 148

Godolphin, Sidney, 252

Goffe, Dr Stephen, 117

Gondomar, Don Diego Sarmiento de Acuna, Conde de, Spanish Ambassador in London, 20, 21

Gonzales, Bartolomé, portrait of Infanta Maria by, 22

Goring, George, Lord, 83

Gramont, Marshal de, 208

Gramont Memoirs, 197

'The Great Condé', 130, 132, 133, 134

Green Ribbon Club, 248, 252

Grenville, Sir John, 174, 175, 177

Grenville, Sir Richard, 83
Grey, Lady Jane, 39
Guiche, Comte de, 208, 220

The Hague *see* Netherlands
Halifax, George Savile, Earl of, 250, 253
Hammond, Colonel Robert, 101
Hampden, John, refuses to pay ship
money, 49, 50
Hampton Court Palace, 44, 59, 95,
99–100, 101–2
Hartmann, Cyril Hughes, 4, 206, 207,
219
Harvey, William, 40, 68, 69
Haslerig, Sir Arthur, 164
Hatton, Lord, 142
Heenvliet, Sieur Johan van, 55, 60, 135
Hellevoetsluis, Dutch port, 61; 'Royalist'
fleet in, 105–7
Henrietta Anne, Princess ('Minette'), 80,
84, 118; birth (1644), 78, 79; left in
the charge of Countess of Dalkeith, 78,
79, 80, 86–7; King Charles I sees her
for last time, 80; sent to Oatlands,
87–8; and escapes to France with
Countess of Dalkeith, 88–90;
Catholicism of, 127, 225; relations
between Prince Henry and, 138; meets
sister Mary for first time, 151; close
relationship and correspondence
between Charles II and, 169–71,
172–3, 175–6, 178–9, 192–3, 195–6,
199, 204, 206, 208–9, 210, 212,
213–15, 216–20, 224, 225; and
Charles's nickname of Minette for,
171; charm and gaiety of, 170–71,
185; betrothal of Philip, Duke of
Anjou to, 190–91, 192, 200, and visit
to England, 192, 193, 196, 198–203;
House of Commons votes present of
£10,000 for, 199; marriage to Philip,
203; Buckingham's unwanted
attentions, 206–7; Louis XIV's
flirtation and friendship with, 207–8;
other admirers, and intrigues, 208,
220; Monsieur's relations with, 207,
208, 226, 228–30; pregnancy and
illness, 208–9; and birth of Marie-
Louise (1662), 209; as unofficial
intermediary between Charles II and
Louis XIV, 214–15, 217, 219–20, 222,
226, 227, 229–33; birth of Philippe-
Charles (1664), 216; birth of
daughter, 229; and death of her
mother, 229; travels to Flanders with
Royal party and visits England,
230–32, 234; and Secret Treaty of
Dover, 232; death (1670), 233, 235–6
Henrietta Catherine, Princess, of
Orange: Charles II's courtship of,

161–2; and betrothal to Prince John of
Anhalt-Dessau, 162
Henrietta Maria, Queen of England, 52,
53, 54, 58, 92, 112, 129, 130, 137, 173,
206, 229; marriage to Charles I, 4,
24–6; and relations with Charles,
26–32, 34, 36–7; Catholicism of, 27–8,
47–8, 127, 141; and 'monsieurs' sent
packing by Charles, 28–30;
Buckingham and, 31–2, 34; premature
birth and death of first child, 34–5;
and birth of Charles (1630), 35–6; and
of other children, 37, 41, 46–7; Marie
de Medici stays at English court, 47;
birth of Henry, 51; and death of
daughter Anne, 51–2; marriage of
Margaret to William of Orange, 56,
57; her unpopularity in England, 58,
199; and departure for Holland with
Mary, 59–62; her efforts to raise
money arms for King, 63–4, 67, 70;
returns by Ship to England and
reunited with Charles, 70–71, 76;
intrigues against Prince Rupert and
squabbles with counsellors, 76–7;
leaves Oxford for Exeter, 77–8; and
birth of Henrietta Anne, 78, 79;
escapes to France, 78–9; Prince
Charles joins her in Paris, 86; and
Countess of Dalkeith brings Henrietta
Anne to France, 89–90; life of penury
at Saint-Germain, 93; her scheme for
Charles to marry Princess Ann-Marie
fails, 93–4; moves back to Paris, 109;
learns of Charles's execution, 117–18;
and retires to Carmelite convent, 118;
domineering attitude to children, 127,
137; welcomes Prince Henry to Paris,
138–9; fails to convert Henry to
Catholicism, 141–6; Princess Mary's
visit to Paris, 150–52; her character
and faded beauty in later years, 186;
betrothal of Henrietta Anne to Duke
of Anjou, 190–91, 192, 200; and visits
to England, 192, 193, 196, 198–9, 203;
her reaction to James's secret
marriage, 196–7, 198; death of
Princess Mary and, 201; and
reconciliation with Duchess of York,
201–2; takes up residence at Denmark
House, 212; and friendship with
Queen Catherine, 212; returns to
France, 223; and death (1669), 229
Henry I, King, 2
Henry II, King, 2
Henry III, King, 2
Henry IV, King (Lancaster), 2
Henry VII, King, 126
Henry VIII, King, 12, 44
Henry IV, King of France, 29

Henry, Prince of Wales (James I's son), 5, 8, 10, 11, 13, 14, 17; death of, 9

Henry, Prince, Duke of Gloucester (son of Charles I), 87, 171; birth at Oatlands (1640), 51; left behind by Charles at St James's Palace, 64, 65; and in custody of Parliament during Civil War, 67–8, 71–5; places in care of Earl of Northumberland, 74–5, 90; moved to Hampton Court, 95; meetings with his father, 97–101; at Syon House, 99, 105, 113, 115, 119; farewell meeting with father (1649), 113–15; imprisoned in Carisbrooke Castle, 120, 136; leaves England for Continent, 136; stays in the Hague, 136–8; Order of the Garter bestowed on, 137; moves to Paris, 138–9; moves to Paris, 138–9; relations with sister Henrietta Anne, 138; Queen Henrietta fails to convert him to Catholicism, 141–6; joins James in army, 142; and his arrogance, 142, 148; sent for by Charles II in Cologne, 146; and stays with Mary in Holland, 146–7, 148; joins Charles II in Germany, 148, 149; and in Bruges, 154; and Breda, 156; Battles of the Dunes, 157, 158; estrangement from Charles, 162–3; plans for new royalist rising, 165; returns to England with Charles II, 176–8; character and appearance at time of Restoration, 185; no suitable position found by Charles for, 187, 189; death from smallpox, 195–6

Herbert, Thomas, 113–14
Hertford, Earl of, 139
Hertford, Marquess of, 65
Hinton, Sir John, 68, 69
Holbein, Hans, 12, 44
Holles, Lord, 215, 217, 222, 228
Holmby House, Northants, 93, 96
Holmes, Sir Robert, 238
Holy Roman Empire, 17–19
Hoogstraeten, Netherlands, 159, 161
Hoskins, John, 41
Hotham, Sir John, refuses King Charles I entry into Hull, 65–6
Hounslerdike, Mary's palace at, 125, 137
House of Commons, House of Lords *see* Parliament
Howard, Sir William, 68
Huddleston, Father John, 259
Hudson, Jeffrey, Queen's dwarf, 58, 79
Huguenots of La Rochelle, 32
Huxley, Aldous, 47
Hyde, Sir Edward *see* Clarendon, Earl of
Hyde, Lady, 136, 193, 195
Hyde, Laurence, 252

Ireland, subdued by Cromwell, 125
Ireton, Henry, 96

James I, King (James VI of Scotland), 5, 9, 35, 50; children, 5–6; proclaimed King of England (1603), 6–7; his relations with son Charles, 7, 11, 17; and entrusts Charles to care of Sir Robert Carey, 7–8; court established in London by, 10, 39; homosexuality of, 10, 11; relations with wife Anne, 11; literary and artistic interests, 11–12, 13; *Basilikon Doron* by, 13; favourites of, 15; and George Villiers, 15–16; seeks bride for son Charles, 17, 19–20; and Charles's visit to Spain, 20–21, 23; declares war against Spain, 23; death (1625), 23–4

James II, King of England (formerly Duke of York), 67, 171, 215, 219, 231, 232, 233; birth (1633), 37; childhood, 37–9, 44–5, 46; Van Dyck's portrait of, 41; wedding of William of Orange and Mary, 57; joins father in York, 65; and made Knight of the Garter, 65; abortive visit to Hull, 65–6; Battle of Edgehill, 68–9; in Oxford, 70, 71, 81, 85; and Oxford surrendered to Fairfax, 90; sent to St James's Palace, 90, 95; and plans to escape, 95, 99–100, 102; moved to Hampton Court, 95; meetings with his father, 97–101; and moves to Syon House, 99; escapes to Holland, 102–5, 108; appointed Admiral of revolted fleet in Holland, 105–6; and brother Charles takes over as Admiral, 106–7; goes to Paris, 118; returns to Holland, but his presence unwelcome, 125, 126; Charles instructs him to return to Paris, 126–7; relations with his mother, 127; conversion to Catholicism, 127–8, 143, 224–5, 226, 237; welcomes Charles back to Paris, 129; matrimonial project vetoed by Mazarin, 132; serves in Army under Turenne, 132–3, 134, 184, 139; *Memoirs* of, 133, 158; Charles II's instructions to, 139; opposed to Prince Henry becoming Catholic, 146; meets Charles and Mary at Meurs, 149; secret love affair with Anne Hyde, 151; Charles II orders him to come to Bruges, 153–4; joins Spanish forces, 153, 154; and his ability as army commander, 154, 156; stays at Breda, 156; Battles of the Dunes, 157–8; estrangement from Charles, 162–3; plans for new royalist risings, 165–8; and Turenne's offer of support, 166–7,

168; offered military command in Spain, 173–4; returns to England with Charles II, 176–8; character, and contrast between Charles and, 184–5, 264; appointed Lord High Admiral, 186–7; secret marriage to Anne Hyde, 193–5, 196–8; death of brother Henry, 196; meets Queen Henrietta in Channel, 198; death of sister Mary, 201; birth of son Charles, 202; declaration signed before Privy Council, 202; Charles II's relations with, 204, 206, 241, 257–8; Second Dutch War, 221; and Battle of Lowestoft, 222; unpopularity and problem of succession, 237–8, 239, 248; commands Fleet in Third Dutch War, 238–9; Test Act passed, 239–40; and resigns all official appointments, 240; marries Mary of Modena, 241, 243; Shaftesbury's hatred of, 243, 248; marriage of his daughter Mary to William III of Orange, 245–6; Popish Plot and, 247, 248; and Rye House Plot, 247–8; exiled to Continent by Charles, 249–50; recalled from exile and sent to Scotland, 251; brought back from Scotland, 252–3, 256; death of brother Charles, 258–9; reigns as James II, 260–64; Monmouth rebellion put down by, 260; dispensation of provisions of Test Act by, 262; and Declaration of Indulgence, 262; and 'Seven Bishops' sent to Tower by, 262; defeated by William of Orange and exile in France, 263–4; causes of his failure, 264; death of (1701), 265
Jermyn, Harry, 156–7, 197
Jermyn, Lord Henry (later Earl of St Albans), 79, 86, 117, 134, 173, 198, 212
Jersey, Prince Charles takes refuge in, 85–6
John George, Prince of Anhalt-Dessau, 162
Johnson, Cornelius, 12, 41
Johnson, Richard, 104
Jones, Inigo, Surveyor of the King's Works, 12, 14; Queen's House, Greenwich designed by, 12, 44; and masques designed by, 12–13, 40; and St James's chapel, 27
Jonson, Ben, words of masques written by, 13
Juxon, William, Bishop of London, 113

Katherine, Princess (Charles I's daughter), 46–7, 52
Kéroualle, Louise de, Duchess of Portsmouth (Charles II's mistress),

233, 244–5, 252, 254, 258
Killigrew, Henry, 197
Kirkby, Christopher, 246
Klein, Francis, 41

Lambert, General John, 164, 165, 171, 172
Laud, William, Archbishop of Canterbury, 47, 57
Lauderdale, John Maitland, Earl of, 226, 238, 240
Leicester, Earl and Countess of, Princess Elizabeth and Prince Henry put in care of, 119–20
Lely, Peter, 182
Lenthall, William, 120
Leonard, Father, of Paris, 35
Leonardo da Vinci, 44
Leven, Earl of, 80
Lindsey, Earl of, 54
Lister, Sir Matthew, 78
Long Parliament (1640–60), 51, 249; members antagonistic to Army arrested (1648), 111; Rump of, 164, 171, 172; return of 'secluded' members to, 173; dissolution of, 174
Longueville, Duc de, 132
Lorraine, Chevalier de, 220, 230, 236; Philip of Orléans' infatuation with, 226, 229; arrested and imprisoned in Château d'If, 229
Lorraine, Duke of, 133–4
Louis XIII, King of France, 17, 24, 29, 30, 79, 92
Louis XIV, King of France, (*Le Roi Soleil*), 92, 130, 132, 151–2, 209, 229, 232, 243, 244, 251–2, 263; court at Versailles, 39, 40, 152, 185–6; betrothed to Infanta Maria Teresa, 169; Philippe d'Anjou's betrothal to Minette, 191, 192; and his flirtation and friendship with Minette, 207; love affair with Louise de la Vallière, 207–8; Minette used an unofficial intermediary between Charles II and, 214–15, 217, 219–20, 222, 224, 227–8, 229–33; Second Dutch War and, 221, 222; and declares war on England, 222; campaign in Spanish Netherlands, 225, 226; and Treaty of Aix-la-Chapelle, 230; ceremonial visit to Flanders, 230–31; and Secret Treaty of Dover, 232; death of Minette and, 235, 236; Third Dutch, 238; Charles II concludes new secret agreement with, 255
Louise, Princess (James II's daughter), 263
Lovell, Robert, 138, 142, 143, 147
Lowestoft, Battle of (1665), 222, 239

Ludlow, Edmund, 164
Lyme, siege of, 78

Maidenhead, Charles I meets children at
    Greyhound Inn, 98
Making, Mrs Bathsua, governess to
    Princess Elizabeth, 73–4
Manchester, Earl of, 54, 214
Mancini, Hortense, Duchesse Mazarin,
    169, 200; as Charles II's mistress, 245,
    258
Mantegna, 'The Triumph of Caesar', 44
Mantua, Duke of, Charles I purchases
    art collection of, 44
Margaret, Princess (James I's daughter),
    5
Maria Anna, Infanta, 19, 20, 21, 27;
    Gonzales's portrait of, 22
Maria Teresa, Infanta, Queen of France,
    169, 207, 235
Marie de Medici, Queen of France, 29,
    30, 35, 55; at English court, 47;
    Rubens's portrait of, 47
Marie-Louise (daughter of Minette), 209
Marlborough, Duke of, 263
Marston Moor, Battle of (1644), 79–80,
    81
Mary, Princess, Princess Royal, Princess
    of Orange, 52, 67, 70, 75–6, 91, 93,
    105, 106, 108, 118, 158, 171, 240;
    birth (1631), 37; childhood, 37–8, 39,
    44–5, 46; Van Dyck's portrait of, 41;
    Catholicism, 48; marriage to William
    of Orange, 55–8; and leaves for
    Holland with mother, 59–60, 61–2;
    reception in The Hague for, 62;
    unpopularity with Dutch, 62, 64, 123,
    125, 126, 182; letter from brother
    Charles to, 62–3; bad relations with
    Princess Amelia (mother-in-law), 64,
    75, 122, 162, 183; Princess Elizabeth's
    letter to, 75; William succeeds father
    as Stadtholder of United Provinces,
    94–5; letter to Prince of Wales, 96; has
    miscarriage, 96; welcomes James to
    Holland, 104; gives banquet to
    celebrate reunion of James and
    Charles, 107; learns of execution of her
    father, 116–17; and death of sister
    Elizabeth, 120; and death of her
    husband, 120–21, 122; birth of son
    William, 121, 122; and dispute over
    his guardianship, 122; temporary rift
    between Charles and, 134–5;
    welcomes Prince Henry to Holland,
    136–7; meets Charles II in Germany,
    139–41, 149; opposed to Prince Henry
    becoming Catholic, 145; and Prince
    Henry stays in Holland with, 146–7;
    Charles II's letter asking for money

from, 147–8; visits Henrietta Maria in
    Paris, 150–52; and meets sister
    Henrietta for first time, 151; joins
    Charles II in Bruges, 153, 156; and
    return to The Hague, 153; Charles's
    quarrel with, 156–7; and friendship
    with Harry Jermyn, 156–7;
    estrangement from Charles, 162–3;
    Charles II's return to England as
    King, 176–8; character and
    appearance at time of Restoration,
    182–3; visit to England, 189–90, 191,
    192, 193, 195, 196, 200; death of
    brother Henry and, 196; and James's
    secret marriage, 198; death from
    smallpox (1660), 200–201
Mary, Princess of Orange and Queen of
    England, 248; marries William III of
    Orange, 245–6; becomes Queen of
    England (1688), 263
Mary of Modena, Duchess of York and
    Queen of England: marriage to James,
    241, 243; birth of son James, 262; and
    birth of Louise, 263
Mary, Queen of Scots, 7, 14
masques, Inigo Jones's designs for,
    12–13, 40
Mathew, Archbishop, 16
Matilda, Empress, 2
Matthias, Holy Roman Emperor, 18
Maurice, Prince of Orange, 55, 76, 78,
    107, 177
Mayard, Colonel, 104
Mayerne, Sir Theodore, physician, 35,
    38, 40, 52, 77–8, 119
Mazarin, Cardinal, 92, 108, 109, 130,
    132, 146, 151, 153, 156, 169, 190, 199,
    200; gives Charles pension in return
    for his leaving France, 139; seeks
    alliance with Cromwell, 139, 153, 160;
    death (1661), 203, 223
Meal Tub Plot (1679), 247
Medway calamity (1667), 223
Meilleraye, Charles de la Porte de la,
    Duc Mazarin, 245
Mende, Bishop of, 27, 30
Mercurius Publicus, 149
Michelangelo, 22
miniaturists, 41, 182
Minette *see* Henrietta Anne
Moderna, Duke of, 241
Monk, General George, Captain-
    General of Army (later Duke of
    Albermarle), 164, 175, 176, 187, 202;
    Royal approaches to, 165, 171; march
    into England (1660), 171–2;
    appointed Captain-General, 173;
    declares himself for Charles II, 174;
    Garter conferred by Charles on, 178
Monmouth, James, Duke of (bastard son

of Charles II), 254; birth in The
Hague (1648), 108; goes to Paris, 225;
his claim to the throne, 248–9, 250,
251, 252; exile of, 251, 257; abortive
rebellion led by (1685), 260
Montagu, Edward, Earl of Sandwich
and Vice-Admiral of England, 176,
177, 178, 193, 196, 202, 232; Garter
conferred by Charles on, 178
Montagu, Ralph, 204, 214–15;
appointed English Ambassador in
Paris, 228, 235, 249
Montagu, Abbé Walter, 142, 143
Montpensier, Princess Anne-Marie,
Duchesse de (La Grande
Mademoiselle), 234; Prince Charles's
courtship of, 93–4; fights for the
Grand Condé in the Fronde, 130, 134;
Minette's friendship with, 231
Montpensier, Marie de Bourbon,
Duchesse de, 93
Montrose, James Graham, Marquess of,
126
Mordaunt, Viscount, 165
Morley, Dr George, 136
Murray, Anne, 103
Mytens, Daniel, 12, 41

Naseby, Battle of (1645), 82, 178
Naseby, HMS, 177, 178; renamed *Royal
Charles*, 178
Nell Gwyn, 244, 245, 254, 258
Netherlands (United Provinces):
marriage of William II of Orange to
Mary (1641), 55–8; and Mary leaves
England for, 59–62; republican
burghers' antagonism to, 62, 64,
122–3; Thirty Years War, 75; leaders'
sympathy with English
Commonwealth, 92; death of
Frederick Henry of Orange, 95; and
William II elected as Stactholder,
95–6; James, Duke of York escapes to,
102–5; part of Roundhead fleet defects
to Charles in Holland, 105–8; death of
William II of Orange, 120–21, 122;
new constitution devised (1651), 123;
and Council of State set up, 123; and
Johan de Witt becomes prime
minister, 123; States General receive
Cromwell's ambassadors, 125, 126;
war between English Commonwealth
and (1652–4), 135–6; and peace terms
exclude House of Orange from
government of country, 136; Henry
Duke of Gloucester's stay in 136–8,
146–7; more favourable attitude to
House of Orange after Restoration,
189; accepts charge of William III's
education, 191–2; Second Dutch War

with England (1665), 215, 216–17,
219, 221–4; Franco-Dutch Pact
(1662), 215, 219, 222; Peace of Breda,
223–4; Triple Alliance with England
and Sweden, 226; Anglo-French
Secret Treaty of Dover against, 232;
and Third Dutch War (1672), 238–40;
Treaty of Westminster (1674), 240; *see
also* Spanish Netherlands
Neuberg, Duke of, 141
Newbury: first Battle of (1643), 76;
Second Battle of (1644), 80
Newcastle, William Cavendish, Earl of,
38, 65, 71, 79, 157
New Model Army, 92, 171;
establishment of (1645), 80–81; Battle
of Naseby, 82; siege of Oxford, 90;
Second Civil War (1648), 105, 108,
109; *see also* Roundheads
Newport, Lord, Constable of Tower of
London, 53
New York, British conquest from Dutch
(1664), 219, 224
Nicholas, Sir Edward, 134, 137–8, 172
Nonsuch Palace, 44
Northumberland, Countess of, 74, 90
Northumberland, Algernon Percy, tenth
Earl of, Lord High Admiral, 97, 113,
128, 186; declares for Parliament, 67;
responsible for custody of royal
children, 74–5, 90–91, 95, 102, 119;
Charles I's meeting with children and,
98, 99; and Prince James's escape,
102–3, 104–5

Oaes, Titus, 246, 247
Oatlands, near Weybridge, 44; birth of
Prince Henry at (1640), 51;
Parliament sends Henrietta Anne to,
87–8
Olivares, Conde-Duque, 21, 23
Oliver, Isaac, 41
Oliver, Peter, 41
Oman, Carola, 152
Orations (Queen Henrietta's priests),
27–8, 30
d'Orléans, Duchesse *see* Henrietta Anne
d'Orléans, Gaston, Duc, 93, 203
d'Orléans, Philippe de Bourbon, Duc
(formerly Duc d'Anjou), 152, 207;
betrothal to Henrietta Anne, 190–91,
192, 200; and marriage at Palais royal,
203; his relations with wife, 207, 208,
226, 228–90; birth of daughter Marie-
Louise, 209; and birth of son Philippe-
Charles, 216; his homosexuality, 226;
and infatuation with Chevalier de
Lorraine, 226, 229; Minette's visit to
England and, 230–31, 232; and death
of Minette, 235–6

Ormonde, Marchioness of, 202
Ormonde, Marquess of, 140, 141, 145, 146, 168, 172, 176, 194
Osborne, Sir Thomas, Earl of Danby, Chief Minister, 241, 243, 245; impeachment of, 249, 250; and committed to Tower, 250
Ossory, Lord, 193, 202
Overbury, Sir Thomas, murder of, 15
Owen, John, bargemaster, 103–4
Oxford (as capital city of Royalists during Civil War), 70, 71, 81; Queen Henrietta's intrigues and squabblings, 76–7; Henrietta leaves for Exeter, 77–8; Charles I diverts Roundhead forces from, 78; Charles I leaves, 85; and surrendered to Fairfax, 90
Oxford Parliament (1681), 254–5

Parliament, 19, 49, 58, 60, 66; of February 1624: 23; Charles I dissolves third (1629), 36; Short Parliament (1640), 51; Long Parliament (1640–60), 51, 111, 164, 171, 172, 173, 174, 249; custody of royal children and, 72–3, 87, 90; Scots hand over Charles I to, 91, 92, 93; Richard Cromwell calls new (1659), 164; dissolution of Long Parliament (1660), 174; and first meeting of new (25 April 1660), 175; dissolution of 'Cavalier' Parliament (1679), 249; new Whig-oriented Parliaments, 249, 252; and dissolutions of, 251, 252, 254; and Charles II's prorogations of, 252; Oxford Parliament (1681), 254–5; and dissolved by Charles, 255–6; House of Commons, 23, 60, 67, 254; Bill of attainder passed by (1641), 53; Charles I's abortive attempt to arrest five members of, 58–9, 215; members antagonistic to Army arrested (1648), 111; and return of 'secluded' members to (1660), 173; England declared a monarchy again and £50,000 gift voted for King by, 175, 177; votes Henrietta Anne present of £10,000: 199; antagonistic to James as heir to throne, 239; financial support for Third Dutch war, 239; demands withdrawal of Declaration of Indulgence, 239; and Test Act passed by, 239–40; Shaftesbury's large following in, 248; first exclusion bill (1679), 251; second exclusion bill (1680), 253; and third exclusion bill (1681), 255; House of Lords, 51, 248; Bill of attainder passed by (1641), 53, 54; Princess Elizabeth's letter to, 72–3; and responsible for welfare of Henry

and Elizabeth, 73; Countess of Dalkeith's letter to, 87–8; second exclusion bill thrown out by (1680), 253
Parliamentary forces *see* Roundheads
Peace of Breda (1667), 223–4
Peace of Westphalia (1648), 132
Pell, John, 73
Pembroke, Earl of, 72
Pepys, Samuel, 222; *Diary*, 175, 195, 223
Perfect Occurrences, 99
Peterborough, Earl of, 241
Philip III, King of Spain, 22
Philip IV, King of Spain, 11, 19, 21, 22, 40, 41, 54, 92, 173, 174; art collection, 22; court ceremonial, 21–2, 39; Charles II's treaty with, 152; death of (1665), 223, 224
Philippe-Charles, Duc de Valois (son of Minette), 216
Plague of London (1665), 223
Pontoise seminary, Prince Henry moved to, 142–3
Popish Plot (1678), 4, 246–7, 248, 252
Porter, Endymion, art collector, 44
Portsmouth, Duchess of *see* Kéroualle, Louise de
Pregnani, Abbé, 228
Presbyterianism, Scottish, 49–50, 125, 156
Pride, Colonel Thomas, 111
Princess Royal, Henrietta Maria's trip in, 70–71
Puckering, Sir Thomas, 34–5
Puritans, 50, 51, 72, 82; *see also* Roundheads
Pym, John, 50, 57; trial of Strafford and, 51, 52–3

Queen's House, Greenwich, 12, 44

Radcliffe, Sir George, 90
Raphael, 22, 44
Rembrandt van Rhyn, 44
Restoration (1660), 175–9, 187, 189, 236; General Monk's march into England, 171–2; Declaration of Breda, 175; Parliament declares England a monarchy again, 175; Charles II's return to England, 176–9; *see also* Royalists
Richard II, King, 2
Richelieu, Cardinal, 47, 92
Richmond, Duke of, Frances Stuart elopes with, 225–6
Richmond Palace, 37, 44, 46, 87
Rochester, Earl of *see* Wilmot, Sir Henry
Roe, Sir Thomas, 62
Roundheads (Parliamentary forces): Sir John Hotham refused Charles I entry into Hull, 65–6; Earl of Northumberland declares for, 67;

Great Civil War begins, 67; Prince Henry and Princess Elizabeth in custody of, 67–8, 71–5; Battle of Edgehill, 68–70; naval forces' attack on Henrietta Maria, 71; Battle of Roundway Down, 76; First Battle of Newbury, 76; Battle of Cropredy Bridge, 78, 79; Charles I's successful Cornish campaign, 79; battle of Marston Moor, 79–80; and Scots come in on side of, 80; Second Battle of Newbury, 80; New Model Army established, 80–81; Battle of Naseby, 82; Bristol surrenders to, 82–3; Charles I surrenders to Scots, 85; Exeter surrenders to, 87; Oxford surrenders to, 90; Second Civil War (1648), 105, 108, 109; part of fleet defects to Royalists, 105–8; trial and execution of Charles I, 111–15; Cromwell's successful campaign in Scotland, 128–9; Battle of Worcester, 129; *see also* Commonwealth

Roundway Down, Wiltshire, Battle of, 76

Roxburgh, Countess, royal governess, 37, 38, 46, 48; remains with Elizabeth and Henry during civil war, 67–8; death of, 71, 74

Royal Charles, HMS, 178, 221, 223

Royalists (Cavaliers), 67–91; Charles I raises Royal banner at Nottingham, 67; Prince Henry and Princess Elizabeth in custody of Parliament, 67–8, 71–5; Battle of Edgehill, 68–70; Henrietta Maria rejoins Charles in Oxford, 70–71; First Battle of Newbury, 76; Battle of Cropredy Bridge, 78, 79; and Charles I's Cornish campaign, 79; Battle of Marston Moor, 79–80; Second Battle of Newbury, 80; Battle of Naseby, 82; surrender of Bristol to Roundheads by, 82–3; Charles I surrenders to Scots, 85; Exeter surrendered to Fairfax by, 87; and Oxford surrendered to Fairfax, 90; Scots hand over King to English Parliament, 91; Second Civil War (1648), 105; part of Roundhead fleet declares for King and sails to Holland, 105–8; Charles I stands trial, and sentenced to death (1649), 111–13; and execution of King, 115–18; Charles II lands in Scotland (1650), 126; Battle of Worcester (1651), 129; and Charles escapes back to France, 129–30; 'The Sealed Knot', 147, 165; prospects of a rising in England (1655), 147–8; Flanders campaign (1657), 152–4, 156; Battle of the

Dunes, 157–8; and Dunkirk surrendered to French, 158; death of Cromwell and, 159, 160, 163–5; and plans for new risings, 165–8; General Monk's march into England, 171–2; Declaration of Breda (1660), 175; Charles II returns to England, 176–9; *see also* Restoration

Rubens, Sir Peter Paul, 40, 44; knighted by Charles I, 40; ceiling painting of Whitehall Banqueting House by, 40; portrait of Marie de Medici by, 47

Rupert, Prince (son of Princess Elizabeth), 60, 71, 81, 84, 94, 186, 198, 232; joins Charles I in Civil War, 67; at Battle of Edgehill, 69; Queen Henrietta's opposition to, 76–7; Battle of Marston Moor, 79–80; Bristol surrendered to Fairfax by, 82–3; Battle of Naseby, 82; appointed Vice-Admiral of revolted fleet, 107; takes over command of fleet, 240

Ruvigny, Henri de Massué, Marquis de, 219–20

Ruyter, Admiral de, 238–9

Rye House Plot (1683), 247–8, 257

St Albans, Earl of *see* Jermyn, Lord

St George, Madame, 27, 29

Saint Germain, Palace of, 93, 109, 134, 229, 230

St James's Palace, 37, 46, 53, 57; chapel, 27, 47; birth of Charles II in, 35–6; and of Charles I's other children, 37, 46; Prince Charles's miniature court at, 38; Henry and Elizabeth left behind by father at, 64, 65; and in custody of Parliament during Civil War, 67–8, 71–4; Parliament orders Princess Henrietta to be taken to, 87; Duke of York joins Elizabeth and Henry at, 90, 97, 100; and escapes from, 102–5, 108; Charles I imprisoned in, 111

Sandwich, Earl of, *see* Montagu, Edward

Scheveningen, Holland, 177–8, 189

Scilly Islands, 85

Scotland, Scots: union with England under James I, 6–7; Charles I crowned king of (1633), 49; Presbyterianism opposed to Church of England, 49–50; Charles I imposes new prayer book on, 50; and First Bishops' War (1639), 50; Second Bishops' War (1640), 51; Charles I opens Scots Parliament, 58; Battle of Marston Moor and, 80; Charles I surrenders to, 85; and handed over to English Parliament in return for cash payment, 91, 93; Charles II lands in

(1650), 125; Cromwell's successful campaign in (1651), 128-9; Charles II's abortive plan to rescue Scottish regalia from Dunottar Castle, 134; General Monk marches into England from (1660), 171-2
The Sealed Knot (Royalist secret organization), 147, 165
Second Dutch War (1665), 215, 216-17, 219, 221-4; Battle of Lowestoft, 222; France declares war on England, 222; Four Days Battle, 222; Medway calamity, 223; Peace of Breda, 223-4
Secret Treaty of Dover (1670), 4, 232, 238, 240, 249, 258
'Seven Bishops', sent to Tower by James II, 262
Seymour, Sir Henry, 112
Shaftesbury, Anthony Ashley Cooper, Earl of, 226, 238, 240, 244, 251; opposition to Stuarts, 243-4, 248, 252; character of, 243; Popish Plot, 247, 248; Exclusion Crisis and 248-57 *passim*; supports Monmouth's claim to the throne, 248-9, 252; and arranges for impeachment of Danby, 249; appointed Lord President of Council, 250; and dismissed from Presidency, 252; acquitted of high treason, 256; and goes into exile, 257
Shakespeare, William, 13
Short Parliament (1640), 51
Soissons, Comte de, 199-200
Sole Bay, Battle of (1672), 239
Somer, Paul van, 12
Somerset, Robert Carr, Earl of, 15
Somerset House, 57; Queen's chapel at, 47
Sophia, Princess, 186
Southampton, Earl of, 139, 194, 195; appointed Lord Treasurer by Charles II, 187
Spa, Germany, 139-40
Spain, 19, 55, 92; Charles's and Buckingham's visit to (1623), 20-23; war with England, 23, 32; and England makes peace with, 36; Thirty Years War, 75, 92; and hostilities between France and, 132, 133; Charles II's treaty with Philip IV, 152, 153; Battles of the Dune, 157-8; Charles II's visit, 168-9; peace treaty signed with France, 169; and betrothal of Louis XIV to Infanta Maria Teresa, 169; Charles II succeeds Philip IV as king, 223; Treaty of Aix-la-Chapelle, 230
Spanish Netherlands, 55, 159; Thirty Years War, 75; Charles II moves HQ to Bruges, 152-3; and joined by

James, Duke of York, 153-4; Battles of the Dunes, 157-8; and Dunkirk surrendered to French, 158; Louis XIV's campaign in, 225, 226; Treaty of Aix-la-Chapelle cedes territories to France, 230; *see also* Netherlands
Stanhope, Lady (later Countess of Chesterfield), 135, 141, 201
Stephen, King, 2
Strafford, Thomas Wentworth, Earl of, 90; as supporter of royal authority, 50-51; and offers King services of army in Ireland, 51, 53; impeachment and trial of, 51, 52-3, 56, 57; and bill of attainder passed by House of Parliament, 53; and execution on Tower Hill, 54
Strange, Lord, 57
Stroud, Ellen, 193
Stuart, Frances, 213, 225; appointed maid of honour to Queen Catherine, 210; elopes and marries Duke of Richmond, 225-6
Sunderland, Robert Spencer, Earl of, 250, 252
Sweden, 226
Syon House, Middlesex, 75; royal children at, 99, 105, 113, 115, 119

Talbot, Richard, 197
Tattersall, Captain, 177
Teiling Palace, near Haarlem, 108, 147, 148
Test Act (1673), 239-40, 260, 262
Third Dutch War (1672), 238-40, 243; Battle of Sole Bay, 239; House of Commons votes money for, 239; Treaty of Westminster, 240
Thirty Years War, 18, 75, 92, 132
Thurloe, John, 138
Tintoretto, 44
Titian, 44; *The Venus of Pardo*, 22; portrait of Emperor Charles V, 22; Charles I's predilection for, 22, 44
Tonge, Israel, 246, 247
tonnage and poundage (import taxes), 49
Tower of London, 102; Stratford imprisoned in, 53; Archbishop Laud imprisoned in, 57; Earl of Danby committed to, 250; and Shaftesbury sent to, 256; 'Seven Bishops' sent to, 262
Treaty of Aix-la-Chapelle (1668), 230
Treaty of Westminster (1674), 240
Triple Alliance (England/Holland/Sweden), 226
Tromp, Admiral Marten van, 56, 70, 71
Turenne, Henri, Vicomte de, 132, 142, 153, 228; Duke of York serves under,

292 *Index*

132–3, 134, 154, 184; his offer of
support to James, 166–7, 168
Turnhout, Princess Amelia's Palace at,
161–2

United Provinces *see* Netherlands

Vallière, Louise de la, Louis XIV's love
affair with, 207–8
Van Dyck, Sir Anthony, 183, 186;
appointed court painter by Charles I,
41; paintings of royal children, 41;
portrait of William and Mary, 58
Vane, Sir Henry, 164
Vardes, Marquis de, 208, 220
Velázquez, 41, 44; sketch of Prince
Charles by, 22
Victoria, Queen, 4
Villeneuve Saint-Georges, Lorraine's
HQ at, 134
Villers-Cotterets, Philippe d'Orléans's
country estate, 229–30
Villiers, George *see* Buckingham, Duke of
Villiers, Lady, 15
Villiers, Lord Francis, 52, 94

Waller, Sir William (Roundhead
commander), 76, 77, 78, 80; Battle of
Cropredy Bridge, 78; Second Battle of
Newbury, 80
Walter, Lucy (mother of James, Duke of
Monmouth), 108, 225, 249
Wars of the Roses, 2
Wedgewood, Dame Veronica, 39
Weekly Intelligencer, 99
Westminster Hall: trial of Strafford in
(1641), 52–3; and trial of Charles I
(1649), 111
Whigs, 248, 249, 255, 262; *see also*
Parliament; Shaftesbury
Whitehall Banqueting House, 56, 115;
Rubens's ceiling paintings, 40
Whitehall Palace: masques staged in, 13;
Charles I's art collection, 44; mob

threatens to storm, 53; wedding of
Mary and William of Orange in
chapel, 57; Prince Henry and Princess
Elizabeth removed to, 74
William the Silent of Orange, 55, 123
William II of Orange, Prince, 70, 76, 93,
106, 108, 112, 118, 161; marriage to
Princess Mary, 55–8; and Mary joins
him in Holland, 60, 61–2, 64; succeeds
father as Stadtholder of United
Provinces, 95–6; welcomes Prince
James to Holland, 104; trial and
execution of Charles I and, 116–17;
death from smallpox (1650), 120–21,
122, 126
William III of Orange, Prince, King of
England, 152, 153, 177, 178, 241, 248;
birth (1650), 121, 122; and dispute
over guardianship of, 122; Mary seeks
advancement of, 123; Order of the
Garter bestowed on, 137; States of
Holland and West Friesland accept
charge of his education, 189, 191–2;
his rise to power in Third Dutch War,
240; marriage to Mary Stuart (1677),
245–6; and his claim to English
throne, 251; visits England, 257;
becomes King of England (1688), 263
Willis, Sir Richard, 165
Wilmot, Sir Henry (later Earl of
Rochester), 76, 138
Wilmot, Lord, 129
Windsor Castle, 59, 111, 253, 256
'Winter Queen' *see* Elizabeth of Bohemia
Wolsey, Cardinal, 44
Worcester, Battle of (1651), 129, 180
Worcester House, Strand; Duke of
York's secret marriage to Anne Hyde
at, 193–4, 198; Charles, Duke of
Cambridge christened at, 202
Wren, Dr Matthew, Bishop of Ely and
Dean of the Chapel Royal, 57
Wyndham, Mrs Christabella, Prince
Charles's affair with, 81–2, 85